Brother to a Dragonfly

BROTHER TO
A DRAGONFLY

Twenty-fifth Anniversary Edition

Will D. Campbell

Foreword by Jimmy Carter

CONTINUUM
New York   London

2000

The Continuum International Publishing Group Inc
370 Lexington Avenue, New York, NY 10017

The Continuum International Publishing Group Ltd
Wellington House, 125 Strand, London WC2R 0BB

Printed in the United States of America

Library of Congress Cataloging in Publication Data
Campbell, Will D.
Brother to a dragonfly / Will D. Campbell ; foreword by Jimmy Carter—25th
anniversary ed.
p. cm.
Originally published: New York: Seabury Press, 1977. With new foreword.
ISBN 0-8264-1268-8 (alk. paper) — ISBN 0-8264-1296-3 (alk. paper)
1. Campbell, Will D.   2. Baptists—Mississippi—Clergy—Biography.   3. Civil rights
workers—Mississippi—Biography.   4. Campbell, Joseph Lee.
5. Pharmacists—Mississippi—Meridian—Biography.   I. Title.

BX6495.C28 A33 2000
323'.092—dc21
[B]   00–031402

Contents

Foreword

The occasion of a twenty-fifth anniversary reissue of *Brother to a Dragonfly* is noteworthy for several reasons. As a true story of family life in mid-twentieth-century Mississippi, the Reverend Will D. Campbell's book has attained the stature of an American classic. Its author has made his own indelible mark as a minister and social activist in service to marginalized people of every race, creed, and calling. Those who read *Dragonfly* when it first appeared around the time of the American Bicentennial celebration in 1976 will be stirred anew by its honest and powerful voice. And a rising generation of readers, discovering the book for the first time, will be getting not only an unretouched picture of life in yesterday's South, but also a clear example of prose writing with enduring and universal qualities.

When I first encountered *Brother to a Dragonfly* some twenty years ago, it had a profound effect on me. It opened onto a landscape with which I was thoroughly familiar: the rural Deep South of the Great Depression. Like Will Campbell, I was born into such a place, and in the same year; like him, I also was raised as a Southern Baptist, went off to war in the 1940s, and came home to a family and a church in a South and Nation that were soon to be thrust into an era of social transformation that would still be in motion at century's end.

I felt that I knew this man. He had grown up in poorer circumstances than I, yet the pictures of life that he painted in his book were so close to my own experiences that they lowered the fences of social and economic class and gave us parity as brothers, in a biblical if not a familial sense. With equal effect, as I subsequently was to learn from others, *Dragonfly* also tore down the walls that separated white and black Southerners. Brother Will, as he was and is called by so many of us who know him, used the force of his words and the witness of his deeds to convey a healing message of grace, reconciliation, and faithful service to any and all who might pay heed.

The sense of pain and loss he felt at the death of his brother Joe, so poignantly recounted in these pages, made all the more meaningful his ministry to my family and me on the death of my brother Billy in 1988. Down through the years, as we have seen our native and beloved South slowly unburden itself of the dead weight of white supremacy, Will Campbell and I have shared the satisfaction and the blessings of that liberating spirit. For as the late Dr. Martin Luther King, Jr., observed in the 1960s, the civil rights movement and the successful legal challenge to racial discrimination freed white men and women who had perpetrated injustice, as surely as it freed black men and women who were its victims.

Brother to a Dragonfly speaks to these complex psychological issues with disarming directness and simplicity. To read this compelling story and realize that it has lost none of its persuasive powers in a quarter of a century is to understand and appreciate its prophetic qualities and its narrative force. It is an affectionate, humorous, loving, and intensely personal story that escapes the confinement of ordinary life to soar aloft as a timeless chronicle.

Brother Will Campbell's abiding gift—to his late brother and the rest of his family, to his small but deeply appreciative audience of churched and unchurched believers, and to us all—is not entirely encompassed by this book of true confession. But *Dragonfly* does stand as his representative letter of faith, no less now than twenty-five years ago.

JIMMY CARTER

As kingfishers catch fire, dragonflies draw flame . . .

GERARD MANLEY HOPKINS

Prologue

His name was Joseph. The name carries no special significance to his story. He was named for a country preacher of the area; not for the Joseph, son of Jacob, sold by his brothers into slavery, betrayed by wife of Potiphar, Saviour of his people, recipient of the blessing of his father. The Egypt was there with him as with Joseph of Hebron and was, as with him, at once his success and final defeat. But unrelated, I believe, to the name. Except that he, Joe, too, was a dreamer. Beyond that I do not know.

I know only that it was his saga and the saga of the times in which he lived. And, yes, mine too. Because the two lives, his and mine, were bound in those days so inextricably together.

Some of these things he was alone in, as was I. Some of them involved us both. Some were the stuff of that brief period in world and national history over which we had neither control nor influence. Yet we were there, Joseph Lee and I, sometimes in a nearness approaching, surpassing illness. And sometimes so far apart that neither could hear the cry of the other.

So far as Joe and I knew, this is how it began. Two lived just down the road. The other two lived in a house several miles away we called "across the river." These four. And more. For they, too, had their history. But these were our history and we didn't bother much with theirs.

Grandpa Bunt:
Never raised his voice, lost his temper,
    lost a fight.
Some thought he had neither of the latter,
    but he did.
Because even Uncle Bunt (everybody called him
    Uncle) was a sinner.

"Have chairs," he said to guests on the day of his
    death.
And then insisted that his baby son not leave him.
    (His baby son was our Daddy. And he came home
    crying.)
    Crying
because Grandpa said at sunset: "You have gone as
    far as you can go."
And Daddy knew.
Knew that Grandpa was
    dying.

And he did die. And slept with his fathers.
But not before he made seventy-one crops.
And progeny plenty—
ten to be exact—
three of whom died ten days apart with
    bleeding flux,
leaving them childless. But the new dispensation
    brought seven more,
        not counting another dead in the womb.

And not before he divided his earth,
giving each child enough for one more,
    one last
generation to survive on the land,
and became a Baptist deacon,
and prayed long and pretty prayers about
    stooping to drink
from the bitter springs of life,
and talked publicly with God about all the bad times.

And the good things promised.

Grandma Bettye:
Grunting every breath, sometimes twice,
    with neuralgia and lumbago.
But smiling, too. Because her lover
    (for sixty-six years her lover)
never once forgot to say: "Mighty fine supper,
    Mrs. Campbell."
No matter what the fare.

And once she cried when he asked if the bread, hon,
was cooked yesterday
    or the day before.
That being as close to irreconcilable differences as
    the years ever knew.

And she talked about the Glory Hole,
meaning the place just above the bridge
where we baptized.
    And where
boys went bathing with her nod,
but girls' bodies made it a naughty sacrilege.
And McComb City was the wickedest place in the world.

Camphor Balm from the Rawleigh Man and
    aspirin from the store
were good for lumbago.
But not as good as salt mackerel
    and knick-knacks Uncle Tiff brought from Louisiana.

She sat on the pew that ran crosswise
    to the congregation.
Right up front. With Miss Emma, Miss Lola, Miss Eula,
Aunt Donnie, Aunt Ida,
not one of them either "Miss" or "Aunt," but old, like

Grandma was old.
For old began at thirty.

And she wore the flannel bathrobe to church
the very first Sunday after Christmas.
Because it was the prettiest thing she
        had ever seen,
        and the Lord deserved the best.
And because it was 1933 and she didn't have a
        bathroom.

Grandpa Will:
Opening the gate,
leading from the barn lot
        to the field of shriveled, crackling
corn stalks, good only for fodder now, because the
drought of '31 had made it so:
"I want the Lord's will to be done
        and I know He knows
        what's best.
But I just can't figure out what He's got in mind."
He called me Jack and gave me nickels.
Taught me how to chew tobacco—said I had worms.
(Though I didn't skid along the floor.)
Let me turn the ice cream freezer, and
let me pick the first watermelon
        because,
I was his favorite.
Because I, of thirty odd, bore his name.

Seventeen stalks of Mississippi Red sugar cane
        stuffed in the rollers of the syrup mill,
snapping the pole that rolled the rollers,
the pole pulled round and round by a pair of
        fine, fat Missouri mules.
"MY GOD, BOY, WHAT THE HELL'S THE MATTER WITH YOU!"
Not to me, but to Joe who silently took
        both rap and rebuke.

Nestled close together, after Grandma died, in a
        feather mattress,
picked from his own geese and stuffed by him in
        the candy striped ticking.
The clock, carefully, slowly wound up tight each
        night, goes off at four.
Two feet, now old, hit the floor,

· 5 ·

followed by a crackling pine knot fire.
And fifteen minutes of aged body bends and push-ups.

Tallow is for tetter (that's a foot disease).
Whiskey is for coughs.
Vicks Salve is for kids.
And Clara is the cook.

And then *Miss Daisy Sandifer came to Grandpa's house*
because,
he said,
"Old rats like cheese too."

And I went home not understanding.

Grandma Bertha:
Long auburn tresses dropping into the sourdough and
teacake batter
like tongues of fire in reverse
        on Pentecost day.
And dark roasted coffee beans,
        parched each morning
and ground by the first hint of day in a cast iron grinder.

"Be kind to the Lillys.
Lice don't make folks trash.
They may be angels
                unaware.
Some folks say I oughten to dip snuff."
"I don't care if he's a darkie.
And I don't care if he stole Albert Carroll's old truck.
He's fourteen years old,
and they ain't gonna beat him."

Buried at Hebron at fifty-nine.
The preacher said we ought to be thankful,
cause in New Orleans,
        death was ugly.
Said four men had to hold the corners of the
casket down with shovels,
to keep it from floating.
Said God meant us to return to dust. . .
        like at Hebron,
and nobody ought to be buried in New Orleans.

This was our history, Joe's and mine.

Of course, we had a mother and a father also. But they are not history. They are a part of now.

Not many people today have grandparents, so they have antiques, anything older than fifty years, effigies of grandmas they never knew, symbols of grandpas they know mainly as Christmas cards, trying, pathetically, to create a history they do not have, or believe they do not have.

But Joe and I had a history. These four. They lived their lives; each one straddled the horse and rode it to the ground, neither applying the spurs nor holding too tight a rein, remaining firmly in the saddle until the end approached—all like a Remington canvas. And each leaving, even then, with a certain hesitation. But without murmur or rustle of thought in opposition to either the roughness of the ride or the imminence of the finale.

And then, ten years ago, long after the last of these in our history had gone, Joe died. Young. But, unlike them, Joe was in some sort of a hurry. About midnight he went into his room and locked the door. From then until eleven the next morning the remnant of what had tried and wanted to be his world sought to break through to him. Then, when it failed, the hinges were removed and he was waiting for it. But waiting dead. Not only willingly but hurriedly. Early. Without the hesitation of those who had gone before us.

Somewhere, something went wrong. I do not know where the street began. I know only where it ended. What were the intersections, junctions and cloverleafs that merged into that one-way lane of traffic? Where were the yellow and red lights, the caution, detour and dangerous curve signs which, if seen and heeded, might have led to a different destination? I do not know, do not ever expect to find out and probably don't want to find out. Perhaps the light was always and only green, frozen, stuck there, never changing and never offering the traveler warning of the pitfalls ahead. I do not know.

MORNING

No, it's further down the path. I know it's further down the path." Joe was looking for something but had not told me what it was. So I couldn't help him find it. He said he would tell me when we got there.

We were walking down a path, through the woods behind our house, in the direction of Grandpa Bunt and Grandma Bettye's house which stood a few hundred yards away. A spring branch flowed directly behind their place and we could hear the rushing waters from the heavy rain of the night before. Joe was seven years old and I was five. And Joe was the leader.

He said we were looking for an experiment. That was all he would tell me. Whatever it was, I knew that it would be successful. Sawbriars, those thin, spindly vines with spines like fish teeth, were reaching out to take hold of whatever piece of clothing or skin they could hook themselves into. I do not know if sawbriars still exist. In 1929 they covered the south Mississippi hills, springing out of the red clay like so many tiny quills, hostile toward everything around them. They were considered a part of the curse, a curse we grew up believing was somehow a part of the Adam and Eve story. We defended ourselves against them with both hatred and reverence. We hated them because one was supposed to hate evil. We revered them because the Bible taught us that it was a part of what we had coming to us on account of someone's long ago sin—sin which was passed on to us and which became our own. Perhaps the sawbriars are all gone and do not exist anymore.

And "stickers" too. Those almost invisible needle points rooted in the ground which had no height at all but spread themselves upon lawns and grassy places like a carpet. They, too, were related somehow to the curse—humanity's sinful condition and history.

As we walked along, bradding the stickers with our bare feet and avoiding the sawbriars as best we could, Joe kept repeating, "I know it's further down the path. I know we didn't pass it yet."

It was early summer and our feet had not become toughened as they would be later on. We stopped occasionally to pull the stickers out, scratching and rubbing where they itched. Joe said this was good training for the "sticker races" which would take place later in the summer.

Sticker races were a frequent game for the dozens of Campbell cousins who gathered at Grandpa Bunt's house on summer Sunday afternoons. They required no equipment and could be played by every size. Training for the races began on the day we began to go barefooted. I do not recall any criteria, such as how many days from the last frost, but somehow it became known that on a particular day all boy chaps would take their shoes off. On that day the tender feet of winter began their perilous journey into spring and summer. First in the yard only. Then timidly onto the stomp—that area between the scraped, packed dirt yard surrounding the house, swept clean with dogwood brooms, and the edge of the fields—and finally into the field, woods, riverbanks and graveled roads. It was not that shoes were looked upon with scorn. We looked forward to the time, generally in late adolescence, when we would wear them all year. It was a symbol of manhood. (Joe would one day have twenty pairs of shoes in his closet and under his bed at once.) Shoes were, in fact, one's most prized possession. They alone separated a man from what was at once his best friend and worst enemy—the earth. Best friend because it produced the corn and potatoes to eat, the cotton to try to pay off the mortgage. And worst enemy because it harbored the cottonmouths and rattlers, the sawbriars and stickers, and snow and ice of winter. The earliest songs we sang had to do with shoes:

> *Mamma, soon I'll be an angel.*
> *By perhaps, another day.*
> *Give them all my toys, but Mother,*
> *Put my little shoes away.*

And years later Carl Perkins and Elvis Presley, swinging, gyrating, twisting, rejoicing to the music and lyrics of "Blue Suede Shoes," a song not about a rich dude from the city who impressed the girls with his daily change of shoes, but a story written in the cotton fields of west Tennessee by a poor boy who saved enough money to pay for the coveted suede, and served notice on the world that it could do anything it would to him but, "Stay off my blue suede shoes!" The wearing of shoes was a luxury dreamed of. The taking them off in spring an occasion which might as well be celebrated as lamented.

The Sticker Race was no more than a contest to see who had the toughest feet. The winner was the one who could run the length of Grandpa's Stomp and "brad" the most stickers. The race was run in groups of four, lined up by age or size. "Bradding" meant that the needle points were broken off by the leather-like soles of the feet with no penetration into the "quick." One was disqualified if he had to stop to pull one out. Those finishing the course were inspected to see if any stickers were present. A tie in the number of stickers went to the one who crossed the line first. When four boys finished a race the winner stepped aside to compete in the finals and four more began. There was never any tangible prize, just the satisfaction of having the toughest feet in the Campbell community.

Joe kept whispering my name. "Dave. Dave. Dave." My name was Will Davis but Joe, and most everyone else, called me Dave until I was seventeen and left home to go to college and announced that I wanted then to be called Will. Joe was the first to make the change saying, "A *man* ought to be called what he wants to be called." Joe was first to declare me a man.

"It's got to be further down the path. I know we didn't pass it yet, Dave." Each time he called my name he whispered it.

I had just returned home that morning from "across the river"— Grandpa Will and Grandma Bertha's house. I stayed with them often when I wasn't needed in the fields at home. I was Grandpa Will's namesake and he made no secret of the fact that I was his favorite. For the favors I had to suffer the taunts and jeers of "Grandpa's little pet" from numerous cousins and even aunts and uncles who were offended at such favoritism. If it offended Joe we never discussed it. His only resentment was that he wanted me at home with him. I had come home that morning because Mamma had been sick the night before and had sent for me.

Before we left the house to look for Joe's experiment, we sat for a long time on the back steps and Joe told me how he had thought Mamma was going to die and how she had made him promise that he would get word to Uncle Boyce to bring me home on his way to

McComb where he worked in the Illinois Central Railroad shops.

Suddenly he found what he was looking for. In a clearing in the weeds and briars beside the path there was a tiny mound of clay. I stooped down and started to dig it up.

"No, waitaminit, Dave. Don't dig it up yet." He had to explain what it was about.

"I caught a 'skeeterhawk Sunday and buried it alive in a Bayer aspirin box. I said I was going to dig it up on Wednesday and if it was alive that would mean you were coming home that same day. If it was dead that would mean you would be gone for a long time."

We had gone up and down the path several times looking for the grave. The heavy rain had settled the earth and washed some leaves over it. In his haste to show me his experiment he had walked past it. When we saw the water in the branch he knew that we had gone too far and when we turned back the last time he walked directly to it.

He had dug the hole in the ground with the blade of his barlow knife and the actual exhuming was brief. We stood touching each other in the damp, eleven o'clock heat of a June, Mississippi morning. The ceremony was not to be rushed, and he must be certain that I understood what was happening.

"I betcha that 'skeeterhawk is alive." 'Skeeterhawk was what we called dragonflies. They had something to do with luck, both good and bad luck. If you were fishing and one lit on the end of the pole, it meant you were going to catch a fish. If one paused, hovered nearby but then darted away, you might as well go to the house. It was bad luck. Someone had told us they caught and ate mosquitoes. We imagined they did it like the big, wide-winged chicken hawks which swept down from the sky and grabbed young chickens from the yard in the spring. We had watched the giant bird soar around and around the chicken pen, stopping dead still in the air. Then, rolling his body into a ball, looking to us like the big steel balls we had seen chain gang prisoners pulling along behind them, he would drop straight to the earth with a force and speed far beyond what its body weight could create. His aim was always perfect, his work quick. With the chicken knocked down from the fall upon it, his beak was sunk into the chicken's head like a flashing spike, killing it instantly. Just as quickly he was gone with his prey. We used to watch a dragonfly to see if he killed a mosquito that way.

"You can't chase a 'skeeterhawk and catch him. They fly all the time. You just have to wait till they light, when they're all tuckered out. Then you can slip up on him and grab him by the tail. Not by the wings though. By the tail. That's the way I caught him."

He held the aspirin box in the palm of his hand.

"I betcha he's alive. I betcha anything he's alive, Dave. I said to myself when I buried him that I was going to dig him up on Wednesday. And if he was alive that meant you were coming home. And you're already home. I betcha he's alive."

Slowly, deliberately, he unsnapped the aspirin box with his thumb nail. The lid was gently raised open. Two brothers stood as close as two brothers could stand, beholding the proof of one brother's experiment.

It did not, could not, have occurred to me that the fluttering of the transparent, gauze-like wings might have been caused by the wind. Joe had buried the dragonfly on Sunday and said that if it were alive on Wednesday I would come home and we would be together. And the wings had fluttered.

He snapped the lid shut, ran quickly and dropped the aspirin box into the rushing and muddy waters of the spring branch.

"Didn't I tell you!"

And two brothers tried to outrun each other, and tried harder not to outrun each other, back to the yard. For there was no thought of ascendancy.

Joe had climbed up a small ladder built along the wall of the corn-crib, looked down at us from the hayloft, and finally made his way to the highest cross piece at the top of the gable of the barn. Aunt Susie's boys, Vernon and Prentiss, were with us and Joe had insisted to us all that he could fly.

"I tell you, I can fly. I've watched buzzards and hawks, the way they do it. All they do is spread their wings out and let the wind blow them along. I can do it too." As he climbed the thirty or forty feet to where he was sitting he kept shouting down to us that he was going to show us he could fly.

It was drizzling rain outside and we had been sitting on a pile of cottonseed in the barn, telling ghost stories. Joe had read Edgar Allan Poe stories and had mastered the telling of many of them: "The Pit and the Pendulum," "The Premature Burial." Later he would memorize and recite—generally only to me—some of Poe's poems: "Annabel Lee," "The Raven."

The old barn was a special place. Not because it was our barn and we knew our Daddy had built it but because it was headquarters for so much learning. And because Joe and I spent so much time together there, usually just the two of us. Joe was the leader here as everywhere.

Once our barn had become infested with large packrats, some of them, tail and all, fifteen inches long. A favorite sport was to take a long handled pitchfork and, as dozens of them lay sleeping where the roof came together forming a sharp gable, go down the line sticking them through the belly with the fork, hearing them squeak and watching them scatter for cover. On one day Joe suggested that instead of stabbing them we try to catch one. I don't recall if we planned to try to make a pet of it or throw it into the pond as we sometimes did 'possums we caught. We would throw the 'possum to the middle of the water and wait on the bank until he swam out, throw him in again and again. Each time he was a little more weary and finally he would be so tired that he couldn't make it out, would sink to the bottom and drown.

His plan to catch the rat was simple. And soon successful. He told me to stand in the corner of the corncrib where there was a hole in the floor. He said that when he bumped on the roof the rats would run for the hole. I was to catch one and not let go. I was not long in waiting. As one ran for the hole in the floor I grabbed him by the stomach. He jerked his head to my left index finger, ripping it from the outer edge of the nail, down and across to the first joint. Blood spurted and the rat, his mouth, eyes and body covered with the salty warm claret, let go. Though he had let go of me I did not let go of him. Joe had said to hold it until he came down and that was what I intended to do. Joe came tumbling down, yelling for me to let go as he fell beside me. But in my confusion I understood him to mean that I should hold on. He grabbed my arm and shook it so hard the rat landed against the far wall, momentarily stunned. The moment was long enough. Joe stomped and cursed and kicked it and finally ground its head to a pulp with the heel of his shoe. Revenge over, he turned quickly to me. The bone could be seen through the flow of blood. Tearing off the tail of his shirt he wrapped and pressed the wound until it stopped bleeding. Several stitches would be required to close such a wound in other days. But then, several weeks of time and healing did as well. The long scar remains as a monument to obedience, trust, love and leadership. Things like that happened in the barn.

Now perched high above us in that same barn, having looked down to the ground and deciding against flying, Joe was telling

Vernon and Prentiss a scary story which had really happened and which we had heard Mamma and Daddy tell many times. When school was in session we could get books to read. At other times we had stacks of magazines given to us by Uncle Boyce and various girl cousins. These were always either *Smith and Street Westerns* or *True Romance*. Other forms of entertainment were simply not available to us. So, idle time was passed by listening to stories of the early childhood of our parents.

The one Joe was telling now had happened when Mamma was four or five years old. She and one of her sisters, Aunt Dolly, were playing in front of their house when they heard yells and screams and pleas for help from the field across the road from their house. Even before they came into sight they knew that it was their neighbors, Mr. Lum Cleveland and his wife, called by Mamma, and thus by us, Aunt Stump. They were both old.

Joe was embellishing the story by making the sounds he supposed each of them was making, dropping his voice as low as a little boy could to imitate Mr. Lum's voice, and raising it as high as he could for Aunt Stump's screams.

"YE—OOOW!"

"*ye—oow!*"

"HELLP!"

"WHE—OOOW! HELP! HELP!"

Now Mr. Lum and Aunt Stump came into vision from the woods that surrounded their house, several hundred yards north of Grandpa Will's house. Running after them, a shotgun in his hands, was a much younger man. The two little girls, frozen in terror, recognized him too. It was Allen Westbrook, son-in-law of the two old people. He was screaming incoherent sounds as loudly as the two he was pursuing. Joe imitated his sounds, or what he imagined his sounds to have been, flailing one arm around, holding onto his perch with the other hand to keep from falling.

Then we heard the shots, Joe pausing after each two volleys to allow time for reloading.

"BOOM! BOOM!"

"POW! POW!"

"BAM! BAM!"

Mr. Lum dropped to the ground and did not move. The screams of Aunt Stump continued. No longer hearing the calls of her husband, she hesitated. Glancing back over her shoulder to look for

her husband, she tripped and fell. Now another shot rang out.
"BOOM!"

Aunt Stump did not get up.

Vernon and Prentiss had not heard the story before. I had heard
it many times but sat in the same rapt attention as they, beholding
now with them two old people lying bleeding on the ground.

The story continued from the lofty roost.

Mamma and Aunt Dolly went screaming to the house, seeing as
they did their daddy running in the direction of the cries of his
neighbors, his own shotgun in his hands. He had heard their calls
from the field where he was working. But he was too late. Both lay
dead in the sun a few yards apart. Allen Westbrook was gone.

The two bodies were brought across the road on a mule-drawn
ground slide and placed on the back porch beside the water shelf.
Most rural porches had such a water shelf. A cedar bucket was
there, a stainless steel or gourd dipper beside it, and a wash basin.
Beneath the shelf would be elephant-ear plants, those stout stem
plants with leaves looking like their name. Water used for washing
hands and faces was always poured onto the elephant ears, the soap
and dirt and moisture making them grow to mammoth size as the
summer advanced to fall and winter. The first frost would bring
them to the ground. Joe continued to garnish the tale, telling us
how the blood of Mr. Lum and Aunt Stump dripped onto and
around the elephant ears, and how they grew so big and so tall that
they had to be cut down with an ax. He told us how the doctor,
summoned to pronounce them dead, had washed the brains of
Aunt Stump before placing them back in her head, and how Uncle
Boyce, older than Mamma and Aunt Dolly, already a young man,
had walked across the field with a piece of head bone to be placed
with the body of Mr. Lum.

Vernon and Prentiss thought it was time for them to go home.
But the story was not finished. Joe told them there was more, and
so they stayed.

The story to that point was what we had heard Mamma tell. She
would usually include some speculation as to why the murders
were committed, but always leaving something to the imagination.

"The daughter was to blame. She's the hussy who should have
been punished. She's the one who always kept things stirred up between them, tattling first to one and then the other. It was her

fault." And Mamma sometimes used the story to explain why her nerves were so bad, and why she was sick a lot.

Daddy's part of the story had to do with the punishment of Allen Westbrook. He was soon captured, or turned himself in, and the trial followed. He was found guilty and sentenced to death by hanging. It was to that event that Joe turned next.

"They killed him on a gallows. Made him climb up this big, tall scaffold, and I'll bet he was as high up as I am now."

He imagined, and passed on to us as fact, that when Allen Westbrook climbed up there he could see all over the town of Liberty.

"Yea, that was the last thing he saw before they put that black hood over his face. He could see the church houses, the school house, Dr. Quin's office and both drug stores. That's what he saw. Everything. He was so high up he could see everything in the world."

And our daddy had been there. The account as it was told to us, and as it was then being told by Joe, began in early morning, before daylight the day of the hanging. Grandpa Bunt got up real early and got his five boys up to go with him. They ranged in age from nine to fourteen years. He already had the mules hitched to the wagon when they got up. They drove the ten miles to Liberty, the county seat of Amite County. It was almost noon when they got there, and that's when he was going to be hung. At exactly dinnertime.

Wagon teams, buggies, and saddled horses were already tied under every shade tree. Allen Westbrook's mother, father and sister waited under a tree far to the left of the jail and courthouse, far enough away that they could neither see nor hear what was taking place. But a clear lane had been considerately left through which they could drive their wagon bearing the casket to the courthouse to claim his body when it was over.

"They told Allen Westbrook he could have whatever he wanted for his last meal. And you know what he asked for?" I knew, of course, but all three of us shook our heads. "No."

"He got fried chicken, rice and gravy and biscuits. He wanted some ice tea too. And some blackberry pie. But they said he didn't eat the pie. But he ate all the chicken and stuff."

He climbed the steps of the scaffold without assistance. The sheriff, a short, fat man named Mann Causey, whom we knew for he had been sheriff again in our time, asked him if he had any last words. He said that he did.

"He made a little speech. He told everybody that if he had listened to his mamma he wouldn't be there on that scaffold. He told everybody to listen to their mamma and they wouldn't ever get in any trouble. He thanked the sheriff and the jailer, said they had been real good to him. That's what he said, and it was the last thing he ever did say."

The traditional black hood was placed over his head. The rope, properly knotted for public display several days in advance, was placed around his neck. Daddy, the youngest of the boys, milled around the courtyard with his brothers and the hundreds of others who had come. Mann Causey pulled a lever which released the trapdoor upon which Allen Westbrook was standing and he came plummeting to justice, stopping short of the ground by not more than a yard. A bubbling, gurgling sound, a few feeble kicks of the feet and legs, feet searching for something stationary in the final moments of consciousness, and then the heavy twisting and turning.

The body was lowered gently and tenderly to the ground and taken inside as if the whole thing had been an accident. Dr. Quin, standing by all the while with stethoscope in hand, leaned over and listened to his chest. Daddy and Uncle Bill, little boys, peered through the window. The doctor said something to the sheriff who then made a circular motion with his arm, motioning to another man stationed midway between the scaffold and the waiting wagon. He in turn made a similar motion in the direction of the wagon, cue to the parents that they could come and take their son home.

The people of Amite County had been heard. Justice prevailed. Grandpa Bunt and his five boys got back on their wagon and went home. Grandpa had said nothing to his boys about why he was bringing them to witness the hanging as they came. He said no more about it as they returned.

Joe, his story finished, climbed slowly and silently down to where we were and sat down beside us. Vernon and Prentiss, heirs to the same genes as Joe and I, wondered why Grandpa Bunt took his boys to the hanging.

"What'd he do that for?"

Their mother was our daddy's youngest sister and was just a

baby when it happened. But she wouldn't have been taken anyway. Only the boys. Vernon and Prentiss kept asking, "What'd he do that for?" As if we knew something they didn't know. We agreed that he had taken them as a sort of lesson against a life of crime.

Later, when we were grown, and the exposure to the man who was Grandpa Bunt was complete, we knew that we had been wrong. We came to know him as a man who opposed violence in any form and for any reason, no matter the justification or provocation. More likely he was saying, "The world is this way but it should not be." He was too gentle a man to have said otherwise.

He was no stranger to either tragedy or violence. In his middle twenties he had buried his entire family of children within a two week period. Little Sophia died. Then Myrtis a few days later. And finally Claudie. Bleeding Flux they had called it, an intestinal disorder which could be cured today with one injection. But one by one his children had died of it until they were all gone. He would describe to us the building of the boxes in which they were buried, how, on each occasion, he insisted upon being the one who would lift the tiny coffin to his own shoulder and carry it the hundred yards from the wagon to where it was to be planted. It was his sorrow, his burden, grievous to be borne. He knew, and passed on to us, that some journeys had to be made alone.

Like the day he died. Near ninety, he had been bedridden for weeks. That very afternoon he had said to all of us gathered, "Y'all have chairs." It was his usual greeting when anyone entered his house. As we were leaving he had asked his lastborn son, our Daddy, not to leave him. But in a few hours he said to him, "Well, Son, you have gone as far as you can go." And the son knew that he was free to leave and did not hesitate nor feel guilty in leaving. In less than an hour Grandpa Bunt was dead.

But as four little boys sat on the cottonseed out of the rain, that day was far in the future. Grandpa would live to see all of us grown, and both Vernon and Prentiss would die before he did. We were just trying to figure out why he took young boys, some of whom were no older than we, to see a man die. We did it in the form of "Remember the time Grandpa . . ." anecdotes.

There were the times he told us of the violence of the Civil War. His first vivid recollection was seeing his daddy in a wooden box, placed in the doorway where the cool air would slow the decomposition of the body until the circuit-riding preacher got there to bury him. His daddy had run away from the Confederate Army at Shiloh because he was sick. Grandpa reported it with neither rancor nor judgment. And with no visible pride that his father had been a Confederate soldier. And such feeling as we had regarding the outcome of a nation divided we got elsewhere, never from him. He was not the Southerner one reads about in books.

It was, in fact, from him that we learned for sure that the war was over and done with. A dozen or more of us were playing on his stomp and had hollered at a black man who was walking down the road.

"Hey, nigger. Hey nigger." The man, John Walker, had recently been beaten by some men for stealing a sack of roasting ear corn. We had heard older boys laughing at the way he told about it.

"Yessuh. Dey got me nekked as a jaybird. Took a gin belt to me. Whipped me 'til I almost shat." We saw no harm in the taunting.

But Grandpa did. Yet he did not scold. Instead he called us all around him. Sitting on a huge tree stump he explained that there were no more niggers.

"Yessir, Grandpa. There's still niggers. We just saw one go down the road. John Walker's a nigger. We saw him."

"No, hon. There ain't any more niggers. All the niggers are dead. All that's left now is colored people."

He knew how to tell a group of his grandchildren in rural Mississippi that the Civil War was over. And some of us never forgot it.

Eventually we tired of telling Grandpa stories and trying to figure out his reason for doing what he did, and turned to other things. Vernon and Prentiss had recovered from the fright of seeing Allen Westbrook hang and no longer wanted to go home. The rain had stopped and Joe began insisting again that he could fly. He wanted to bet us a dime that he could fly from the highest peak on the barn to the ground. None of us had a dime so all of us took the bet. Then he said, "Now I didn't say *how* I was going to do it."

We didn't know what he meant by that, but however he could get from the top of the barn to the ground without climbing down we would accept as flying and we helped him carry out his scheme.

A half-inch cable had been left at the house by someone and Joe went and got it. He also had with him when he returned a pulley from a well windlass and a short piece of rope. By now we were beginning to understand how he was going to fly but continued to do his bidding. The cable was more than a hundred feet long. He climbed back to the top of the barn and fastened the cable to the top rafter under the overhang, letting it drop to the ground. Next he stretched it as far as it would go away from the barn, the slant of the cable forming about a forty-five degree angle with the ground. The pulley was placed on the cable and the cable was then secured to a heavy iron stake driven in the ground. A short piece of rope to hold onto was tied to the pulley. Then there was the problem of how to get the pulley from the ground end of the cable to the starting place at the gable of the barn. This was accomplished by tying two plowlines together and pulling the pulley up the cable after he climbed to the top of the barn.

After the hour of preparation, the flight was about to begin. But first he decided to have a test flight with a burlap sack filled with cottonseeds to see just how fast the pulley would come down the cable. From his perch at the top of the barn he pulled the sack up to him, then released it. The sack came down with such speed and such force that it split open when it hit the ground, scattering cottonseed all over the barn lot. The rest of us joked and laughed about how Joe's seeds were going to be scattered when he came down just like the seeds from the sack. But he had bet us he could fly and it was obvious that he intended to do it, scattered seeds or not. First the iron stake had to be driven deeper into the ground so that he wouldn't hit it for he said that was what had busted the sack. Then he determined at what point his feet would first touch the ground as he approached the end of the cable from the top of the barn. He said if he hit the ground running, and let go of his grip on the pulley rope there would be no sudden stop and he could make it.

Back at the top of the barn he pretended to be Allen Westbrook.

"If I had listened to my mamma I wouldn't be here today. You boys always listen to your mammas and you won't ever be in any trouble."

And then, imagining, I suppose, that he was seeing what he had imagined Allen Westbrook saw from the gallows, he spoke again as he took his grip on the pulley rope, speaking in a shout. "I can see all over the world from up here. I can see everything in the world. I can see Mr. Scott Nunnery's store and all the way to Uncle Bill's house. I can see to East Fork! *I can see all over the world!*" Then with a wild scream he kicked his body away from the roof of the barn and in not more than two seconds the pulley brought him down the cable to the ground. Rolling over several times as the force of the flight continued to carry him forward, he bounced quickly to his feet and bowed politely to each of us, holding his hand outstretched for the dimes he knew did not exist.

"I told you I could fly!"

Joe loved those woods, those two sections of land lying to the south of our place which we called the Moore Pasture. It was really not a pasture at all, but cut-over timber land. It belonged to the Crosby Lumber Company and in exchange for our fighting their forest fires, fires which invariably came on the windiest days of March, they let us graze our cattle there. Years earlier a man named Delton Moore had surveyed and fenced this land, sealing it off forever from the older settlers who had homesteaded the Territory of Mississippi, heirs now only to the knowledge that they had once owned it. Resentful of this, perhaps, they refused to call the land by the company name, preferring the name of the surveyor who served as buffer between them and the timber barons.

Joe and I often talked about what that forest must have looked like before the dummyline came. Once the teacher read to us some lines beginning

> This is the forest primeval, where the murmuring pines
> and the hemlock . . .

and Joe looked at me and smiled. And I knew what he was thinking. Knowing, it became my thought too. That's it. That's what the Moore Pasture looked like before the dummyline came. That is what that man was talking about.

The dummyline was a railroad spur, joining with the Illinois Central Railroad, but built and owned by the lumber company which had somehow come to own the timber rights to thousands of acres of land. And later, the land itself.

Long before the assassination of some European archduke—unknown and unheard of by those heirs around the Moore Pasture—had started the First World War, the powers and principalities of

American commerce knew somehow that there would soon be reason for great stockpiles of lumber. The southernmost part of the country was a good place to begin. The resource was there, the labor was cheap and plentiful and the climate made it a year-round enterprise. And so the dummylines came. Not just to these woods but everywhere around. The operation of the dummyline was more memorable than the felling of the trees and so it was remembered and talked of longer.

Older people, our daddy among them, told us what the forest had looked like before the trees became pieces of ship decks, bulkheads, barracks at Fort Dix and Camp Shelby, gun emplacements at Belleau Wood and Chateau-Thierry, Liberty Bond platforms for Douglas Fairbanks. But by the time we were born they were all gone and we could only imagine. We knew that the trees were big, some so big that two men could not reach around them. We had supposed that they were all the same size and we supposed that they stood in rows like crops in a field. Virgin timber. That's what the old folks called it. "Ain't no more virgin timber in this country. It's all gone." Heart pines with needles eighteen inches long. Longleaf pine trees. Now they were all gone, cut down by big smelly black men with crosscut saws and broadaxes, supervised by white men with different smells who pulled them from their stumps with ox teams and loaded them on flatcars of the dummyline.

Grandpa Bunt remembered well what it had been like. As we covered every acre on foot or on horseback in the late afternoons looking for our milkcows, he would point out where the camps had been, two little temporary towns, one for white and one for colored, rows of shacks which housed the workers and their families during the two or three years it took to cut everything standing to the ground.

Grandpa was a tall, lean man. Yet we thought of him as big. He was an unsoiled man in body and mind, toadied to no one and spoke harshly of no one. We thought he looked like the picture on the Prince Albert cans from which he chewed tobacco. No one else chewed Prince Albert tobacco. That was smoking tobacco to everyone except Grandpa. As we tramped the woods, always at a leisurely pace, listening for the cowbell, he talked. And Joe and I listened and agreed.

"You know, hon, we always pick the cow to put the bell on with great consideration of her character. All the other cows follow the one with the bell. So we never pick a fence breaker or a fighter. She's the leader. The bellcow is always the leader."

And we knew what he was telling us, knew that he was saying that if we couldn't become leaders we would have no choice but to follow someone else's bell.

His voice was matter of fact as he talked of the dummyline, and he always pointed out whatever value in it he could find. He had had the contract for removing the manure from the ox pens. And with the tons of ox dung he had fertilized ten acres of corn, making more in one year than he had previously made in three. Yet we knew that he knew something wasn't right.

Only vestiges of the big trees remained, nothing alive. Pineknots, those whorled, hard as concrete pieces of roots and limbs, flammable as turpentine, could be found everywhere upon the ground. Pile them around a wash pot for a roaring fire to boil clothes on washday. Or around the rendering pot on hog-killing day. Fires not as hot as oak or hickory but quick-burning, throwing flames high and evenly around the pot to boil the water in a hurry, water to throw the hogs into so that the hair could be scraped off with butcher knives. Because these pineknots were still plentiful, some folks used them in fireplaces to heat their houses or in cookstoves. But this was considered trashy, something niggers did. Proper people used hardwood for burning, using the fat "liadard" only as kindling to start and keep it going.

Later, in our own time, a military use was discovered for these remnants the dummyline had left. Pineknots were piled and hauled away. Stumps and even taproots were dynamited and pushed and pulled from the ground by the Hattiesburg Hercules Company when naval stores were in the same demand, as Pearl Harbor approached, as the original timber had been in the first great war. But by now the Tennessee Valley Authority had given us electricity for heat and light, so we helped load the wagons and pickups and bobtail trucks without hesitation or twinge of nostalgia. Loss of virginity is but one step from debauchery.

While the dummyline was in operation a huge pond had been dug in the middle of the forest to supply water for the ox teams and the steam engines. It had remained for a while after the lumber company had moved on. Then one night someone dynamited the levee and with a net caught all the big catfish and lamprey eels, leaving the smaller ones, and the perch, the turtles, the minnows, to die as the water soaked into the ground below the levee.

It was to the old pond area, now growing the unvirgin slash and loblolly pines which grew faster and soon shaded out any issue the few remaining longleaf trees brought forth, that Joe and I were going. It was a cool day in the fall and a cousin from New Orleans was visiting us. Joe said I was not to tell him where we were going. He was in his early teens—several years older than either of us. I went, not because I did not want to be with the cousin, but because Joe said it was time for me to go. He had with him a little rope halter he had made from a worn-out plow line. As we walked along he began to say words I knew only as ugly words, words used by older boys when talking about girls. One of the words had once been written by a girl on the inside of my notebook but as soon as I had seen it she quickly jerked it away and tore it to shreds. And once Grandpa Bunt had made us remove a big Vicks Vap-O-Rub sign from the side of his barn because someone had scrawled that same word onto the metal sign with a pocket knife.

Joe explained what we were going to do and I was scared. But he instructed and assured me. He stationed me on the side of the old levee and said for me to wait there, that he would be back directly. I had not known this feeling before, this willingness and unwillingness, hesitation and eagerness, prurient steam extending and expanding tiny veins and tissues, lust and passion not even words yet. I was only imagining what we were about. But he returned, as he had promised, leading a gentle and pubescent bovine, and suddenly I knew it all. He turned his head away from where I stood, whistling, humming and then mumbling words of a tune, casual and discreet, leaving me to cumbrous instinct.

Going into the forest I had been as the forest itself had been when the dummyline came. And leaving now as the forest had been left when the dummyline was gone. Joe said not to worry about it. And not to tell anyone. I suppose we had read Leviticus 20, but never mind. We never discussed it.

It was not the last time we would go together into those woods. And for many purposes. We were both beginning to feel the pressures of the world and the Moore Pasture was our retreat. It was the middle of the great depression and Joe and I knew something wasn't right. Daddy had accepted a W.P.A. job but the rigidity and the discipline of it was more than he could take. He had never had someone tell him when to pick up a shovel before, when to put it down, which rock to move, when to begin, when to quit. When the rural poor, like the reservation Indians before them, were poured into a mold not of their own doing, one which made no sense except to foreman and timekeeper, they failed—and were known thereafter as lazy, shiftless, no-initiative "rednecks." For whatever reason, Daddy failed, quit, or was fired.

That left no alternative but direct relief, handouts, welfare. It was something he had tried to avoid. He was a proud man, a man who was no stranger to hard work, and had never been without resources before. Now, in addition to being poor, he was sick. Dr. Quin found a heart murmur and told him not to work. So he did what many did during those years—he asked his government for help.

The system required one to go before a board and "sign up," a process which required the revealing of things of a financial nature which earlier would have been considered so personal that they would not have been shared with closest friends. All property and all personal belongings had to be listed.

Daddy had a gold watch, a railroad watch, twenty-one jeweled Illinois timepiece, symbol of manhood and symbol of status. It must be sold. A gold watch might be enough to disqualify one for assistance. The system, like all systems, was inefficient, senseless, and began at the wrong end of need. Before one was eligible for cash vouchers, little slips of paper which could be used as money to purchase necessities and staples we could not produce, he had to accept commodities they offered—little pieces of fatback while we had whole sides of bacon, hams and link sausage hanging in the smokehouse all year; powdered milk, with three cows milking every day; dried beans, with bushels of them already stored in the barn; and grapefruit. Lots of grapefruit. We had never seen it before, it was bitter and we didn't eat it. But all those things had to be accepted if one expected to get the needed money. So we accepted it, made jokes about it, threw it away or gave it to someone else who had even less than we.

Because Daddy was sick, Joe ran the farm. He was eleven years old, and all of us helped, but he was the leader, plowing, planting, cultivating, harvesting.

For one year we had a wage hand, Leon, a twelve-year-old Negro boy, big for his age. Larger farmers had tenants and sharecroppers. A wage hand was someone who worked for pay but got no proceeds from what was produced. His daddy let him work for us for five dollars a month and we paid his daddy, not him. Generally the pay was in the form of produce—meat, butter, potatoes, eggs. He slept in the smokehouse on an old cot and in the hottest summertime would wrap himself up head to toe in quilts, hiding perhaps, knowing and not knowing that he was a slave, rented, not bought. For five dollars a month. Mostly, Leon and we worked together. But at other times we fought, played, dropped knives, had pet sayings to each other like, "Ain't it a bitch!" and pet names for each other like "Brother Mother." Joe, from time to time, as overseer and master, decided that Leon must be whipped and saw it as his responsibility to administer the punishment. But Leon was seldom the resigned chattel and this effort most often led to a fight between the two of them.

And sometimes Joe would let him go to the Moore Pasture with us to walk and dream and talk about what we would be someday far off. Joe wanted to be a writer and would spend hours outlining for us the stories of his books. I had the intent of becoming an actor; we had seen the senior plays the high school did and we had read of professional theater in books and Joe said he would write plays for me. Leon wanted to move to McComb and have his own shoeshine stand in the McColgan Hotel. None of us became what we intended but it mattered little at the time.

We had no friends, only cousins, who were, of course, friends as well. But we did not think of them as friends. Cousins. Aunt Clara was mother to eight of them, all of whom we liked and loved.

She had been left a widow with two daughters and six boys when Daddy's oldest brother, Uncle Jessie, was shot in the leg by a deranged country storekeeper. He was actually the best friend the old man had. His fields were near the store and several times a day he would stop and visit—a drink of water, some smoking tobacco, any excuse at all. Some of the neighbors found it sporting to report things Uncle Jessie was alleged to have said of the old man, watching him go into an incoherent fit of rage, his mental condition making it impossible for him to know what they were doing. One afternoon when Uncle Jessie jumped up onto the store porch, Mr. Mitchell stood ready on the inside with his loaded pistol. Uncle Jessie survived for a few weeks, but gangrene in the injured leg took his life.

Uncle Jessie should have lived and we should have known him. But he didn't and we didn't. I was two and Joe was four when he died. But we knew his widow and loved his children, in many ways the most remarkable of all our kin.

Hubert, the eldest, secretly married May Dee Cleveland, the storekeeper at East Fork who died of leukemia.

William, called Sorghum, married to Frankie Barron, no children, logger and farmer.

John, the one who cut our hair with hand clippers, married to Kathleen Hutchinson, Mississippi State Trooper, now retired.

And Robert Lee, renamed Tunney, perhaps after the fighter, though he was the most passive of us all, very intelligent, killed while flying a bomber over Germany.

Ross, known as "Munch," later as Benny, closest to Joe, tough, often defended me against hostile cousins, experienced months of combat hell in World War II, lives in his mother's house, bearing the unseen scars of war without murmur or complaint.

Delton Reed, called Peter, baby of them all, playmate, classmate, buddy. Father of five boys, singer, could laugh louder than anyone in school, now farmer and factory foreman.

Reba, firstborn daughter, married to Lamb McElveen who lost his hearing in World War I.

And Mary, other daughter, gentle and understanding, kind to us all, married to Jamie Brumfield.

And all of them, excepting Robert Lee who lies buried in England, live in the same county. Something about Aunt Clara, and one another, kept them close. Now Aunt Clara is dead. But it is too late for them to scatter now. They will remain. Uncle Jessie planted them well. Uncle Jessie. A man of great courage. A man who walked out of the churchhouse one night when the Ku Klux Klan came in and presented a pulpit Bible and some money to the congregation. Only a brave and strong man would walk out on the Ku Klux Klan in 1925.

Sometimes his boys, or some of them, were with Joe and me in the Moore Pasture. They were with us the day Joe taught us about community organizing and how we could protest against Federal encroachments. Some others were with us too.

For years we had a place at school called "down the hill." It was a grove of trees a few hundred yards behind the school house where we went at recess time for toilet purposes. There were no plumbing facilities in the building and not even an outhouse nearby. So we used the woods, each little clique having their own favorite place which the members would use and guard with fervor and dedication against any who dared threaten their territorial rights. But a W.P.A. project had recently built a "facility" for our use and we were told never to relieve ourselves outside that structure again because, it was carefully explained, such a practice led to the spread of the dread hookworms.

We saw this as oppressive in itself, but the day a technician from the State Health Department visited the school with a program to detect who among us already had hookworms we were morally outraged. All the girls were marched into the study hall first. Then the boys. The study hall, a large room with dozens of handmade tables, slanting downward on either side from the middle, with benches to seat five pupils on each side of the table, served as assembly hall, and could accommodate the entire enrollment at one time. Bob Stuart, a stocky little man with red face and hair, and a head that looked like a pink volleyball, who saw himself as a strict disciplinarian, was the principal. When we were all seated, all of us hurrying and scampering to make sure we were seated in our own little grouping, for we knew something exciting was about to take place, he introduced our guest and told us all to pay close attention, that what we were about to hear was very important.

First the man explained that he was operating with a grant from Washington. This, we supposed, to indicate the magnitude of what he was about to say. He said the purpose of the grant was to rid our community of hookworms, adding that the South was backward, not so much because of the Civil War, but because of malaria and hookworms. (We had not known until then that we were backward and therefore had not pondered the possible reasons for our backwardness.) He passed out a mimeographed, one-sheet set of instructions, rolled around a small tin can looking then like a snuff can and looking now like a container for filmstrips. Total silence was required for five minutes while we read what it was we were expected to do.

"Are there any questions?"

There were no immediate questions because no one understood enough of what he had read to evoke a question.

Now the principal spoke. "Now if any of you have any questions you had better ask them now because every last one of these specimen cans must be returned tomorrow."

This did elicit a question and one of the high school boys asked it for us all.

"What is a specimen?"

"A specimen is . . ." The principal glanced at the visitor who appeared relieved that the question was not directed to him. Mr. Stuart continued.

"A specimen is . . . a specimen is a small amount of something."

Now we knew how much but we didn't yet know how much of what. The instruction sheet had said to place a specimen of feces in the container, write our full name and the names of both our parents on the label, and return it to school the following day. But "feces" was no more a word of our vocabulary than "specimen."

Gradually it began to dawn on us in the form of a very vague notion that the entire operation had to do with what we called "taking a crap." But it had not yet come into clear focus for any of us. And did not during the whispering and mumbling that was going on throughout the hall, not until one of the smaller boys, thinking that he was speaking softly enough so that he would not be heard by anyone except himself, said, "I know. He's telling us to go home and shit in a snuff can."

What he said was heard by those immediately surrounding him. They in turn shared it with others and in not more than a minute howls and uncontrollable laughter had spread over the auditorium like the fires that came to the Moore Pasture in early spring. More than a hundred boys, ranging in age from six to eighteen, were guffawing, snickering, shrieking, hollering, roaring as one.

The embarrassed representative of the State Health Department stood glowering at the principal, arms folded tightly across his chest. The rage of the principal was so obvious to us that the noise subsided as quickly as it had begun. Now the hall was a sea of compelled silence, all the boys sitting with teeth clenched, lips drawn tightly together to hold the thundering mirth churning and tearing at our insides, bellies almost bursting from our efforts to control muscles which would not be controlled. And when the principal, seeing that the tortuous restraint would not hold for long, said, "That's all," every voice exploded and there was pandemonium. School was out.

Now we were far back in the Moore Pasture woods, laughed out, not finding any of it funny anymore.

All of us resented the idea that the government had the right to know what our "feces" looked like. And we found no humor in this demeaning act of having to bring ourselves to such close contact with our body waste. Still we knew that it must be done.

But Joe, lagging behind the rest of us, reading again the instruction sheet, found a means of protest.

"It says, 'place *a* specimen of feces' in the container. It doesn't say, 'Place a specimen of *your* feces' in the container." The creative dissenter was right. Of course! One boy could provide the specimen for us all.

But which one? Joe said since it was his idea he should be excepted and asked for a volunteer, looking straight at me in a manner that told me I should not offer. When no one volunteered he suggested that we say, "eeny, meeny, miney, moe. Catch a nigger by the toe. If he hollers, make him pay, fifty dollars every day." Joe had earlier shared with me the method he had of making that come out wherever he wanted it to. There were many combinations but by first counting the number of persons and starting the rhyme with the person on his immediate left, he knew in advance which one would be chosen.

As is so often the case with social protest and community organizing there was a problem we had not reckoned with. When the laboratory report was returned we learned that our common donor *had* hookworms, meaning we *all* had hookworms and all of us were required to undergo the treatment or confess to our misdeed. We chose to swallow the pills, big pills, almost the size of bird eggs.

Joe, who was later to become a scientist himself, raised a question about the scientific method which had not occurred to me. He wondered why the researcher did not find it strange that while *all* the Campbell boys had hookworms, not *one* Campbell girl was found to be similarly infested.

There would be other times when we would go to those woods to discuss and dissent and take counsel together. In addition to building us an outdoor john, the W.P.A. had also built us a lunchroom. For four cents one could buy a hot lunch each day. That excluded us, for sixteen cents a day amounted to three dollars and twenty cents a month, more than we had. Another category allowed parents to exchange produce for their children's meals. Corn meal, hams, eggs, or whatever the lunchroom listed as being acceptable. This did not carry the status that paying cash did, but it was not seen as disgrace. We could have arranged for the exchange but the rules of the system said that those on direct relief must be given their lunches free. That was the unhappy category in which we found ourselves.

The embarrassment was intensified by the manner in which Mrs. Myrtis Cruise, the manager of the lunchroom and other New Deal programs, took the head count of those to be served. Each day she began by asking all those who were buying their lunch to raise their hands. These were eager to be counted and continued to hold their hands outstretched long after she had passed them and moved on to the next row. Those in the produce class were not quite so anxious but offered no resistance. And she appeared to count them with pride. But when she announced finally, voice saccharine and patronizing, "And now, all the little relief children, hold up your hands," the thought of Evie Lee McKnight, the prettiest fourth grade girl in the world, object of my dreams and fantasies, seeing me acknowledge that I was a relief child was almost more than I could bear. I would sit with my hand in my lap, watching from the corner of my eyes exactly which row the count was on and waiting until she was but one person removed from me before quickly, but only partially, indicating with one finger that I was among those to be counted.

Joe felt that I was imagining the problem to be bigger than it actually was but offered a suggestion anyway. The fifth grade met with the fourth. So we were in the same room. He said he had noticed that Miss Myrtis always came to take the count when his grade was having geography lesson. His suggestion was that I ask to be excused to go "down the hill" just as they were beginning that lesson and that I could wait in the W.P.A. john until she had made her rounds. For the first few days he would glance across the room and nod to me when he felt it was time for me to go.

This worked, but the mystery of the john and my imagination as to its construction led to a situation even more troubling than being counted as a relief child. There being no plumbing, the twenty-hole outhouse was built over a rectangular trench dug in the side of the hill. With no light it was impossible to see the bottom of it and I wondered what kept the frame structure from simply falling into the hole. On this day, as I waited, I decided to find out. Generally there would be a dozen or more boys there, for it was the social gathering place as well as toilet. But for once I was the only one there. Older boys went there to smoke, though it was against the rules, and I found a kitchen match and a piece of newspaper, a necessity since tissue was not furnished. With these items I would explore the abyss beneath me and know what no one else knew. I had not considered the fact that there would be layer upon layer of used paper at the bottom of the pit. Suddenly I realized that the paper I had lighted was sharing its fire with other pieces of newspaper, leaves—also used for such hygienic purposes—and notebook sheets. The thought of being known as the one who burned the W.P.A. john to the ground overshadowed the humiliation of being on relief.

Back at my desk I was near panic. I looked at Joe and he smiled, indicating that I had missed the headcount. But he didn't know that now I had a more serious problem. As we sat there the pride of Bob Stuart, the twenty-hole W.P.A. john, was burning to the ground. By raising one's hand and saying, "May I speak?" a student could get permission to go and talk briefly with another. I considered doing that and telling Joe what had happened but decided that it was too risky. I might be overheard. And the teacher sometimes exercised her right to ask the person spoken to what they had talked about for it was supposed to have to do with school matters. The only view of the area was from a window beside the pencil sharpener. Permission did not have to be asked to sharpen a pencil. I took all the time I could, breaking the point and starting again. I could see no smoke, no fire. Well, it was too soon. The paper fire had not yet reached the upper portion of the structure. Or maybe it had been discovered and extinguished. No! In that case they would already be looking for me. Justice would have to be done whether it burned down or not. I returned to the pencil sharpener several more times until the teacher, Miss Fiveashe, a woman with square build who had short hair, wore nothing but skirt-suits and looked like a man, called out, "Having trouble with your pencil, Dave?" Maybe she knew already and this was just a stall until the principal came to take me away. I was certain that my life was ruined and made a lot of promises to the Lord about all the deadly and secret sins that possessed me if He would spare me.

When the bell rang for recess I did not go in the direction of "down the hill." That might look suspicious. I remained inside the building and talked with the teacher about some bit of trivia. It was not until the end of the day and Joe and I were far back in the woods that I told him what I had done and asked him if he had been there during the afternoon recess. He assured me that my fears were unfounded, thought it was funny and said that he wished it had burned on down. The enforcement of its use was considered by him to be further interference in our business, further repression. He didn't like the stuffy and cramped conditions, and having to stand in line just to pee. It didn't make any sense. But none of his words, words meant to relieve my anxiety, were taken as encouragement for me to return and complete the act of arson.

Joe loved those woods and used to tell me that one day, when he had written enough books, he would own them. And I always understood that when he owned them I would own them too. He would seek out the smooth barked beech trees, no matter what size, and with his knife carve both our initials on them. He kept count of how many times he had done that and said that by the time we were grown he wanted our initials on every beech tree there. He thought the tiny carved initials would grow with the tree and when the trees were big the letters would be a bold proclamation to the world that they belonged to us.

Sometimes it would take a long time to cut through the tough bark with J.L.C. and W.D.C., and it was while he was about this one day that I told him I was going to join the Church. I was seven years old and had not been baptized. Joe had joined a few months earlier, the night Mr. Claude Cruise, husband of Miss Myrtis, had come stumbling into the churchhouse crying that his house was on fire. It was at the very time the preacher was telling of the horrors of eternity in a burning hell.

He advised me to wait another year or so, explaining that while he knew I understood what it was all about, there might be some who would laugh, feeling that I was too young. But he said no more to dissuade me, adding that if I really wanted to do it he would sit beside me that night so that I would not be afraid when it came time to go down the aisle during the invitation hymn. He explained what the preacher would whisper to me. He said, "Brother Hunt will ask you if you repent of all your sins and want to follow Jesus in baptism." He instructed me to say yes. Someone would then make a motion that I be received into full fellowship and receive the right hand of Christian fellowship. That made me a candidate for baptism if the vote was favorable which, he said, it always was.

On the appointed night Joe sat beside me on the third bench from the front. He said if we were further back, where boys our age generally sat, it would be harder to do. On the first word of the invitational hymn Joe nudged me and I moved quietly and quickly past him and down the aisle. With Joe as catechist I had no trouble fielding the questions. Yes, I repented of all my sins, intended to lead a new life, and desired to follow Jesus in baptism.

Because my conversion came in early spring there would be a waiting period before I could be baptized. This was done only during the summer months when the river was warm. The waiting period gave us time to order new clothes, white linen pants and white shirt, from the Sears Roebuck catalog. Almost always when an order was placed in the mail on Monday it would return by Friday. But my size was not available and there was an exchange of correspondence about the order. It was to be the first test of my vow to lead a new life. As the baptismal Sunday approached and the new clothes had not come I became more and more impatient. And when they did not come on Saturday it was obvious that I would have to be baptized in clothes from the previous summer, and I exploded.

"I *hate* Sears Roebuck!"

Joe explained that he knew how I felt but that since hating was a sin and I was the one to be baptized I should try not to get mad. He agreed that we had been done a grievous wrong but said that he would hate them for me.

So on a Sunday morning in June of 1931, with the congregation gathered on the bank singing,

Happy day. Happy day,
When Jesus washed my sins away . . .

I waded into the crystal clear waters of the east fork of the Amite River, capsule of piety. Joe stood on the bank, off to the side of the rest of the group as he usually was, sulking and seething at Sears Roebuck, a propitiation for my sins, vicariously taking the rap as the preacher told us in the sermon Jesus had done for us all.

That afternoon, in the Moore Pasture, he told me that he was proud of me.

By role, designation, category and assignment Joe was the worker. I was the sickly one and therefore something of a drone. Sister was just that—Sister. Daughter with three brothers and thus special. Paul was the baby. We lived that way and if those categories and designations and roles seemed unfair to any of us we never discussed it. That's who each one was. One did not ponder identity. Everyone knew and understood, without being told. Without asking questions. *This* is who I am. *That* is who you are. The question, "Who am I?" need not, and did not, come up. That's the way we lived.

I think Joe was just under four years old when we moved from the "Old Place." The "Old Place" was a few hundred yards up the road from where we were all raised to leaving-home age. Daddy and Mamma had moved there about a year after they were married—he at nineteen, she at seventeen. They lived the first year in the house with Grandpa Bunt and Grandma Bettye. Then Grandpa gave him forty acres of land and he bought about that much more. It was our place from then on. That's where we lived and worked and did everything that families do except go to Church and school and occasionally visit kinfolks.

We had to move from the "Old Place" because it didn't have a well. They tried, more than once, but there didn't seem to be any water beneath the ground. They carried water, two buckets at a time, from Grandpa's house. I just remember the stories—Sister and Joe crying for a drink of water, Mamma finding Sister drinking out of a small washpan where all three of us had just been bathed, and catching rain water dripping from the eaves of the house.

It would be some years before it occurred to our father that we were poor. He could go to his backyard and draw up a bucket of water from a sixty-five-foot-deep well whenever he pleased or the need arose. That was a luxury. One with luxuries is not poor.

It was only when the depression came that we discovered we were, in fact, poor people. We were not destitute, not with cured hams and sides of bacon hanging in the smokehouse all year, chickens to lay eggs and to eat, cows to give us milk and butter, fields in which to grow food. Country people were not impoverished. They were simply poor.

Those neighbors and uncles around us were not quite so poor because they had been in the War. And because veterans were eligible for a small pension if they had been disabled by their service experience. The way Dr. Quin saw it, everyone who had to leave home and family and go to war had been disabled by it. So he was the county's biggest industry. It was he who must do the examination and report to the government his findings. He always found something to report. So every man who had spent any time at all in World War I received a pension.

For that, and other reasons, Dr. Quin was well thought of. He looked and smelled like a doctor was supposed to look and smell. Slight of build, short cropped mustache, small twitching eyes, the air of chloroform and mercurochrome, which he called "monkey blood," following him wherever he went. He gave us chewing gum, which he called "touloo," and little wooden boxes that hypodermic syringes came in with tops that slide on and off on a groove.

Our poverty became a reality. Not because of our having less, but by our neighbors having more. For our daddy was not a veteran.

I suppose, in the beginning, it would not have occurred to us that we were poor because we saw our mother dole out our rags to another woman from time to time. We had heard the story, just whispers here and there, of why the black man shot her husband and what had happened to him after he did it. For some reason the white man's wound never healed and there was an open drain in his side. We later learned that, by our standards at the time, they were rich. But still they needed something we had, our rags. So every few weeks for years the woman would stop at our house and before she left Mamma gave her a paper sack filled with worn-out sheets and pillow cases, tattered underwear, shirts and blouses too far gone to patch. Though she came in an automobile, something we didn't have, we knew the story of the rich man and Lazarus, and assumed that we were the Dives of the story. We were giving her rags and that meant something.

I do not recall our being unhappy as children. And I do not recall our being happy. A family of six, living on a small cotton farm during the depression, growing no more than five or six bales of cotton a year which sold for a few cents a pound, did not think in those terms. Even married couples did not think in those terms. Happiness was not something promised. Happiness was not a part of the contract. If it came, we experienced it without naming it. If it didn't, we couldn't complain, not aware that we were due it or that it even existed. No one ever said, "I'm not happy living with you so I'm leaving."

Sister: Only daughter and firstborn. There was always partiality to the oldest child. If that child was a girl that was an added reason. And if only daughter there was never the slightest question about it. If that were the way things were supposed to be and we grew up knowing that was the way things were supposed to be, what harm could come to the psyche?

She was named Lorraine. But we could no more have called her "Lorraine" than we could have called her "Henry." She was *Sister.* She grew up in the fields with the rest of us. Daddy once brought her a little red rocking chair. She rocked Joe in her little red rocker, and sang to him and told him stories about times "Before me and Mamma and Daddy married." And she rocked me, and Paul called her "Mamma" for the first years of his life. She was destined to be the one, the only one, to remain near the old home place to look after our parents in their old age, and her own large family as well.

Sister was that—Sister. Oldest. And thus special.

Paul Edward: Joe called him "Bunyon" at an early age. He was the baby. Because of a mild polio attack at an early age his left shoulder never developed. He was, however, strong. And feisty. He could whip any of us in a fight, and often did. Still he was called afflicted, especially by Mamma, and was exempt from much field work because of his affliction.

His temper sometimes brought further exemption. Tease him in the field to the point of anger and he was free to throw down his hoe or cottonsack and go to the house. If we complained that his leaving made additional work for us we were told that we should have left him alone.

We were picking cotton far back in the field we called the "old flat." Sister, Joe and I would break into shrieks of laughter each time he came near because he smelled bad.

"Bunyon. You stink!"

When he had had enough of that he left his sack in the middle of a long row and went home. We knew he wouldn't be back so we finished the row.

The next morning he smelled no better. "Bunyon stinks! Bunyon, you stink!" We blamed it on everything from his breath to his feet. But again it was soon enough to send him screaming home, heart broken but with the reward of not having to come back.

The third morning the smell was even worse. We no longer found it funny. Joe decided to give him a summary examination to learn the source of the offense. Bunyon was not at all in agreement with that notion and resisted by grabbing the water bucket, an eight-pound lard can, and swinging it round and round whacked Joe with all the force he could muster. Getting hit with the water bucket would normally have been no more than token defense, a gesture, having no bearing at all on the outcome of the encounter. But Joe fell to the ground, screaming and with convulsion-like movements. We were both baffled and scared by his outcry and gathered around to see the extent of the injury. As Joe quieted down he carefully unbuttoned the side of his bib overalls, exposing a sickening sight.

Summer boils, risins we called them, were common to us all. They probably resulted from a poor diet but we blamed blackberries, tomatoes, or the acid in wild plums. A big one, deserving of the name carbuncle, had plagued Joe for weeks. Usually when they came to a "head" they would be gently squeezed, or punctured slightly with a needle, sterilized by a flaming kitchen match, and the core would pop out and healing could begin. But Joe's was a more stubborn case. The squeezing and puncturing didn't work and every day it got a little bigger until it was nearly the size of a lemon. And about the color. The well-landed and well-directed water bucket had accomplished what other forms of coaxing and persuasion had not. Joe's boil had been well-popped for sure. The hard ball of pus, hard as green apple, was hanging out of its nest by yellow and red strings of corruption. The hole it had left in the skin was a nasty sight but the pressure it had relieved made Joe quick to forgive.

Paul, stunned and remorseful, glad that his violent deed had resulted in some good, now offered to submit quietly to the proposed examination. Joe was gentle and thorough. At first not touching, walking instead round and round Paul as he stood erect in the middle of the steaming cotton field, moving in, now closer, quieter, sniffing the breath, his hair and ears. Bending for a second time, subtle and polite, in the direction of the rear end. Running one finger between the big and index toe, backing away with no hint of verdict, looking him over as if he were about to make some monetary bid on his person. Without a word spoken he moved now to the actual search. Back pockets first. Then front. Nothing there. As he unbuttoned the small pocket in the bib of the overalls his glance at us told us the truth was about to be revealed. Reaching the thumb and index finger into the pocket he pulled something out and quickly threw it to the ground. He stepped back and pointed at it, bowing low as he stepped.

"Aw heck. I remember. The other day when I went to the house to get some water I caught a lizard and was going to make a pet out of it." The lizard had been dead for five days. There was a lot of laughter all around, Paul joining in. He was accepted back, recess was over and the cotton picking resumed. And for the rest of the day four Campbell children—Lorraine, Joseph Lee, Will Davis, Paul Edward were a community.

Paul was the baby. The only one who would have an identifiable adolescence—coming home drinking a few times, stealing the big number seven school bell and dropping it into the Amite River, staying out late at night, things that adolescent boys do but Joe and I didn't. Mamma would stop the boozing by pouring his bottle of liquor down the drain. And she learned how to bring him home on time by tying a string across the door, the other end looped to a bucket of water on the ledge above, so that when he came in she would be awakened by the crash of the bucket and the splash of water. And the school pranks were soon cured by the patience and wisdom of a country school principal.

And he was the one who dropped out of school after the eleventh grade to work at Camp Van Dorn, a temporary army base during World War II named for a Confederate general who was defeated at Pea Ridge and again at Corinth.

The next year Paul, baby and afflicted one, returned to become valedictorian of his class at Liberty High School, the big consolidated school which had swallowed up the satellite rural communities by taking their last bit of identity. Places like East Fork, Mars Hill, New Zion, Glading, Robinson, Hebron and Thompson had once been well-known and the people gathered at their schoolhouses for annual Stunt Nights, Cake Walks, Senior plays and graduation exercises with speakers from town. After consolidation they ceased to exist as community centers.

Their graduates, or drop-outs, had once become the next generation of farmers, storekeepers, log haulers. Now they moved on to New Orleans to work in the ship yards, or to Baton Rouge to seek their fortune in the oil refineries. Paul chose the former, getting a job and rising from delivery boy to Retail Sales Manager while going to night school at Tulane University, gaining two degrees.

And to New Orleans he took Freddie, a beautiful teen-ager from Liberty. She the one who after more than twenty years of marriage, bearing two daughters, packed up all her belongings one Sunday morning and left their elegant Arabian horse ranch, never to return, leaving behind the broken heart of baby brother Bunyon, who had assumed until a few weeks earlier that theirs was the storybook union. He did not then turn to drugs or booze but joined the Church of God, actually joined what we as children had called the "holy rollers" and considered children of the devil. But the split-level Baptists, now grown rich, could offer him nothing but a weekly appointment on the counselor's couch with a young Th. D. probing his psyche. The "holy rollers" could, and did, offer him a place where he could cry out loud to an empathizing audience who would cry with him because they loved him, a place where he could laugh out loud and shout God's goodness out loud and roll on the floor and scream in either agony or joy when he felt like it. And the "holy rollers" could, and did, offer him ex-prisoners to take home and care for, and homeless boys to whom he could, and would, give his land and houses to be their own ranch and home, bringing life and laughter to the barns and meadows neither the barns and meadows, their giver, nor the homeless boys had ever known before.

To heal the brokenhearted: "Freddie is coming back to me and the door will be open. But if she doesn't it is because God doesn't want her to come back and I'll be just as happy." The Th. D.s could analyze and even put such feelings in intellectual perspective. But they couldn't understand. Because they couldn't, and because someone else could, he found deliverance, a good woman named Betty to share his life; and survives and flourishes.

Yes, Bunyon was the afflicted one. And the baby.

And I, named Will Davis but called only Dave, was sickly. Not afflicted but sickly. And the one marked early to be the preacher.

Our daddy was nicknamed "Preacher" and called little else by his neighbors and brothers and older nephews who were near his own age. The name went back to a time shortly after he was married. He came from the field one day and said that he was going to become a preacher. But he finished no more than the sixth grade of school and already the public relations of "Fulltime Christian Service" was beginning to lean heavily on the academy. Already, even in rural Mississippi in 1918, the notion was getting around that the Jesus story was so complicated that only the learned could convey it. So Daddy did not become a preacher but was called "Preacher" by his friends and neighbors. And still is.

And before him there was Preacher Baham, our great grandmother's second husband. We never knew much about Preacher Baham except that he had moved to Mississippi from Tangipahoa Parish, Louisiana, married our great grandmother, was a successful farmer, and was considered strange because he could be heard talking to the Lord and preaching as he followed the plow. ("Lord, I'm ready to go. Or I'm ready to stay.") Years later I would relate to my mother-in-law, in an effort to please her, that my Grandpa Baham had come from the same Louisiana Parish as she. Not overwhelmed by the news she responded wryly that all the Bahams in Tangipahoa Parish were colored people. But our Grandpa Baham was, in Amite County, Mississippi, a white man. And a preacher.

With these as precedent, I was marked, or called, at an early age. And except for a few times—rebellious from parental punishment and thinking of being a railroad man like Uncle Boyce, or a Merchant Marine like Addison Sinclair as a way of revenge—I never questioned my vocational future.

Sickly, too. And thereby special. Not special as Sister was special, but special in that when there was family quarreling it was I who was told by Mamma that I would be the one to bring the family back together, meaning, I gathered, that I would die early as punishment for the bickering of others who would thereafter live in peace and harmony. Though I had difficulty in seeing that as inducement to pursue my ministerial status and career, it did lead to a degree of deference which I do not recall resisting.

When I was five I had pneumonia. And was, on that occasion, given up for dead. It was an epidemic winter and many people, young and old, died of it. The medical procedure was a poultice of mustard, kept constantly over the entire chest area. Although the doctor was summoned, his job was nothing but one of diagnosis, and if he chose, prognosis. Mine, he said, was not only pneumonia, but double pneumonia. I was frail to begin with and I learned later that I was expected by physician, relatives and neighbors to die. A local woman, Cousin Flora Callendar, known for being good with sick people, came by to look and visit. Daddy followed her outside and asked her what she thought.

"Lee, you want the truth, don't you?"

"Yes, I want the truth. If I hadn't I wouldn't have asked. He's my boy and I want the truth."

"Well," she said, "pneumonia goes in a nine-day cycle. Generally on the seventh day the fever breaks. That's when they go through the crisis. Dave has been sick three days. If he keeps going down for the next three days like he has the last three, when the fever leaves him, well Lee, he'll leave with it. He's just too weak."

The next day I was still living, lying in bed with a roaring fire in the fireplace and all windows closed as tightly as they could be shut. Any sort of draft was thought to lead to sudden death.

Daddy talked with Uncle Curt and Aunt Dolly, Mamma's sister and favorite kin. They agreed that the only hope was nursing care and together they went to town in search of a nurse. Miss Beleau, a young woman recently out of nursing training, said she would come for twelve dollars a week. Daddy had ten of it which he gave her then, promising the remainder as soon as possible. They drove her home and she immediately set about the salvaging job she was employed to attempt. First she opened one of the windows, explaining that there was not enough air in the room. Next she removed some of the covers from the bed and instructed that the fire was to die down to a flicker, that it was burning up some of the available oxygen. There was to be absolutely no company. Only herself and one other person was to be in the room at any one time.

Mamma was for immediate dismissal. This hussy had come into our house, exposed a sick child to a killing draft, offended the neighbors who were there to be of help, and let the fire go out. But

Daddy had made the decision to hire someone to do a job and he was not one to tell them how to do it. The nurse would remain.

Part of her equipment was a glass drinking straw, bent at about a twenty degree angle three-fourths of the way up. It was about the most intriguing thing I had ever seen, and some degree of consciousness was maintained because of my preoccupation with it. Whatever she offered me to drink, generally canned blackberry juice, a little hot soup, or lemonade, was taken with enthusiasm. Before, it had been refused. That much accomplished, she went about the task of routine nursing chores, taking the temperature and pulse, alcohol rubdowns, enemas, and preparing for the approaching crisis. By now the news of her strange and arbitrary behavior had spread throughout the community. But Miss Beleau was undaunted. She was doing what she was trained to do. And what she had come to do.

Only Delton, or Peter as we called him, Aunt Clara's baby son, my age, broke the no-company barrier. I awoke one afternoon to find him leaning over my bed, whispering in my ear.

"Hey, Dave. Dave. Dave. Dave. Hurry up and get better. Hey, Dave. Hurry up and get better."

Of all people, children were not allowed, because children were thought to get the disease from other children. But Peter, after having harangued Aunt Clara for days, had slipped off and walked the mile to our house. The nurse made quick work of his visit when she returned to the room and discovered that he had come through the side door when she had not been looking. It was probably good therapy.

The crisis passed. The fever left but I didn't leave with it as Cousin Flora had predicted. Miss Beleau went away at the end of her one-week contract.

Several weeks later I was allowed outside the house for the first time and Joe was waiting with a nice and well-prepared surprise. He had dug a pit in the ground, deep enough to stand in and not be seen. He had made a cover out of old barn lumber. A door, just big enough to drop through had been carefully sawed out and framed. He said he had made it as our secret hide-out.

He related how long it had taken him to dig it, apparently unnoticed because of concern for the sick one. He said he had been real scared.

"Dave, did you know you had pneumonia?" I had not been told

and, because I was familiar with the high mortality rate, the news gave me something of a fright.

"But you're okay now. You're well. But I was real scared. You're okay now though. Honest!"

We sat together in one corner of his dungeon, the closed door shutting out all light. He hugged me close and began to talk again.

"I heard'um talking. I heard Miss Flora tell Daddy that if you kept going down for three more days like you had been you'd die. I cried and went and asked Grandma Bettye if it was the truth. She told me to stop crying and start praying."

He said that was when he started digging the pit, that he didn't want them to take me way up to the East Fork Cemetery and bury me. His plan was that if I died he would immediately announce that he already had a grave dug and maybe they would keep me there where he could visit me every single day. When I began to get better he changed his plan and put the wooden cover over it for a hide-out.

"And I heard'um talking when you went through the crisis. They thought I was asleep but I was awake listening. I heard Miss Beleau say to Daddy, 'He passed through the crisis at midnight.' That was when the fever left you. I heard her say, 'When the fever left him his lips got all blue and he was pale all over and his pulse was mighty weak. But he made it and he's going to be all right.' I heard her say all of that to Daddy."

We sat huddled together for a long time after that in the darkness of Joe's secret grave, neither of us speaking a word. I, perhaps, reflecting with childish thoughts upon my near death, Joe rejoicing in the resurrection.

The secret hide-out was soon to come to an end. Mamma, or Sister, one came calling. We tried to make it out undetected, but failed.

"You know better than to take that child in that cold hole! Don't you know how sick he's been? Now you cover that hole up this minute. And, Dave. You go back in the house by the fire!" No amount of begging could change the order. No promises that I would not get back in the hole until summer. The pit had to be filled up.

When I was about eight, it was a shot in the eye with a rock from a slingshot. (We never called that particular weapon a slingshot. It was made from a forked twig with two pieces of innertube tied to a piece of leather from a shoe tongue. It was called a "niggershooter," and liberation from such thought patterns is not easy.)

Scott and Sam, Joe and I were playing war. Daddy had sold a sizeable tract of timber for crossties. It had been great excitement to watch the trees being felled by the crosscut saws of powerful big black men. And the manner in which they took their near razor sharp broadaxes and hewed them into shape was an art long since lost. They camped in the woods and were there for weeks, going home only at Saturday noon. Joe and I used to stand and watch them cook the big, round and thick flapjacks over an open fire, stack them eight or ten high and pour sour smelling P.O.J. molasses onto them, and sidedress it all with fried hogmeat half an inch thick. That was what they ate every day about three o'clock. I think it was their only meal of the day.

The slabs they left from the pine logs would be an envy to any creative housebuilder today. But these were left on the ground to rot. We dragged some of them into a pile, stacking them end on end into a square which we called our fort.

The war began with broken corn cobs which we agreed would not do serious injury when an enemy soldier was struck. And the object of the game was to strike the enemy. As in all war. Sam and I, the younger two, were on one side. Joe and Scott on the other. Someone, I never remembered who, suffered a smarting blow from a good sized piece of corncob. He must have been the one who made the decision that rocks were in order as ammunition. Whatever happened, whoever fired first—and whoever knows who fires first in war?—the rock battle was on. Though for purposes of gaining as much sympathy as possible, and in order to assess as much blame as possible, Sam and I never admitted that we were not only similarly armed but had actually divided our army into fighting and supportive troops. Sam's job was to gather ammunition as rapidly as possible, and mine was to fire as rapidly as possible. I had reached my hand around the side of our fort to pick out a choice rock from the store Sam was piling, Wham! An enemy rock struck a nearby tree, bouncing straight at, and to, my right eye. The war was over. Scott and Sam decided to go home as I made my howling way to the house to report that Joe had deliberately and purposely conspired with Scott, to hurt me bad. The pain was soon gone and I do not recall any punishment for anyone because the details were too vague. But a week later the white of the eye was red and the pain was becoming unbearable. Aspirin held me for another week when Daddy decided that he ought to take me to the doctor. I remember well the stern lecture the McComb E.E.N.T. specialist, Dr. Cotton, gave my father. "Now you have probably waited too long. The boy will probably never be able to see in this eye. Just look at it!" And with those words he placed the mysterious, mirror-looking light over Daddy's head and I watched Daddy as he pretended that he was looking through the tiny round hole in the contraption and could thus see something he had not already seen with the naked eye. The doctor continued with his scathing denunciation of my father, whose only response was "Well, Doctor, you just don't know how it is with a poor cotton farmer." And I am sure he was right. For the deep compassion the doctor had hinted at was never reflected in the bills which continued to come for years until the last dollar was paid.

Again I was to lie in bed for six weeks. This time it had to be motionless, flat on the back without even a pillow. A cold patch was to be kept on the eye at all times and paregoric administered every few hours for the pain. That was in such quantity and for such duration that I cannot hold a bottle of it in my hand today without a strong impulse to drink it.

I am sure now that the greater pain was Joe's. Even if no one spoke to him of blame, he assumed and felt it. I do not remember any conversations we had that summer. He was quiet, withdrawn, and his bedwetting, with which he had been plagued since infancy, increased.

Daddy and I had to ride the jitney, a three-seated car which Mr. Frazier and his wife drove to McComb from Liberty every afternoon to get the *Jackson Daily News*, which they delivered to houses along the road on the return trip. This was so Dr. Cotton could check the injury. The only excitement I recall Joe showing during that episode was one afternoon, shortly before we were to catch the jitney, when he came flying into the house from the cotton patch behind the house where he had been plowing. He had found a fifty cent piece! Actually we knew when it had been lost and who had lost it. But whatever ethical consideration there was of returning it to the loser was quickly dispelled by Joe's determination to "give it to Dave." "Here. Here. Buy something in town." And that was that. It was, I now know, more an act of generosity than of penance.

I was the sickly one.
And Joe was the worker.
Not chosen to preach.

But more than worker, though worker is enough. When one is productive it is assumed that he is happy, or content, does not need fretting over. Save the fretting for the one who sits detached and unproductive. Fawn over him. Give him a nickel and take him to the store with you. Let him visit Grandpa a lot. Give him first helping at the table. Take him to the doctor to make sure his health is all right.

More than worker. For he protected me as best he could. From hurt. Once when the school house burned down—it burned twice while we were there—the first four grades met in the lodge hall of The Woodmen of the World. The Woodmen Hall was a small, two-room building which we always liked. We had heard stories about grown men riding a goat in there.

We carried our lunch to school in a little lard bucket. Joe called it our "teet" bucket, his contraction of something "to eat." It was socially more acceptable to take one's lunch in a brown paper sack but sacks were not always available to us. So Joe and I generally shared the same bucket. Lunches were kept in a small room, where some sort of Woodman ritual took place, located between the two larger rooms where classes were held.

Our lunch was usually biscuits with fried ham, a baked sweet potato, or sometimes a piece of corn bread with some kind of vege-table. Or it might be biscuits with a small jar of molasses. When this was the lunch we would gouge a deep hole in the biscuit with our finger and pour the syrup in the hole. (All this was before the coming of the Federal lunch room program.) Such a school lunch was not a thing of pride. Those who had light bread and bologna sandwiches tried to eat where everyone could see them. The ham and biscuit crowd ate as far from everyone else as they could, usually beneath and behind a big beech tree, far enough from the Woodmen Hall not to be noticed. (Today ham/biscuits have been franchised throughout the South, and sell for a respectable price.

But now was not then. Then ham and biscuit was the lunch of the poor.)

At recess time one could go to the little room and get part of his lunch, enough to hold him until dinnertime. On this day our lunch was in a paper bag and at recess I told Joe, with uncertain pleasure, that I had eaten half of a bologna sandwich from our sack. He looked at me funny and asked me to show him which sack was ours. When I did he confirmed that that was our place and said nothing more. His silence gave me doubts. And at lunch time, when he hurriedly led me, not to our usual spot, but out of sight of all the other children, I knew. Joe knew that I would not willfully steal someone's lunch. And he could not tell me that I had done so by mistake. The two of us sat with a paper sack between us and ate bologna sandwiches made out of light bread, and an orange which we halved, and two cookies. Apparently the teacher explained to the owner of the lunch that it had been taken by mistake for we never heard it mentioned. And we never mentioned it to each other—not even when we lived to see ham and biscuit elevated to the rank of delicacy, light bread and bologna relegated to still dwindling status.

I hated some of the chores assigned to me and sometimes wished that I could be the main worker so I wouldn't have to do them. I especially dreaded the job of taking chickens to the store. The barter system was used more than cash and when we went to Mr. Will Wilson's store—the same store where Uncle Jessie had been shot, and now, several years later, Mr. Will ran the store and was married to Aunt Clara—we took hens, eggs, or fryers to exchange for what we needed. It was only a mile, but with a hen under one arm or in a sack it was a long mile. I didn't know who might pass and see me, or what they might say when they saw me. I cursed the job to Joe one time and he suggested that I walk through the woods. It was three times as far but that way I could be certain that I would not be seen. He also offered to go in my place if he were not working in the fields at the time. And many times, he did.

Worker. And shield.

Joe seldom entered into group activities. About twice a year Uncle Clifton came home from Coushatta where he taught school, and later worked for the Department of Agriculture. We looked forward to those visits for he was a compelling storyteller and entertainer, and we also considered him rich. He had left home in his middle teens because he hated working on the farm, had struggled his way through high school in Hattiesburg, almost a hundred miles away, at what is now the University of Southern Mississippi. He was a tall man, square jawed, muscular but not fat. We loved him.

The Sunday afternoons of his visit were always given over to a talent show. Every niece and nephew was expected to enter. Each one got a prize, though they varied in value, and Uncle Clifton was the sole judge. The grand prize was a dime or, at times, as much as a quarter. Most received pencils, pens, trinkets, a ruler with "Coca-Cola" written in red letters down the side, a comb, chewing gum or candy. I learned to play the harmonica and the year I played it and danced a jig at the same time I won first prize. Once Elaine, one of Uncle Luther and Aunt Cornie's girls, went behind the house and cried because her prize was a pencil with the lead broken off. We told her it could be sharpened but the fact that it had been handed to her with the lead broken was taken as a personal insult and a slur on her performance.

I don't recall Joe ever performing. He encouraged me, would sit on the steps and clap his hands but he never sang, danced or recited.

Worker. And shy.

And creative too. The red clay from banks, washed from our gullies along the old dummyline and on old road beds, would have been the envy of any potter. For most of us it was something to roll into balls and throw at each other, or to squash and squish between our toes when it rained. But for Joe it was something to shape into various objects, cups and saucers, busts with an amazing likeness to Abraham Lincoln and George Washington. When they were finished they were placed in the sun in summer and by the fireplace in winter to dry. No one paid much attention to them. They were just trinkets Joe had made, and none of them remain.

Perceptive.

Uncle Luther's boys told us there was a side show coming to McComb and that Uncle Luther was going to take a school busload to see it. No one knew exactly what it was but that didn't really matter. We knew that it was coming in on the train and that it cost a dime. We went at night, after all the chores were done, and when we got to the railroad station we could see two boxcars pulled onto a siding. We got in line, paid our dime and the man told the group that we were about to see the biggest whale ever caught in the north Atlantic Ocean. About all we knew of whales was that one had once swallowed Jonah and vomited him up three days later. The viewing of the whale was something of a fiasco. Though we were close enough to touch it we couldn't get far enough away from it to see it in perspective. The guide took us all the way around it, announcing as we went something about flippers, flukes and things. All of it looked pretty much the same and one might as well have been looking at the side of the boxcar itself. We noticed that the guide kept whispering something to the men and a lot of them were hurrying toward the door. We soon did the same but were turned back when we reached the entrance of the other railroad car. It was just as well for we saw that the men were handing the attendant another dime and most of us didn't have another dime to hand him. We began to pair off and gather in small groups speculating on just what the mysterious second car had inside it.

Joe pulled me to the side and said he knew what was in it.

"I heard what that man told them. He didn't think I did but I did." He said the man told them it was the whale's penis, and then quickly explained to me what a penis was. We had other designations.

"He said it was twenty feet long. Boy, that's a big'un, ain't it?" I said yes.

"Don't tell'um!" Joe said. So he and I drifted on back to the bus, knowing something that only the men knew.

And builder.

Ingenious bird traps, built by no special pattern but with Rube Goldberg trigger mechanisms designed to catch the bird alive when it came in and began to peck at an ear of corn fastened to the end of the trigger. A fiendish contraption he imagined looked like the gallows on which Allen Westbrook had been hanged—trap door, noose, and steps leading up to the scaffold. Lizards, toadfrogs, or fieldmice were forced to climb the steps to be hanged. His private executions ended when he once tried to hang a chameleon. When he sprang the trap door open the weight of the thing was not enough to break its neck. It just kicked and danced in mid-air at the end of the noose. A small stick was tied to its hind legs but still he wouldn't hang. Finally half a fence rail was tied to it and when he came down the weight popped both his eyes out of socket. The realism was enough that he dismantled his gallows.

And bizarre.

He never loved but one dog. Rover just showed up one day. We didn't know what kind it was but it was handsome, a big dog, almost silver colored. It looked like it might be a breed all its own. Joe said that because it was new to us and we had found it, it would be a Newfoundland dog. We just called it Rover. From scraps of boards and whatever could be found Joe built a house for it, looking in miniature like the one we lived in. Two years later it disappeared as it had come. We thought we heard a thud and then a yelp during the night but we never found its body. Joe said that it was dead and we lay awake almost all night when Joe declared it dead, talking about all the things he had done. Once he had howled all night and Joe said when a dog did that it was a sign somebody had died. The next morning a neighbor came and told us that a tree fell on Mr. Will Newman and killed him.

Kind too.

Mamma was sick a lot. We always assumed that she had stomach ulcers for Dr. Quin had once said that anyone who washed dishes with Octagon soap was apt to have ulcers. We used Octagon soap because the wrappers had coupons on them. Although she was in her twenties and thirties at the time we considered her old, for she considered herself old, we believed with her that she would soon die.

On the nights when she had stomach pains there was a routine pattern to be followed. It generally commenced shortly after everyone had gone to sleep. She would awaken Daddy with cries and groans and tell him to send for the doctor, that she was dying. There was no telephone, no car and the doctor was twelve miles away.

Joe was always the first of us to go to her. He would get the wet rag to place on her forehead for that was thought to comfort nausea. Daddy would sometimes coax him back to bed, or ask him to go in the kitchen and mix a spoon of baking soda with a glass of water.

"Here, wife. Take this, It'll settle your stomach. It was probably what you ate for supper." Sometimes Mamma would drink the sodawater, sometimes not. In either case it was a stalling tactic, a part of the all night drama.

By midnight the vomiting began. The night jar had to be emptied and that was my job. Sometimes everyone would go back to sleep but always to be soon jolted by the piercing screams of agony. When there was no more fluid in the stomach there would be a period of dry heaves, the soreness in the abdomen becoming more and more intense and more and more localized. This was the point at which all the pillows in the house would be brought and Mamma would be propped in a sitting position. By now everyone was involved, following the script we had learned from earlier nights like this one. Joe was always standing or sitting beside the bed.

By three o'clock Mamma was in a state of hysteria, crying, writhing, sending last messages to living relatives, reaching out for the spirit of departed ones. Daddy's words were those of assurance. "No, wife, you're not dying. Now, wife, turn over on your side and try to go back to sleep." All of it was a part of the scenario, well-timed, programmed and planned to get us to daybreak.

Uncle Sewell was the mail rider. He was not our real uncle but he had been married to the daughter of Mr. and Mrs. J. Scott Nunnery who ran the general store at East Fork. Mrs. Nunnery, whom we called Miss Fannye, was the aunt of our Aunt Cornie, mother of six cousins—Scott, Betty, Sam, Elaine, Irma, and Burnette. They lived a few hundred yards down the road from us and, because we heard them call the mail rider Uncle Sewell, we called him that too. At five o'clock he left his house to go to Liberty to get the mail and begin his route. Four o'clock was the cue for Daddy to say to Joe, "Joseph! Go tell Sewell to tell Dr. Quin to come out here." Joe would walk the mile to Uncle Sewell's house and hurry back. By seven the doctor was there. The examination was always brief and the Doctor always motioned for Daddy to follow him outside, talking to him in medical terms which Daddy did not understand but did not need to understand because he knew already the meaning and reality of chronic hypochondriasis. The medicine was always green, always in a six-ounce bottle. And by eight o'clock Mamma was always asleep.

When Mamma and Daddy quarreled, as they did often for a few years, it was Joe who was upset the most. Their differences seemed somehow dated from the time Paul was born. At least that was a date often mentioned as being the point at which Mamma "got sick." Though still in her twenties, that, it seemed, was the beginning of old age. And the beginning of geriatric continence. The quarrels were often severe, generally over trivia, and they often resulted in Mamma hiding in the woods for hours at a time. I do not recall being especially upset by this. But Joe persisted in calling and looking and crying until he found her and they returned to the house.

Joe was kind to his mother. And loved her to his life's end.

And Grandma Bettye. She seemed to single him out from the herd of grandchildren the way Grandpa Will Parker had singled me out. In my case it was because I carried his name. The relationship of Grandma Bettye and Joe was something else. She appeared to know something about him no one else knew. She was concerned about what he was thinking, what he was feeling. She consoled and assured him all during the summer I was in bed from the eye injury, explaining that it wasn't his fault, and that he shouldn't worry about it. She took aspirin tablets, lots of them, for lumbago and neuralgia. And when Joe complained to her with one of his frequent headaches she shared her aspirin tablets with him and gave him some to bring home. She had one of the first radios in the community and invited Joe to come and listen with her as often as he could. One of his favorite stories had to do with Grandma Bettye and that Philco radio. They were listening to a sermon on Sunday morning. Twelve o'clock was approaching and she hadn't made the cornbread for dinner. She told him she was going to turn the radio off while she went to the kitchen and made her bread and he was not to turn it on until she got back because while the bread was cooking she wanted to hear the rest of the sermon. Joe was too kind to explain to her that a radio was not like a phonograph.

And he didn't know, and none of us knew, that the radio was ushering in an era when nothing could be put to sleep as it once had been, an age of motion as well as sound—motion and sound which could not be controlled. Could not be stopped. Turn it off and it goes right on. And you can never pick up where you left off.

Joe was all these things. But not called to preach.

J oe and I had walked the six miles, across the river, to Aunt Dolly
and Uncle Curt's house. They had no children. Uncle Curt got a
veteran's pension and drove the school bus, owned a big cotton
farm, and Aunt Dolly was a good cook. About twice a year Uncle
Curt and some of his friends went to the Homochitto River on a
camping and fishing trip. We were never taken on one of those
three day trips, but when Uncle Curt went we were invited to
come and stay with Aunt Dolly. And that was good enough for us.
The big buffalo fish, lamprey eels and blue cat, some weighing as
much as seventy-five pounds, tasted like nothing we ate the rest of
the year. And hearing the adventure stories—hemming the big catfish up in a hollow log and catching them by hand or with grabbing
hooks, campfire antics like putting fresh chicken mess on the hand
of a sleeper and then, tickling his lips with a feather to make him
wipe his mouth in a quick and unsuspecting fashion—was almost as
good as being there.

Their house smelled with the fragrance of apples all year like
ours did only at Christmas time. Uncle Curt looked all the time, no
matter how he was dressed, like the army picture of him hanging in
the blue, oval frame above the mantelpiece—tight-laced leggings,
overseas cap fitting just as tightly, tilted to the side, standing at
rigid attention, staring directly ahead. We had heard his war stories
so often that we told them to each other. But we never tired of
hearing them from him.

It was a Sunday afternoon and he was to leave as soon as we finished dinner. Aunt Dolly had prepared his favorite dishes, fawning
and humoring him as if he would never come back. Flaky, brown-
crusted chicken and dumplings, English peas picked that morning
and floating in a sauce of freshly churned butter and heavy cream,
potatoes boiled in the same pot. Hot biscuits, too. And iced tea. It
was all there and we were hungry for it but no one began until everyone was seated and we "asked the blessing." Uncle Curt didn't
pray out loud and that ritual was observed only when they had
company.

When a new pastor came to a church one of the first things he learned was who prayed in public and who didn't. It was considered a social error and a sacrilege to ask one to lead in prayer who was known by everyone as one of the ones who didn't pray in public. Those who did pray in public were considered no better than those who didn't. But the categories were established early in each generation and Joe had already been placed, or placed himself, in the same category as Uncle Curt. He had learned to say, "I beg to be excused," if someone who didn't know asked. So I knew that I would be the one called upon and had already composed and memorized a short table blessing. It was not the same one as our daddy used. That was his prayer and nobody else prayed it. We had heard it three times every day since we were born, though for several years we couldn't understand the words and thought he was reading it from the blue, to us indistinguishable, writing on the back of the plate and, in fact, thought that was why plates were always turned upside down.

> *O Lord, look down on us with mercy.*
> *Make us thankful for these and all other blessings.*
> *Pardon and forgive us our sins.*
> *We ask for Christ's sake. Amen.*

That was Daddy's prayer. It had been his since he got old enough to visit someone else's house and become established as one who could be asked to say the blessing. It seemed more awkward to me to have to say, "I beg to be excused," than it was to go ahead and do it. I once suggested that to Joe but he pointed out something I had not thought of. He said you wouldn't have to say, "I beg to be excused" but a few times and everybody would know not to ask. If you went ahead and said the prayer you would be the one singled out from then on. I didn't have any choice in the matter anyway since I was going to be a preacher.

Just as Aunt Dolly was saying, "Dave, will you ask the blessing?" there was a frantic hammering and yelling at the door.

"Mr. Curt! Mr. Curt! Noon Wells been shot. Mr. Curt! Noon Wells been shot!"

Noon Wells was a black tenant and the news was not heard as if he had been white. Uncle Curt talked to the man who brought the news and, seeing that he was not immediately needed, sent word that he would be on up there directly, that he had company and was about to eat dinner. With that we returned to the table, I asked the blessing, we ate and listened to Uncle Curt grumble over the loss of a good field hand at cotton picking time, and complain, too, about the preempting of his fishing trip.

The man said it had happened at Leona and Pearl's house. Leona and Pearl lived together on a neighbor's place, were not married and their house was a popular gathering place. We had heard whisperings of what went on there but were never told outright. When we finished eating Joe and I were allowed to go with Uncle Curt to the scene.

Beside Leona and Pearl's house was a small, two-room building which had once been a schoolhouse for white children—before the progress of consolidation had closed it. The children who had previously attended it were now sent on buses to one of the larger schools in the area, there being no opposition in rural Mississippi in 1933 to that recently urbanized practice. Hundreds of these structures still dot the countryside and they seem invariably to be used for storing hay. This one was no exception.

The body of Noon Wells lay in the front opening, his feet and legs outside, his heels resting upon the ground. His shirt was unbuttoned and pulled open and a single bullet hole could be seen near his left nipple. An open knife lay nearby. Flies crawled in and out of his open eyes and mouth, and walked over the crusted blood which had drained from his nostrils. The other black men who had been present sat under a tree and waited for "the Law." They spoke and Uncle Curt asked them what had happened. One man had obviously been chosen to do the talking. He said they had been in a crap game, that Noon and John White got in an argument over some money and Noon had come at John with a knife. John backed away, hollering at him to stop. When he didn't, he shot him.

John White lived on Mr. Earl Moore's place but Uncle Curt had driven by his house without stopping. Later, Mr. Earl drove up, spoke, indicated to Uncle Curt that he was sorry, that the sheriff had asked him to bring John to Liberty so he could put him in jail, that the sheriff would be out to investigate the killing before night church services, and that if Uncle Curt got in a bind on his cotton picking he would lend him as many of his "hands" as he needed. Uncle Curt acknowledged his presence, but made no comment on any of the things he said. Mr. Earl soon left.

Joe and I had never seen a dead body before. Except in a casket. (Of those we had seen plenty. The schoolhouse at East Fork was not more than fifty yards from the churchhouse. And despite the rigid Baptist tradition of separation of Church and State, when there was a funeral it was considered a school function. Not extracurricular and not voluntary. Every child from the primer to the twelfth grade was lined up and marched into the churchhouse, seated to listen to the funeral service, marched past the open casket for the viewing of the remains and then to the cemetery for the burial.) As for this dead man, we took our cue from those about us, looking upon the situation in an almost casual fashion. And in an atmosphere approaching carnival.

But in less than an hour our mood was altered by approaching sounds we had never heard before. At first they were far away and could not be recognized as human sounds, rising and fading in elastic fashion, coming from no certain direction and from everywhere. Slowly and deliberately, they drew closer and gradually we realized what they were. The black men formed a group under a giant beech tree, sheltered from the sun, each one hunkering on his calves, saying nothing. The whites hunkered in the same fashion, but in a separate group. Joe and I sat on a tree stump, ignoring the heat and far enough away from both parties to be considered a part of neither.

As the volume and intensity of the sounds became greater, one of the Negro men looked at another and said, "That's Noon's mamma." And that was all anyone, black or white, said about the sounds.

As the woman and her train of attendants came into vision, Joe and I tried not to look. Yet we did not know what the proper, the expected, thing was. The mother was surrounded by an entourage of a dozen or so women, mostly her own age. They were supporting her from falling and part of the time almost carrying her. The dominant sound we heard was the wails, the moans, the shrieks, the whimpering of the mother. It could not be described as crying at all. Those sounds were backed up by the more subdued ones of her supporters. It was as if they knew they were playing supporting and not starring roles, that they should let her be heard loudest and farthest of all. Their pace did not quicken as they came closer to the body. Nor did it grow any slower. And the sounds did not change except to take on a more specific direction. And for the last hundred yards or so a few words could be distinguished from the rest of the lament.

The mother shouted.

"LORD!"

Those surrounding her picked up with their refrain as in a litany.

"Lord."

"JEESUS!"

Now the echo. Softly. "Jesus."

"LORD!"

"Lord."

"JEEESUS!"

"Jesus."

"GOD LORD JESUS!"

"Lord Jesus."

"LORDY GOD!"

"Lord God."

"TAKE ME ON TO GLORY!"

"On to Glory."

"O JESUS, MY JESUS. OR BRING MY BABY HOME!"

"Bring 'im home."

The women surrounding her picked up and duplicated each sound and each word as they were uttered, the mother giving them time after each word and each sound to complete their own faded replica of her words and sounds. They were thrusting her more and more to center stage. As her incantations became louder, their response was more and more hushed.

It must have been half an hour from the time the first faint noise was heard until the women reached the old schoolhouse. Because the road had been built to skirt a certain property, miss a tree too big to be pushed or pulled down, or go around a rock too large to move, there would be times when it seemed they were almost there. But as the road turned, the party would move in the opposite direction, taking them almost beyond hearing again. None of the men commented or acknowledged their presence when they finally did arrive. Both groups remained in silence, hunkering in place, staring or poking their fingers at the ground. Joe and I remained on the stump, high enough to see the proceedings to follow.

The tone changed abruptly when all the women formed a semicircle around the door opening where the corpse lay. All sounds and all words stopped completely, as if by some prearranged and rehearsed signal. For several seconds there was absolute quiet. As the mother, alone now, took the one step up into the building the silence was ruptured by a vastly different sound. Now it was unmistakable crying. Sobbing, wailing, shouting, screaming, yelling—the broken heart of a mother and her sister, and her sisters, calling their hurt to the world. And then quiet again, everyone stopping as one.

The mother squatted beside the body of her son, not crying now. No more wails, moans—the ululation gone. With the corner of her apron in one hand, she tenderly daubed at the caked blood from his nostrils, fiercely shooing the flies away with the other hand, as if they were doing him harm. And as if the cleaning of his nostrils would bring him life again. She sat for a very few minutes, rubbing his forehead, patting his now stoney chest.

"They didn't have to kill him. They didn't have to kill my boy." Just those words over and over for as long as she was there. "They didn't have to kill my boy." Somehow she seemed to know when it was time to go. And when that time had come, not more than ten minutes from the time they had arrived, she quietly stood erect and held her head askance, shaking it slowly from side to side, looking down at a body that was once alive in her own body, had cooed and sucked and slept at her then lithe and plump breast, now wilted and sagging. A body that now lay dead in a schoolhouse door, a door which would have been closed to him when it stood as a place of life and learning.

Her step from the building indicated to the other mourners that she had accomplished what she had come to do, and the recession began. The going was in exact reverse order of the coming. As were the sounds. First there was the unmistakable crying. Then the indistinguishable sounds which had been heard at the beginning, the modulation the same.

They moved as slowly going as they had coming. Down and around the curving and twisting of a tiny dirt road, as whorled and meandering as the history which had brought them, and us, to that day, a road that would later merge with a bigger one that led to the city. They would, of course, not go to the city. At least not yet, but would stop at the site of their own habitation, remaining for at least another generation on the land to which they had been brought. And leaving then only when they were driven off, not by blatant bigotry and designed exploitation, but by a machine, analogous to the one responsible for their being there in the first place. The mechanical cotton picker, first designed by a black man named A. P. Albert, would take them away in the same manner as Eli Whitney and his machine had brought them—against their will, with neither technologist meaning them any personal harm, for they were both honorable men. And Joe and I would be similarly taken away.

We watched them until they were out of sight. And listened until they were out of hearing. And we listened for a long time after that. At those sounds. Whether the sounds we were hearing were those of a buried or modified culture, merging with another as the dirt road merged with the bigger one leading elsewhere, it would not have occurred to us at the time to ponder. But later we would remember them as the articulation and recitation of two hundred years of pathos. An emancipation which still had not reached them, or us, if in fact it had reached anywhere at all. A manumission inferred by Christian proselytizers, but undelivered by the steeples and structures they represented.

Whether West African or European, Nigerian or Mississippian in origin, they were the pleadings of an African peasant woman to the son of a Jewish peasant woman to be with her in her travail.

They were Jesus sounds, absorbed from a nation and a culture Jesus was alleged to have had a hand in founding and forming, drawing, too, on a nation and a culture where he had not been known at all, yet meaning more to that which was African in this scene than he had ever meant to that which was American in it.

And they were sounds which would not soon depart from us.

While the mother was with her son the sheriff had arrived. But he remained inside his car until she had gone and until she was completely out of sight. And until the sounds were beyond hearing. We were anxious to see a real lawman at work, for we had recently sent two cornflakes boxtops to Battle Creek, Michigan, and had been made Junior G-Men. They had sent us a little badge, which we wore proudly to Sunday School and everywhere. And we had certain crime-solving information not available to just anyone. Of particular interest to us was a code building set. We had learned that criminals often wrote letters to each other in this fashion. The scramble—CBOL SPCCFSZ UPOJHIU—would mean nothing to the ordinary citizen. But the G-man would suspect a code. And moving each letter back the *c* becomes *b*, *b* becomes *a*, and so forth until the code is broken. CBOL SPCCFSZ UPOJHIU becomes instead "bank robbery tonight." Joe and I had cautioned each other about sharing this information with others. We watched carefully to see how efficient our own county sheriff was.

He noted the knife beside the body of Noon, measured the distance it was from his hand and then carefully wrapped it in his own handkerchief. He asked Uncle Curt to help him remove Noon's shirt and then sitting down, taking the upper part of the body in his lap, he removed the bullet with his knife. With these two pieces of evidence he left. We soon did the same.

By circulating through the group which had gathered at the old schoolhouse, Joe and I had learned that the story the man had told Uncle Curt was not the way it had happened. We were little boys and the black men who had been present did not hesitate to talk to one another in our presence. The crime had actually been an execution. Noon Wells was young and handsome and perhaps more virile than some of the older men and they had become enraged that he had enjoyed more than his share of the favors of the two women. When he had become quite drunk two of them held him up by each arm and led him into the yard. As they held him up, John White steadied his pistol against a tree, and with careful aim, shot him through the heart. He fell backward into the door opening and his own knife had been taken from his pocket and placed beside him.

But that version was not reported at the preliminary hearing the next day, a hearing presided over by Mr. Elisha Barron, the local Justice of the Peace, sitting behind a glass counter in Mr. Scott Nunnery's store. The counter was regularly used for displaying bolts of cloth. Mr. 'Lish opened and closed the brief hearing with gentle raps upon the glass counter with a wooden mallet, the kind used for pounding a wood chisel. The sheriff testified that Noon Wells had obviously approached John White with a knife in a gambling dispute and that John White had no recourse but to kill him. The man who had given the account to Uncle Curt at the old schoolhouse repeated it. And Mr. Earl gave a statement as to the good character of John White as a tenant. When they finished the Justice of the Peace said that it was, in his judgment and by his ruling, justifiable homicide and that it would not be taken to the Grand Jury. Mr. Earl took John White home.

We were learning that crimes of black against black were not as serious as white against white. And certainly not as serious as black against white. Years later, when I was to learn of the impotence of law, I discovered that, despite the motivation of those meting out that hierarchical double standard of justice, the inequity was, in fact, not evil at all. For it did not, I discovered, lead to an increase in crimes of violence of black against black any more than the stringent punishment of black against white crimes led to a decrease in such crimes. At least, for whatever reason, the black captives were released as Jesus had proclaimed release for all captives.

The events of the night would be remembered as long as those of the day. Because Uncle Curt would have to appear at the preliminary hearing the fishing trip had been called off. Instead of staying at their house as planned, we stayed at Grandma Bertha's. We generally felt secure in her house. But on that occasion there was little sleep.

A summer thunderstorm blew in not long after we had gone to bed. We were down the hall, and across it from the room where Grandpa and Grandma slept. The rain beat upon the tin roof and rattled the windows. Lightning flashed, cracking, striking in the distance. But it was not the noise of the night that kept us awake, but the recollections of the day. Long after the storm had passed we both lay awake, as still as a quahog nestled in the sand, not speaking a word. A huge clock stood on the floor in our room. It was the same clock which Grandma had used to call time on those who came courting her daughters. (Wanting to indicate that it was past the midnight curfew on one occasion she made it strike thirteen times, to the delight of those frolicking in the parlor.) The clock no longer ran, but the wind kept bumping the pendulum against the side, causing the chimes to make sounds reminiscent of those we had heard in the afternoon. Still we did not speak. It must have been well past midnight when Joe said in a low voice, "Hey, Dave. Are you scared?" I, as softly, replied, "Naw. I'm just about asleep." He turned on his left side, slid his right arm around me and we lay there until far into the morning hours when we fell asleep. Years later, if the words, "Are you scared?" were heard, one of us would always answer, "No. I'm just about asleep."

MIDDAY

Typing cost extra at East Fork. So did piano lessons, Glee Club, private voice lessons, quartet, even "public school music"—an arrangement in which an entire class went to the music room and learned songs like "Can I Sleep in Your Barn Tonight, Mister?" and "Give the World a Smile." Joe had no interest in taking music, said he wouldn't get up on the stage at the recitals because they were all just making fools of themselves. Certainly another reason was that all of us knew that we couldn't afford what it cost, and Joe was sensitive enough never to bring the subject up.

The family attitude toward typing was different. Daddy believed that typing was the answer to poverty. If one knew how to type he would never have to go hungry. So the year the school bought six or eight typewriters and hired Mr. Spurgeon Lewis to teach students in the eleventh and twelfth grades how to operate them, Daddy was among the first to sign up. The money would come from somewhere.

It was Joe's first flirtation with status. Until that time music had been at the top of the social scale. Everyone knew that it cost money to take music. So if one were seen going and coming from the music room, or seen in recital or concert it said to the other students whatever it is that money has to say.

The typing room became a place of its own, too. Those who "took typing" formed something of a clique. The special room became a hang-out for those within the privileged circle. They could go there during recess and could even eat their lunch there. They were expected to practice as much as possible and, since the teacher could not always be there, the typing room was used for social purposes also, and rumors and gossip began to build as to what went on in there. The clacking of the keys and the sound of the carriage being shifted rapidly back to the left hand margin added to the romance of it all.

If one had to explain the events of history in one word that word would have to be *roads*. It was a road that ended the depression for us. It was the same road that provided the cash for Lee Campbell to enroll his children in typing classes. And, just as he had said, typing would form and fashion Joe's life in the immediate future and to a lesser extent my own. There had been talk of the road for years. We had always lived on Highway Twenty-four. It was a gravel road and dust from passing cars and trucks was one of the plagues with which we had to contend. Every two years, when new legislators were being elected, we were told that the hard surfacing of our road was a certainty. The term used was "Farm to Market Roads." We would get a new road so that farmers could get their produce to the market town. It was not until 1937 that we got the promised road. As one traveled south from Jackson or Memphis or even Chicago, he could turn west at McComb on Route Twenty-four and travel much fewer miles to get to Baton Rouge, Lake Charles or Houston than by continuing south to Hammond or New Orleans and then heading west. But little commercial traffic had done that when the road was gravel. In 1937 we did not know what the principalities knew—that there was a war coming soon and that a new road would open up a speedy access to and from the oil refineries in Baton Rouge, all of southwest Louisiana and the Texas coast, to the soon to be built Camp Van Dorn in Centerville, and provide rapid troop movement to the vast Louisiana Maneuvers to be in operation within three years. We really believed that the promise had been fulfilled to *us*.

And with the road came the largest sum of money we had ever had at any one time. Because the macadam road would straighten a long curve when it reached our place, taking with it a sizeable slice of our farm, Daddy was paid five hundred dollars. The advantages of the macadam far outweighed any worry of what cargo they would carry.

There were other benefits as well. Our house and many others along the highway had to be moved and the housemoving crews had to have a place to sleep and eat. For the first and only time we had boarders. The drama of moving a house from one place to another, and in such a way that "the cream on the milk won't even be broken" was excitement we had not known before. I missed most of it because it came at the time when I was living with Grandpa Will after the death of Grandma Bertha. I was not there long—less than six months—because Grandpa married Miss Daisy Sandifer. She had nursed Grandma during the closing weeks of her life. Some of her relatives were considered "trash." But it was the brevity of the mourning period which caused the scandal and led to the hostility from his daughters and the feeling that he was being disrespectful. But Will Parker was not one to be controlled by protocol, or whims of prideful daughters. He assigned me the task of going home one weekend and finding out what the daughters were saying about him. When I reported that it was less than favorable he said, "Well, Jack, old rats like cheese too." And he went to New Orleans to bring his new bride home to Hebron.

By that time the road had been nearly completed, the house had been moved and I had missed most of the fireside stories told by our boarders. So Joe related most of them to me as we hiked through the woods of the Moore Pasture, worked in the fields, or squatted in the shade or shelter of the barn. Some of the house-movers were from the North Mississippi town of Purvis. They told the story of Will Purvis, a man accused of murdering a neighbor as he rode by on horseback late at night. On the day of the scheduled hanging something happened which they interpreted as Divine intervention. It was reminiscent of Allen Westbrook but with a dramatically different ending. When the sheriff pulled the lever to release the trap door the rope broke and Will Purvis tumbled to the ground unharmed. Whether by custom or law, Mississippi would not hang a man a second time, so Will Purvis was set free. Joe was not sure that it was an act of God to protect the innocent and suggested the possibility of the rope having been tampered with—by the sheriff who had been bought off, by another who might have been guilty instead of Will Purvis, or some relative.

The road paid for the typing lessons and the typing led to Joe's first job.

We had known about the CCC Camps for there was one at what was later to become Percy Quin State Park. It was for veterans but we also knew that there were camps for young boys, and long before Joe graduated from high school he had decided that he would join.

Civilian Conservation Corps. Randolph Kennebrew had been in the C's, as it was called, several years before. He had gone to college after getting out and Joe and I had watched him stand on a platform at the Glading Fourth of July Political Picnic and make a fine speech about how he was going to improve our lives with electric lights. He was running for the State House of Representatives and we were proud that his brother was married to our cousin. And there were other success stories and an aura of drama which surrounded the C's. They planted trees, built fire towers, dug lakes, lived in barracks, had uniforms, and got paid thirty dollars a month. Of that, the enlistee kept five and the rest was sent home. In the case of a veteran it was sent to his wife and family. With the younger ones it was sent to the father. Those who could afford it gave the money back to the son when he was home on the weekends. Joe had talked of enlisting when he reached sixteen, but decided to wait a year, until he finished high school. It was the second of the New Deal programs in which Joe had participated.

The NYA, National Youth Administration, made funds available for various types of teen-age employment. The school principal had three or four jobs and Joe was given one of them. For a few dollars a month he did several hours of work each week around the school house and grounds. I inherited the NYA job after Joe left and was assigned the task of building fires in the school heaters during the winter months. It was a good job. I could go to Miss Fanny Nunnery's store at recess time with Evie Lee, Gladys, and Elaine and offer to pay for the cold drinks just the same as any of the other boys. I could buy valentines for everyone in the class on that festive occasion and when there was a class party and ten, fifteen, or even twenty-five cents was assessed each member, I did not have to make excuses about not going. It was, in general, a more comfortable time than the ham and biscuit days.

Despite all the excitement and anticipation, the actual departure of Joe for the CCC Camp was not a happy experience. Mr. Nolen Hutchinson's boy, Barney Lloyd, had signed up also, and Mr. Hutchinson had a pick-up truck and was going to take his boy to report to Brookhaven, thirty miles away. They had said that Joe could ride with them. It was cool for April, and raining. They were to leave about daylight. Joe had been told that he would get two uniforms, plus shoes, a cap, and other accessories upon arrival—so there was no point in taking clothes. What he did need had been placed in a paper sack, along with some cherished articles which he had received as graduation presents: a desk fountain pen, a book, *The Ramparts We Watch*, by George Fielding Eliot—given to him by our cousin in Baton Rouge, Emmett Webb, who had made a lot of money selling insurance, enough to care for his mother in style and keep his sister in a private mental hospital for two decades—the first non-school book any of us had ever owned except a Bible which was not considered *a* book. Mamma had cooked his breakfast and Daddy was taking it all in his usual stoic fashion. Paul was asleep in the back room and I was still in bed, though not asleep, in the front room where Joe and I slept together after Sister left home.

I heard the old truck horn sound, heard Mamma mumble something to Joe and give him some kind of quick kiss on the cheek, and Daddy said that we would see him in a week or two.

"Bye, Dave."

"Bye, Joe."

I looked through the window from where I lay and saw that Joe was not getting into the cab of the truck but was instead climbing onto the back. Apparently, Miss Ruth, Barney Lloyd's mother, and the mother also of Kathleen who married our cousin, John, had decided to go along, so there was not room for Joe in front. But he did not hesitate. He put his paper sack down beside him and sat down against the cab of the truck, facing backward so that he would be partially protected from the rain. I remember the beam the headlights cut through the dawn, I remember the sound of the motor as the truck trudged into the early morning rain, taking with it my brother, in a sense taking him forever.

Though that was not what I was thinking, it must have been what I was feeling. I was fifteen years old, but we had never worried about what age a boy or man stopped crying. Somehow I knew. The family was dissolved. Though we were to have far more fun together in the years yet to come than we had up to that point, it was certainly the end of an era. And it was the beginning of the end.

The first letter we got from Joe said that he had been made Company Clerk. We didn't know exactly what that meant, but he said that he sat at a desk all day—typing. Others in the CCC Camp had to dig ditches, cut down trees, use pick-axes, man crosscut saws— nothing new or adventuresome for them. But Joe had made it big in one week.

It was the beginning of a new life for Joe. And for us all. The olive drab uniform, cap looking like those worn at American Legion conventions by veterans of Argonne and Belleau Wood, were just about the prettiest and most romantic thing I had ever seen. I wished to be old enough to join up too.

Knowing that Joe was sitting behind that desk with a typewriter at his fingertips day or night, we knew there must be a telephone near by. I had once talked on a telephone, but that was when they had phones in the Hebron area "across the river," and Aunt Dolly and Grandpa Parker had them. I vaguely recalled standing on a kitchen chair where I talked all the way from Grandma's house to Aunt Dolly's to let them know that I was there and would be there for perhaps another week. The two places were three miles apart. I was, I suppose, five years old at the time. But those phones had long since been removed by the depression and I had not talked on one since. Now having surmised that Joe was probably sitting near one we decided, or Daddy decided, that he and I should go to Liberty and call Brookhaven and see how he was, tell him that we got his letter, and ask him when he was coming home.

We walked up the stairs to the Liberty telephone exchange. Mr. Bennie Tarver had been paralyzed when a pile of logs from a truck he was loading rolled down on him, and his wife had been given the job of telephone operator.

Mrs. Tarver sat in front of something I had never seen before. She knew Daddy, and as soon as he told her what we were there for, it took no time to reach the Brookhaven operator.

She had told Daddy that whoever was going to speak to Joe should get inside a small room which she pointed to (later I was to learn that the little room was a telephone booth) and wait for her to reach Brookhaven and the proper number. She explained that it might take some time for them to locate him at the camp but that we should be ready. Daddy had motioned me inside the little glass room. While I had no notion what I should do to make talking and hearing between the two of us possible, I was not going to reveal that to Mrs. Tarver. Or to Daddy. I picked the horn-looking thing from off the hook and could immediately hear Mrs. Tarver's voice coming from one end of it. If her voice came from that end I reckoned that Joe's voice would come from the same end. I put that end against my ear, glancing at Daddy to try to read the accuracy or inaccuracy of what I had done. But Lee Campbell is not an easy book to read. He sat motionless and unrevealing. He had put me on my own.

I heard the Brookhaven operator ring a loud, long, ring. Even before the sound had stopped there was a voice. "CCC." "Long distance calling Mr. Joseph Lee Campbell." "Speaking!"

"Speaking?" Whatever it meant it was my own brother saying it. So I interpreted it to be my cue to speak also. Small talk mostly. "How are you, Joe?" "Fine, Dave, how are you?" "Aw, very well, I guess. When are you coming home?" "Well, maybe this weekend. But Daddy or Mamma will have to write me an excuse so I can get a pass." I didn't know what that meant but remembered to report it on the way home. "How do you like your new job?" "Just fine." "Do you ever see Prentiss or Bobby Gerald?" "Yea. I see them every day." And so went our first telephone conversation.

Joe not only had a typing job—my god, he answered the telephone for the whole camp. We believed he was an important person for the CCC.

Joe was never to be poor again. He had vowed daily, during every crop year, that he would escape the drudgery of the farm and never return. The day he climbed into the back of that pick-up was the last time he would ever do any type of physical labor. The others of us would spend the middle years of our lives trying to get back into some sort of farm-related living. But Joe's distaste for it lasted.

At first he came home every weekend. But the weekends soon got further apart. We learned that he had a girlfriend, his first. She was a Brookhaven girl, an adopted daughter of prominent merchants who shared the fear and prejudice of the CCC invaders but had taken a liking to Joe, partly because he "seemed like such a nice young man," and partly because of the status he enjoyed as Company Clerk. And maybe because they did business with the CCC.

At eighteen Joe had become a handsome man. As a child he was referred to as "knotty," wormy looking. As an adolescent he was thin and gangly, sensitive about the pimples on his face and the way his shoulder blades stuck out. Now he stood over six feet tall and had what people called a "filled out" look about him. His skin was a Latin tan, his hair jet black, coarse and wavy. While he had been shy and unassertive as a child, as a young man he was gregarious and compelling.

On those weekends when he came home there was local courting to do and he began taking me with him. And there were stories of life which he began to share. He, of course, had more to tell than I because he was a big man in the CCC and I was still an East Fork boy with limited experience.

But whatever successes I had Joe heard with pride. I had entered an essay contest sponsored by Sears Roebuck and the 4-H Clubs of the state. Sears would give away six registered Duroc Jersey gilts to those who wrote the best essay on "The Cow, Hog, and Hen Plan of Farming." It was an effort to diversify agricultural pursuits in the area since everyone, except the farmers, was in agreement that the state was slowly choking itself to death by planting nothing but cotton year after year. The assistant county agent, Red McCelvin, had asked Uncle Leo, by then a successful turkey and cattle farmer, if he had written the essay which I had turned in. Since Uncle Leo had not even known that I had submitted one, and since he did not take kindly to having it implied that he had aided a nephew in wrong-doing, he soon convinced the assistant county agent that if the essay were good enough to evoke such a question it was good enough to be declared a winner.

Joe was proud, said so, and laughed with me when I told him of the trip to Natchez where the banquet to award the pigs was held. Troy Laird's boy, Tommy, had also won one of the pigs and we had agreed to let Tommy ride with us to get them. It was sixty miles to Natchez and to get there by noon meant leaving early. While we had been told that only the winner and his father could attend the banquet, it provided an opportunity for others in the family to make the trip. So Mamma, Daddy, Paul, Sister and her husband and little girl, and I loaded up for the trip. When we stopped to get Tommy it was raining and his daddy said that because it was too wet to plow he had decided to go with us. Nine people and two pigs on the return trip was something to share with Joe. As we fixed one of several flat tires, one of the pigs got out of the crate and we had to chase and coax it through the Homochitto swamps for nearly an hour. Joe thought that was the funniest part of all. So I laughed about it too.

Joe and I had become friends, sharing dreams, ambitions, romances, and all the things friends share.

My plunge into the preaching world came suddenly and without much warning. The word had made the rounds that Dave was going to be a preacher. But there had never been anything formal about it. I had mastered the art of public praying and for the past two summers had impressed some of the more pious ones at revival meetings—Hebron, Glading, Thompson, and, of course, East Fork—with long and well-worded prayers which, they had said to one another and to relatives, sounded for the world like a preacher praying. "That boy can pray as sweet a prayer as you ever heard!" Our East Fork pastor, J. Price Brock, had taken an interest in me and would sometimes take me on his preaching circuit. The hour of preaching at each church was arranged to fit the convenience of the preacher. One at nine, another at eleven. Across the county line, thirty miles of dirt road away, still another church would meet at two in the afternoon. Then back to the last by seven that night. He introduced me to his congregations and began to insist that I read certain books. The first was a little handbook on personal timidity. He had noticed that I never talked to anyone on his church fields unless asked a question, would not go to the dinner table until specifically asked, did not shake hands unless the other's hand was offered first. He did not outright say that I had to overcome my shyness if I were going to be a successful preacher but I got the message. Such practical and social habits as that seemed more important than what I might believe about one theological point or another. Interesting that I should find the same thing true throughout years of theological training. The training was for success, not faithfulness to Christian orthodoxy.

Since Brother Brock went to school at what was then called "Baptist Bible Institute," now the New Orleans Baptist Theological Seminary, and must ride the train each weekend the hundred or so miles, his wife and two babies were left alone in the new East Fork parsonage. So I was asked to stay with them during the week and go to school from their house. That was, of course, considered an honor and each morning I would stand, yawning, on the front porch as all the school buses rolled by going to school. Then at the last minute Mrs. Brock, actually not many years older than my own sixteen, would drive me the quarter of a mile to the school house. I tried hard to time it so as to arrive just as the bell was ringing, for that meant that everyone would be in the front of the building as I was saying good-bye to the preacher's wife.

But my debut as a real preacher man had nothing to do with my relationship to the pastor. It started as a joke. In April the eleven members of our graduating class had gone the hundred yards from the schoolhouse to the churchhouse to practice for our forthcoming baccalaureate exercises which, as always, would be held in the East Fork Baptist Church. Mr. Ray Turner was in charge of the rehearsal. His wife, the meanest woman I had ever encountered, and the best English teacher, was assisting.

Someone had played the Washington and Lee March on the piano as we filed down the aisle, and we had remained standing to sing "Follow the Gleam." Something had gone wrong and it must be repeated. Somehow I had made my way to the dais and sat on the double chair reserved for the preacher. It was a holy position and I felt presumptuous and insecure sitting there. I had borrowed from Holland Anderson, one of our classmates, his big, black hat, looking like those worn by Italian priests and it, two sizes too large, covered my head and ears. When the class finished the singing of "Follow the Gleam," they were supposed to sit down. At the precise moment they sat, like a jack-in-the-box, I stood up, placing my hands firmly on the pulpit and looking down at them in judgmental fashion. I had intended to be cute, but not funny. At least not as funny as it apparently was. As they roared with laughter my ears burned with embarrassment. And yet I was more than pleased that I had made them laugh. I glanced quickly in the direction of the principal and his wife. I feared I had committed an act of sacrilege. But they were bursting with uncontrollable guffaws. I was a hit! There was no stopping me then. I went into contortions and gyrations, flailing away at the pulpit, making the veins stand out on my neck. It was a pantomine which would have been a credit to Billy Sunday at his best.

Walking back to the school someone, Gladys Anderson I think, suggested that we should ask Brother Brock to let us have a youth day service at church. Based on that performance, everyone thought it would be a good idea. So in five minutes it was all planned. I would be pastor, Evie Lee would play the piano, Delton as song leader, and so on through the list of church functions including collecting the offering, a job reserved for the deacons.

The youth day was set for late June and until the day came I spent more time practicing my sermon than doing anything else. I continued to work in the field, but if plowing, the sermon outline was tacked on the rung between the two plow handles where I could preach to the rear end of the horse. And I did it with varying enthusiasm. At times I wished that I had never appeared behind that pulpit. But most of the time I felt that I could not wait until the day arrived. Daddy asked on more than one occasion if I would be ready, stating that he had rather I not plow another day than to fail in my first preaching endeavor. He also pointed out one night when we were having our daily Bible readings that my voice was not very strong. I told him of a preacher secret I had heard from Norma Jane, Brother Brock's wife. She had told me that when they were first married she had him drink a glass of pineapple juice before he went into the pulpit on Sunday morning. I had already planned to have a can of pineapple juice on hand that Sunday morning as part of my last minute preparations.

Joe would, of course, come home from the CCC Camp for the occasion. Grandpa Will Parker would be there for sure, Aunt Dolly and other kin from "across the river."

The sermon was called "In the Beginning." The Scripture reading was, appropriately, the first chapter of Genesis, or at least major portions of it. The sermon told of how this was a beginning for us, of how our class could be compared to the creation story. The majority of it dealt with the fact that the Biblical account said, "In the beginning God created the heavens and the earth . . ." and that the rest of the Bible had to do with earth and what happened there and not with heaven. I was a sixteen-year-old fundamentalist, but for some reason which I have never understood I had never taken much to preachments about other worlds—above or below. It was, in many ways, heretical and modernistic for East Fork. But on that occasion I could have denounced Christianity as a capitalistic myth cunningly designed to keep the masses under control, and our youth choir could have sung Ukrainian folk songs, and our Sunday School superintendent could have lectured on "The Origin of Species," and all the people would have said "Amen." Never had they been so proud of us. I chided the oldsters and chastised them lightly for being irregular at Sunday night services and this was the most appreciated part of all. It meant that Dave was not to be a preacher who would tolerate sin, and would denounce it no matter how unpopular it made him. (Somehow the pride of some of those in attendance that day went sour when the little preacher years later turned to denouncing social sins.)

Everyone in the graduating class had some part in the service. And we were all roundly hugged and congratulated and commended for having done so splendidly. Uncle Hilary, or "Uncle Fork" as we called him, Grandpa Campbell's half-brother, father of my buddy Thaxton, or "Snooky," and the one who was considered a drunk though he was in fact a moderate drinker, allowed to all standing around after the service that they should remember that day for they would be hearing much from the little preacher. Ray Turner, a great teacher in any age, simply whispered, "Plow deep," the R.F.D. version of "Right on." Aunt Ida, not really Aunt but sister to Aunt Donnie, wife of Uncle Fork, who lived with them and was considered rich because she lived on some kind of mysterious disability insurance policy, kissed me and cried. Joe made no comment but gave me the kind of look that told me he had been extremely proud of what I had done. For I had stood up, laid my dollar Ingram watch on the pulpit—an act which had nothing to do with when I began or stopped for it was all written down, a fact which brought the only criticism from one aunt, which Mamma dismissed as jealousy because one of her boys was not making a preacher—and said my piece.

Somehow I did not feel as awed in the presence of Joe after that. His success as a company clerk, his being the one providing the bulk of the money, both in the family needs and when the two of us were out on social occasions, his uniform and his poise in the presence of girlfriends, had been enough to keep me in a state of wonderment.

Now I could claim a success of my own.

For I was a full-fledged preacher, entitled to buy Coca-Colas at clergy discount.

J oe was not long in utilizing my new status and vocation. He said they had a chaplain who lived in Jackson and served the CCC Camp in Brookhaven and the one near Meadville, twenty-five miles to the west. He indicated that the chaplain was not the most dedicated and conscientious of ministers and that he probably would readily agree for me to preach for him at one camp or the other so he wouldn't have to do it himself. In a week or two Joe wrote and said I was to speak on the following Wednesday. I assumed that it was to be at the Brookhaven camp and hitchhiked there in the early afternoon. I found Joe busy with his duties as Company Clerk, but he took the time to explain to me that there had been some confusion, suggesting that there always was when the chaplain was involved, and told me that the chaplain was speaking there in late afternoon because an inspector from the Fourth Army Corps was there, and that I was to be the preacher at the camp at Meadville that night. Joe was arranging to have me transported there in a staff car when the chaplain decided at the last minute that he would go with us.

The staff car assigned to him was the latest model Dodge sedan, painted army brown. I had never ridden in a vehicle so new or fancy. There was an awkward moment as we were about to depart. The chauffeur opened the door and the chaplain took his usual place in the back seat. The driver did not know whether to open the other back door or the front door opposite his seat for me. He stood waiting for some sign or indication from the chaplain who was similarly uncertain of the protocol in such a situation, perhaps not having been instructed on this particular circumstance by the CCC Chaplain's Manual. I was not about to risk a social error by choosing the wrong seat in a CCC automobile. It must have been a full minute before the chaplain said, "Maybe you had better sit back here with me." His hesitation made me feel just a bit unwelcome. Then the chauffeur expressed further bewilderment and was not sure if he should come around and open the door for me as he had for the major or if I should open my own door. Thinking, I suppose, that everyone should risk something, I opened the door myself and climbed in.

Finding, upon our arrival, that the inspector had in fact preceded us, the chaplain made a quick decision that he should do the preaching. He had told me as we rode along that he would begin the service with a few words of welcome and then turn it over to me to conduct as I saw fit. Instead he did it all, the hymns, prayers, Scripture readings and finally a sermon. He told his congregation of not more than a dozen boys that he was not going to deliver the sermon he had prepared for the occasion because of something he had heard one of the boys say as his car was driving into the camp. He indicated that it was so profane, so obscene, so offensive to chastity that he could not repeat it from behind a pulpit but instead wrote it down on a piece of brown paper bag and carefully buttoned it inside his uniform pocket, saying that anyone who wanted to see it could do so after the sermon. The discourse which followed was filled with examples of what such language could lead to, from drunkenness to crime to the electric chair. The boys appeared more confused than persuaded. When he finished he announced that there was a guest present and that he would now come forth and say a few words. I had not come prepared to say a few words but rather to deliver, for the second time, the exact sermon I had given at East Fork a few weeks earlier. I knew at the time that a full length homily was not indicated for the situation but didn't know what else to do. I had it all typed and inside the looseleaf binder I had used the first time. So I did what I had come there to do—read my Scripture and give my sermon. Neither the fact that I had done so nor the content and quality of my remarks were commented upon during the ride back.

When we arrived back in Brookhaven the chaplain showed the first gesture of kindness of the entire experience. At least, I interpreted it to be a gesture of kindness. Instead it turned out to be a cynical prank intended to further embarrass the green and inexperienced preacher boy who had gotten in his way and, according to Joe, ruined his own plans for the evening.

As we were driving into town, knowing that I had not come prepared to spend the night but intended instead to preach in the afternoon and then return home, he said, "Brother Will, where are you going to stay tonight?" At first I assumed that he was going to offer to find me a bunk at the camp. But he continued, "You know, it's against the rules for civilians to stay overnight at the camp." I timidly replied that I would probably try to hitchhike on back that night. "No, that's too risky. I'll tell you what. There's a nice little tourist home [this was before the days of motels and motor inns] right here in town. Why don't you just stay there tonight and go on back in the morning?" I had no idea what staying in a tourist home overnight would cost but was certainly not going to tell him that I had only two dollars in my pocket. But he had already sensed that. "It won't cost you but four dollars. And I'll tell you what. You've been mighty nice to come all the way up here at your own expense." He ceremoniously placed a five dollar bill in my hand as the driver pulled into the drive of what had once been a large and gracious residence.

I noted with curiosity, yet with special pride, that the woman who came to the door to admit me paid more than passing attention to the Bible and looseleaf notebook I held in my hand when I entered. The Bible was my badge and I wore it with honor and did not see my public display of it as any more ostentatious than a doctor coming into a house with a stethoscope in his hand. It was not a matter of flaunting it but rather a testimony to one of my favorite Scripture texts: "For I am not ashamed of the Gospel of Christ . . ."

It was a strange night I spent there. People seemed to be moving around, coming in and going out all night. And there were new sounds, noises which I had not heard before. I connected it all with the noise of the traffic on the streets—the ways of city folks. I slept very little and was glad when the morning sun indicated that it was time to leave. Joe explained what I had not understood when he asked me later that weekend where I had spent the night.

"That son-of-a-bitch! That son-of-a-bitch!"

I had spent my first night as a circuit riding preacher in a whorehouse.

I felt betrayed and disgraced and somehow defiled. Joe saw the anger rising from within but quickly moved in before it could be expressed. "No, Will. You're a preacher. Just leave it to me."

When he had taken my own sin upon himself at the time of my baptism it was by standing apart from the crowd on the river bank, angry and sullen at Sears Roebuck for not sending my white britches on time. This time he would use his personal affability and charm, as well as his position, to influence those to whom the chaplain must give answer.

From time to time he would report with considerable satisfaction on the progress of the vendetta he began against the chaplain. Once he insisted that the Commanding Officer, who by then had become his close friend despite the wide gap in age and rank, go to chapel with him so he would observe first hand that the "Man of the Spirit" was almost a man of the spirits. At other times he would add to the morning report, which he had to prepare as Company Clerk, a not so subtle reference to the effect that "the chaplain made his usual weekly appearance despite the fact that he appeared ill and had trouble walking and speaking." But he would never let me even voice approval of what he was doing. It was *his* sin and I was to remain obedient to the vow of purity—a vow he had taken for me more than I had taken for myself. Despite my fundamentalist commitment, I was not, even then, as pietistic and moralistic as Joe insisted that I be and assumed and accepted that I was.

One Sunday afternoon a middle-aged couple stopped at our house and I could hear them exchanging excited greetings with Mamma and Daddy. They sat on the porch for a long time while I, still shy and fearful of strangers, stayed in the bedroom. After they had talked, Daddy came in and said Mr. Sharp from Baton Rouge wanted to talk to me. Tom Sharp, I was to learn, had grown up near Grandpa Parker's place, close to where Mamma and Aunt Dolly had watched as Lum and Stump Cleveland had been killed. He had drifted away, and was then chief financial officer for the Esso Corporation of Louisiana. This was the first time he had been back in many years and he had been present that morning when I preached at the Southside Baptist Church in McComb. He had asked his host, Jewell Parker, a first cousin to Mamma, who I was and where I lived. When Jewell, responsible for my being the supply preacher that morning, told him that I was one of Lee and Ted's boys, he had driven out to talk to us.

He came right to the point. "Where are you planning to go to school?" I had not given it much thought because such a decision did not require much thought. If one went to college from East Fork it was always, no exceptions, to the Southwest Junior College in Summit, a small town about fifteen miles away. I replied, "I guess to Southwest." "How would you like to go to one of our fine Baptist Colleges?" I had learned of Mississippi College in Clinton and hoped to transfer there after two years at Southwest. I told him of that plan and he said that would be fine, that Mississippi College was a good school, but "How would you like to go to Louisiana College now instead of Southwest?" (I assumed that he was speaking of L.S.U., with which we were all familiar because that was where Uncle Clifton had been captain of the football team for two years after finishing at Hattiesburg, and we had relished his stories over the years of how he had—in addition to playing football—fed the hogs for the university to work his way through school. Being an outstanding athlete was not so rewarding in the days immediately following World War I. He had also been the one appointed, perhaps with some small stipend, to guard the money collected at games, until the banks opened on Monday morning. We had re-lived with him his stories of putting the money in a large canvas sack and using it for a pillow on Saturday and Sunday nights.)

I told Mr. Sharp that I had not given that possibility any thought but, yes, I would like to go. Then he asked me how much money I had. I told him the truth in figures while Daddy softly chuckled the truth from his end of the porch. I had a job for three months work-ing in the cemetery and they were paying me fifteen dollars a month. In addition, I was taking care of the school principal's bird dogs while he was doing further study at George Peabody College for Teachers in Nashville. He had not told me how much I would be paid, but we knew him to be a fair and honorable man, and I was sure that he would pay me something. Mr. Sharp said, "Well, we won't worry too much about the money," but gave no other assurance. Instead he asked Daddy if I could come to Baton Rouge the following weekend.

On the next Saturday evening, after Mr. and Mrs. Sharp had taken me to register at the college, we drove to one of their friend's residence, a porticoed mansion with crystal chandeliers, stairways and bannisters, hard-wood floors, doors and windows of ornate abundance, and furniture such as I had never seen before. The meeting was held in the library, a room almost as big as our entire house. Maps, charts, and diagrams lined the room and a huge outline of the Great Pyramid was on an easel facing the double row of chairs.

A Brunhilde-like matron approached the front and began to fill in names of the various chambers, rooms, corridors, galleries and passageways of the pyramid. To this she added the assemblage of the evening. She reviewed what had been covered in earlier sessions, pointing to the king's chamber and what period of history it symbolized; likewise for the queen's chamber, and several other compartments, carefully dating each one as she approached the area she would discuss on that occasion. And that particular compartment foretold the Second World War which was also, she informed us, to be the last of wars. The milennium was approaching when Christ would return to rule the earth for a thousand years.

Some of that was not new to me. We had talked about it in Sunday School a few times, although haltingly and without the authority she evidenced there, and without the documentation of such an impressive array of graphs and charts. And we had listened to the fulminations of Uncle Charlie Baham after the Jehovah's Witness book salesman had traveled through and captivated his head and heart.

But there was an added dimension here. Though a lot of it was vaguely familiar, the real point she was making I had not heard before. In her review she had indicated that in an earlier lecture she had established and documented beyond doubt that the Anglo-Saxons were for a fact the lost tribe of Israel. This meant, among other things, that *we*, and not the Jews (as we had been taught), were God's chosen people. It was my first excursion into that elitist world, and I found myself rather liking it. But one thing bothered me as the lecture proceeded. More and more we were brought to see that Hitler was not all bad, that Franklin Roosevelt was bordering on anti-Christ, in league with the Devil to try to keep the world from coming to its intended end.

I had never known a Jew. There were a few families, merchants in McComb, we referred to as "the Jews" and mocked their accents and talked about how they ate bananas when they were too rotten to sell, and were rich and stingy. But Uncle Boyce had long since explained to us that the Calebs and the Mickels were not Jews, but Methodists whose ancestors had come from Sicily. It was all too much for me to comprehend. I knew it was not the orthodoxy of East Fork, yet in this setting of elegance and charm it was attractive. And it was impossible for me to fault two people whose kindness and generosity had already been expressed in such a magnanimous fashion.

I knew that Joe would have some opinion on the matter, so I remembered what I could of it and shared it with him. They had given me a handful of tracts and magazines all dealing with a notion called Anglo-Israel. I gave these to Joe and he did little more than thumb through them. "Sounds like a bunch of dopes." I told him that, on the contrary, they were smart people, good people, living in big houses, driving big cars, and had offered to send me to college. He thought about it a while longer, took another, though still cursory, look at the articles. "Sounds like a bunch of *rich* dopes."

What, then, was I supposed to do about the money they had already invested in me and indicated they would be sending from time to time. "Sniff it out. Take a good long smell. Check the strings. If they ain't too tight . . . keep the money." I took his advice and it was to be a relationship which would last for no more than a year and they never mentioned the Anglo-Israel Movement to me again. Whether it was just a fad with them, which passed as the nation was swept into war, I never knew. I did, however, learn that I was flirting with the demon of anti-Semitism in its most dangerous and sinister form—rich people, powerful and good people, not really meaning any harm, who probably meant it when they said some of their best friends were Jews.

When I arrived at Louisiana College to begin preparation for the ministry, the campus clearly rendered more to Caesar than to the lowly Galilean I had followed there. The archway which served as entry to the grounds was guarded by two sections of machinegunners. As one rounded the drive and approached the administration building, the fire streaking from giant anti-aircraft guns, shooting at low-flying planes could be seen. Tanks rumbled along the periphery while uniformed soldiers, forbidden to play cards on these Baptist grounds where their tents were pitched, made poker, canasta, and pinochle sounds from small groups across the fence, and haggled with sandwich and soft drink vendors as they made their rounds. It was the Louisiana Maneuvers, the biggest wargame ever scheduled, a rehearsal which was soon to become as real as death it-self in places like Bougainville, Iwo Jima, Casablanca, Salerno, and Normandy Beach.

Though classes were not taken seriously and I was ill prepared for college, I did learn to diagram a sentence under patient instruction of Miss Hall, that cereal comes from Iowa and beef from Nebraska in Professor "Squatty" Strouther's Civics class, a few things about *Beowulf* and the Venerable Bede from Dr. Carson, and a lot of things about the Bible and life from a comical and saintly old man named Brother Brakefield who would, in obvious annoyance at the rat-a-tat-tat of the machine gun outside, pull all the blinds, then open one of them long enough to peer briefly outside and yell, "Roll on civilization!"—that being the first indication he ever gave us that he realized the irony and incongruity of all that was going on around us. The other indication came when he chose as text for his sermon on the evening of December 7, 1941 the following passage: "Every man to his city, and every man to his own country. So the king died, and was brought to Samaria; and they buried the king in Samaria. And one washed the chariot in the pool of Samaria; and the dogs licked up his blood; according unto the word of the Lord which he spake." His words were not a call to arms but a call to repentance. He made little mention of the war. The point he made, and made well, was that America was in deep moral trouble. He left no doubt that the military victory would be ours. "But," he thundered, "the victors have a strange way of accepting the gods of the vanquished." How could he have known? If we had asked him, which we didn't, he would have given his usual response: "It's in the Book."

IN the midst of the flood of patriotic fervor that ensued after Pearl Harbor, Joe remained indifferent, even antagonistic.

He had participated in both the NYA and the CCC, as well as eating at the trough of one Federal program or another since childhood. But this had not prepared him for war. He had no systematic or ideological rationale for his position, and it would not have occurred to him to seek conscientious objector status. It was just in his bones. A part of it was simply his stubborn resistance to authority of any kind. He did not like to give or receive orders. And despite the fact that he had succeeded and actually thrived in the CCC, he hated any kind of regimentation. He sought, and got, the position of Company Clerk, he said, not so much because he would rather type than plant trees, but because as Company Clerk he had private sleeping quarters in the headquarters building and did not have to sleep in the barracks with a hundred other people. A part of it also was his conviction that "this war won't do any good."

Joe visited me not long after the war began. I met him at the bus and after holding me in a long embrace he blurted, "Well, Brother, they've called my number." It was the first time he had called me "Brother" since we were children.

When we were little, Cousin Ed and Cousin Melissa Campbell lived for a while in a house Uncle Bob and Aunt Susie had built when they were first married. It was on Grandpa Bunt's place, behind where we lived. They were distant cousins and we really didn't consider them kinfolk. But Grandpa did, and let them live on his place during the depression years when there was nowhere else for them to go. They had two boys, both older than we were, and for some reason we considered them different. The oldest one was named Vernon Lee and was married to a woman named May. We thought she looked like a mail box.

Their youngest boy was named J. W. but everybody called him "Brother." Cousin Melissa had a lisp and called him "Buh'ther." Joe used to call me "Buh'ther" when he wanted to tease or humor me. Before the war Cousin Ed took his family back to Fernwood and they all worked in the box factory. And shortly after Joe joined the CCC Camp, Vernon Lee and May were involved in a car wreck and Vernon Lee was killed. They brought him back to East Fork to bury him and the preacher held up a whiskey bottle at the funeral and said if it hadn't been for that Vernon Lee would still be alive. Within a few months J. W. married May, and, because they had all lived in the same house all along, it was considered scandalous.

Joe had not called me "Brother" since. Now, as he embraced me, he called me "Brother." But we both knew that it meant something different then. It was what he would call me from then on. It became the rule. It was violated only when there was some strain between us.

By then, I was preaching twice a month in a country church not far from Huey and Earl Long's home, working twenty hours a week at B. Ginsberg's clothing store, was assistant business manager of the college newspaper, and had just met Brenda Fisher—a factor far outdistancing the others in interest and in time. But Joe wanted to talk about the war. His objection to going had become an obsession. My thinking had got no further than equating my religious convictions with duty to country.

Joe had moved beyond that: "I'm not going. I'm not going! I'm not going!" I expressed some of the prevalent sentiment of the day about freedom and patriotism. He still wasn't going.

"Freedom? How am I free if they won't leave me alone. You think I'll be free in the chickenshit Army? Hell no! There ain't no freedom there. I've already seen it, man. It's dog eat dog, and the big dog does all the chewing." I said something about Hitler taking over the world and none of us being free.

"Brother, nobody *is* free. Freedom is how much you're willing to do to get people to leave you alone.

"And patriotism? That's just something they sold us. How can you love a country? A country is nothing but a big piece of geography. I love that eighty acres of land up there in Amite County where we were raised. But I can't love three million square miles."

When we began to talk about what he proposed to do to stay out of the Army he stated with resignation, "Nothing. I'll have to go.

"Well, Brother, to hell with it. Let's go to a movie." I wanted to take Brenda but he insisted that we go alone. "The poor ye have with you always. You can see her from now on. Let's just me and you go."

The movie was *Sergeant York*. Joe picked up a line from Gary Cooper which would be a favorite expression for him through many a crisis. "I'll be acoming back, Ma." He practiced until he could say it with the same drawl and inflection Gary Cooper used. "I'll be acoming back, Ma." He said it over and over the rest of the weekend and at the bus station he waved through the crowd and said it again. "I'll be acoming back, Ma." They were words I would have cause to remember.

There were a few delaying tactics but nothing more. He was deferred for two months while he and his Company Commander traveled around the state phasing out and closing up the few CCC Camps still in existence. "Discharging 'em and enlisting 'em," Joe called it. Virtually all of the enlistees in the CCC program went directly into the Army. He tried, after that, to enroll in one of the V-5 or V-12 programs, college training sponsored and paid for by the military for those with unusual technical or mechanical aptitude, but he failed the exams.

Shortly before he was to be inducted he was stricken with a near ruptured appendix and we both assumed that the disablement would lead to at least a temporary exemption. The incision failed to heal properly and both he and the surgeon appealed for a delay. But one month after the surgery he was ordered to report. He phoned and said that he had been properly selected by a board of his neighbors and friends, to go to war. He managed at the last minute to be assigned to the Army Air Corps (which he saw as better than the other branches), and was sent to Jefferson Barracks, Missouri.

I went home a few days before he was inducted. He was supposed to be at the Liberty Courthouse at eight o'clock, but it was almost twelve before the chartered bus came to get the thirty new soldiers from Amite County, Mississippi. It was the same courthouse where Allen Westbrook had been hanged. We talked about that while we waited. It was the courthouse in which records of deeds to our property, mortgages, birth certificates, hunting licenses, draft numbers, marriage and death certificates of kinfolk were stored. We talked about that too, Joe lamenting and complaining that the government knew too much about us. "You know, Brother, if the damn government hadn't ever been told I was born I wouldn't be waiting here now for a bus to take me somewhere I don't want to go."

Joe teased Mamma about the lunch she had fixed for him. "What you got in the 'teet' bucket, Myrtis?" It was his pet name for her. As the bus pulled away, seeing that Mamma was about to cry, he stuck his head out the window, grinning as best he could. With a "chin up" motion with one hand, he beat on the side of the bus with the other as the straining noise of the big diesel engine almost drowned out his words. "I'll be acoming back, Ma."

I knew that I would soon follow him. Despite the fact that we had not been together on any regular basis for almost two years, I felt a certain loneliness and uneasiness knowing that he was miserable and I was enjoying life. Since I was studying for the ministry, I was classified 4-D and would not be drafted. I was failing in school, bored with the routine, and coasting in my social life. It seemed a good time to enlist.

But enlistment was not easy in my case. I spent far more time trying to get in than Joe had spent trying to stay out. I tried the Navy recruitment office, but they said I would have to have a 1-A classification before they could consider me. I suspected that my hundred and seven pounds was no more impressive to them than the number on my draft card. The Marine folks just looked at one another and said they had their quota for that quarter, but that I could come back in three months if I wanted to. The Army took the same position as the Navy.

That meant I had to appeal to the local Draft Board which was even more frustrating and confusing than trying to explain my case to the military. Seeing that I was not only a ministerial student, but ordained already and pastoring a church, they admitted that they had not had a case such as mine come before them. When one of them asked why I didn't continue my training and become a chaplain, I replied that one had to be twenty-four years old to be a chaplain and that I was only eighteen and feared the war would be over in six years and I would miss it. They indicated with their looks and sighs that it would be no great inconvenience to them if I missed the war. After saying they would have to seek legal counsel, they said they would be in touch. About a month later they wrote that my status had been changed to 1-A.

I never knew how Joe got the news that I was planning to enlist. We never discussed the possibility of my going and in every conversation about his going he would conclude with, "Well, thank god, *you* don't have to go." After I got the notice I withdrew from school, or simply quit going to class, but continued to live in the dormitory and work at the store until I could be inducted. Joe began to call two and three times a day, and to write daily letters. "Don't do it, Will. Please. For my sake. For Mamma's and Daddy's sake. For God's sake. Dammit, Will. Please don't get into this mess." He was still in basic training at Jefferson Barracks, the incision in his side still draining. Sometimes he would call late at night. On several occasions he called me while I was at work at B. Ginsberg's store.

"But I've got to go now, Joe. I'm 1-A. It's just a matter of getting drafted. Now I'm just like everyone else."

"Hell, no. You don't. You're a man of the cloth. You're ordained. You can get the damn classification changed back. Please, Will." Over and over. Every day until late December when I told him I was reporting to Camp Beauregard on January 7.

For the most part it was, for both of us, an uneventful war. He was sent to the Panama Canal Zone to be an Air Corps clerk, and I, after training to be an M-1 rifleman, was sent to New Caledonia, Guam, and Saipan to be a medic, working most of the time as a surgical technician, an assignment I tried hard not to accept. But my ministerial status again betrayed me. The Master Sergeant, who was interviewing us at the replacement depot on New Caledonia, routinely assigning us all to the 45th Division, then engaged in heavy combat with the Japanese, asked me two or three questions about basic training, whether I thought I was ready for combat, checking my service record at the same time. Suddenly he stopped what he was writing and said, "I see you're from Mississippi." I replied that he was correct. "I see you're from Liberty, Mississippi." I told him that was our post office, but that we lived several miles out of town. "Toward McComb?" "That's right. Toward McComb." "You ever hear of somebody named Shorty Campbell?" I told him that I had an Uncle they called Shorty, but his real name was Clifton Collinsworth Campbell, but that he didn't live there anymore. "Yea. I know. He lives in Coushatta, Louisiana, and I was in the Rotary Club with him and lived just down the street from him before I got drafted."

He had already put my record in the file, but reached into the basket and pulled it out. He studied it for several minutes. "I see you were at Louisiana College studying for the ministry." I told him that was correct. "Why weren't you 4-D?" I chuckled and told him my enlistment story. He shook his head and turned the paper over and over, staring at it and at nothing in particular. "Do you plan to be ordained?" When I replied that I had already been ordained he pushed his chair back and stood up. "Look, little buddy, you don't even have to be here. We had a case like this through here two months ago. I'm sending you home!" "No! I mean, please . . . I can't do that. I want to go on up with my buddies. We've been together a long time and I'm going with them." "You've been together three months. Now shape up, man. I can get you out of this hell. You don't know what you're talking about. I've been up there. I went through Guadalcanal and Rendora. I know what it's like. And I'm lucky as hell to be alive. Now, all I have to do is fill in a form, get it signed, and the next boat that's going that way, you'll be on it. It's that simple."

I tried to explain to him that my brother had been drafted, that all my cousins and friends from home were in one part of the world or another, and I didn't feel justified sitting in Pineville, Louisiana doing nothing. But I saw that I had to do better than that. So I lied. He remained standing, hands folded across his chest, glaring at me, a man fully as big as my uncle, his friend. "Sergeant, I'm going to tell you the truth. I knew a lot of boys at Louisiana College saying they were going to be preachers just to keep from going into service. I'm going to be a preacher all my life. And twenty years from now I don't want anybody wondering why I decided to go into the ministry just as the country was going into war."

He probably knew I was lying, but it was enough to effect a compromise. "Okay, Private Campbell." He sat down and tore up the assignment card he had started. "But I tell you what. I just got a call from the 109th Station Hospital here on the Island. They need some orderlies. How do you think you'll like being a medic?"

I protested some more. "I want to go up in combat with my buddies. That's what I'm trained for. I don't know anything about being a medic." "They'll teach you all you need to know." I tried once more. "How about being a combat medic? I could be a litter bearer." It was too late. He continued to write. "I owe your uncle a favor, Private. I think he would like the way I'm evening the score. Now, dismissed!"

Brenda and I sat in front of a late December fire in Daddy and Mamma's house talking of marriage. I had been home from the war for one week. Though we had not seen one another for more than two years, we had written to each other every day during that period and probably knew each other better than most couples who had been together constantly. We would be married at her parents' house in two weeks.

Suddenly there was a banging and bumping on the front door and loud talking. Before I could reach it, the door opened and there stood Vernon Anderson, a big, loveable cousin of ours, holding Joe in his arms.

"What's going on? What's the matter with Joe?"

"He can't walk. He can't stand up. Help me get him to the bed."

Joe, at twenty-three, was over six feet tall and was well built. Vernon carried and dragged him to a nearby cot and when we stretched him out he turned over and didn't move. I checked his pulse and respiration. Slow, but stable. I frantically examined him for other signs I had learned to recognize during two years in a wartime operating room.

"You guys been boozing?" "No, Will. I swear to God. We went to the picture show and took these girls home and Joe said his leg was hurting. We stopped and got a Coke and he took some of his medicine. When we got to the house he couldn't get out."

"What kind of medicine?"

"I don't know what it is. Some kind of capsules. And some little pills." Vernon ran to the car, got Joe's coat and showed me the bottles. One contained several one-and-one-half grain nembutal capsules. The other about an equal number of half-grain codeine pills. Both bottles bore the label of the Camp Shelby hospital, where they had been prescribed for Joe's injured leg. Both were safe drugs unless taken in large doses and in that combination.

By shaking, slapping, and half standing him up, we got him awake enough for me to ask him how many he had taken.

"I didn't take but three, Will. They won't hurt me." His voice was soft and his speech slurred.

"Three of what?"

"Nembutal."

"How much of the codeine?"

"Two."

Not enough to hurt a man of his size, and not enough to incapacitate him beyond the point of walking. But he had indicated to Vernon that he couldn't stand. Next morning he asked me what Mamma thought about what happened and when she entered the room he smiled at her and said, "I'll be acoming back, Ma."

News of his injury had come to me in a circuitous and suspenseful manner. I was sitting on my bunk in our thatch barracks on New Caledonia, reading a stack of V-Mail letters. They were all pretty much routine, news from friends in the States and from Army buddies. Toward the middle of the stack was one from Paul, our younger brother. It began, "It sure was too bad about Joe and Prentiss. We were all very sad, but everyone is beginning to recover." The remainder of his letter was trivia. His flowers were doing well. He had a new girlfriend. He was working hard and saving his money. But no further word about Joe and Prentiss.

I knew Joe had been transferred to Brookley Field in Mobile, Alabama. And he had told me in his last letter that he was supposed to go home on furlough. Prentiss, Vernon's brother, was in the Navy, but we didn't correspond. I didn't know what the news was, but I knew it wasn't good.

Brenda wrote every day, but sometimes eight or ten letters would come at once. The next day was such a delivery. I hurried through every letter, hoping that she had received word from Mississippi. She occasionally visited our parents, riding the bus from Louisiana College where she was still a student.

"I was real sorry to hear about Joe." Just that. None of the other letters mentioned what it was.

There was an American Red Cross unit on the Island, and I took my problem to them. Within three days, but quite long days, they had the story for me. Prentiss and Joe were both on furlough. Prentiss, with his Navy wife of two weeks, and Joe had been out for the evening. Prentiss had lost control of the car a few hundred yards from home as they were returning. Prentiss had been killed instantly. Joe had a serious concussion and a broken leg. The wife was unhurt. That was the Red Cross report. It was a sad relief.

Joe lay unconscious in the McComb Hospital during the days it took the military to go through all the channels to transfer him to the nearest Army hospital at Camp Shelby. News was hard to come by. By then New Caledonia and the entire South Pacific was not taken as seriously as it had been earlier in the war. Ships and planes were going directly to the Marianas and other central Pacific islands where the buildup for the anticipated invasion of Japan was taking place. That meant that we were short on mail, low on food, and even lower in morale.

Joe recovered from the concussion, but the leg would not heal properly. It was a compound fracture of the femur, up near the pelvis, but should have been a routine case in orthopedic circles of any competence at all. Because of a continuing fever, some hallucination and reversal of personality, he was thought for a time to have a fat embolism, an extremely serious development in fracture cases, but this was eventually ruled out. Long after the bone should have been well knitted, an X-ray showed that it had moved apart and out of line. Months later, when it did appear healed and the cast had been removed, he refused to stand or attempt to walk. When the physical therapy department failed to gain his confidence and cooperation they brought in a psychiatrist. When that produced no results the chief of orthopedic surgery threatened him with court martial for malingering. Rather than face that, he agreed to try. As soon as they stood him up he fell, breaking the bone in the same place. What had earlier been a soldier's willful disobedience of an order became, in the military pecking order, "Who the hell made this man stand up?" His position had been vindicated, but his leg was broken and seven more months of treatment and convalescence was indicated. Years later he confided to me that he had unloosened the straps on the brace the technician had put on him shortly before they stood him up. When I asked him why, he said, "I told them bastards I couldn't walk and I proved it." It seemed an extreme measure to make a point. But by then I think Joe would just as soon have been lying on a hospital bed as enduring the senseless military regimen.

Now he lay on a cot in our mamma's livingroom, an honorable discharge in his pocket, one leg almost an inch shorter than the other, insisting once more that he couldn't stand up.

We talked a lot during the days that followed. For the very first time I began to feel a hesitation on Joe's part in being my leader. During all the years of the past he was always willing, and generally anxious, to answer my questions, support me in my uncertainties, give his opinion. I was not only on the eve of getting married, I was planning to go to Wake Forest College, a place several hundred miles away. I needed and wanted his approval. But he wasn't so sure it was a good idea. "I don't know, Will. That's an awful long way off. Maybe you ought to think about going back to Louisiana College." It was not what I had hoped to hear because I had some uncertainties of my own. More and more he began to question me as to what I thought *he* should do, now that the war was over, no more CCC or Army, and jobs hard to find. He told me that he had always wanted to be a pharmacist, ever since we used to stand on the tips of our toes and look into Dr. Quin's abandoned office at all the mysterious bottles and mortars and pestles. But he wasn't sure he could make it. All that chemistry and math—subjects he had not mastered very well in high school. Over and over he would ask me what I thought. Over and over I told him I thought he ought to try it.

During the long months while Joe was in the hospital and I was in the jungles of the South Pacific he had written many strange and distressing letters. One of those letters was not as strange to me as it was surprising. The Army was as rigidly segregated racially as society back home. More so, actually, because black soldiers were in different camps and bases and the only sight each had of the other was in town. In my case that meant there was no contact at all since New Caledonia had but one small town and there was seldom occasion to go there. If I had thought anything at all about race relations it was certainly not along the lines Joe was talking in his letter. I certainly did not think of myself as a bigot; I just found no occasion to violate the behavioral norm of my Mississippi upbringing. Such was obviously not the case with Joe. He wrote in long and anguished details of the suffering of black people since slavery. A lot of "did you knows?" were added about the contributions and accomplishments of Negroes. But mostly he urged me to find and read a book he had recently completed. He said, "It'll turn your head around." He added that he knew I could find it in the Post library because it was one of those which had been selected by the Council on Books in Wartime, an independent agency which, in cooperation with the Armed Services, made certain books available in small, convenient, and economical form. He even listed the Armed Services Edition, T-26, he was so anxious for me to read it. I did find the little book and read it. It did, as Joe had predicted, turn my head around.

The name of the book was *Freedom Road*, by Howard Fast. A historical novel, it was the story of an illiterate former slave named Gideon Jackson. The setting was near Charleston, South Carolina, and the time was the reconstruction period. Gideon Jackson was elected as a delegate to the constitutional convention, had, with great pain and sacrifice, learned to read and write, and was eventually elected to Congress. His family's economic situation sounded at times like our own family history of that period. With great patience, wisdom and insight he had succeeded in getting poor whites organized politically and economically in opposition to the gentry and plantation class. Fast, in the book, very graphically depicted the purpose and activities of the Ku Klux Klan—an organization I remembered primarily for presenting the pulpit Bible in our church—and described in detail the manner in which the Klansmen were used to destroy Gideon's alliance between poor whites and Negroes. The climax came when President Rutherford B. Hayes withdrew the Federal troops that had occupied the area since the Civil War. A great battle concluded the book in which Gideon, his family, and all their compatriots in the alliance were slaughtered as they sought to defend themselves. One of them, the son of Gideon who had become a doctor, had agreed to go to the encampment of the Klan where one of their troops had to have an injured leg amputated to save his life. When he hesitated to say "Sir" after the operation was successfully concluded, he was shot and killed.

Though it was a short book, I was a slow reader, and it took me all night and into the hot Sunday morning of the South Pacific to finish it. They were the most powerful and compelling words I had read in my nineteen years. The poor whites, the Abner Laits, the Will Boones he described, were my people. And I knew that the black men and women—Marcus, Jeff, Rachel and Jenny, and Brother Peter—were those we grew up thinking we had to oppose. I had never questioned why we were so taught before, that it was because for us to do otherwise would constitute a threat to those who ruled us before the Civil War and who had in just one decade after the war succeeded in ruling us again. Sitting in the tropics, I read the final words my brother in a hospital bed almost all the way across the world had recommended to me.

Gideon Jackson's last memory as the shell struck, as the shell burst and caused his memory to cease being, was of the strength of those people in his land, the black and the white, the strength that had taken them through a long war, that had enabled them to build, out of the ruin, a promise for the future, a promise that was, in a sense, more wonderful than any the world had ever known. Of that strength, the strange yet simple ingredients were the people—there were so many of them, so many shades and colors, some strong, some weak, some wise, some foolish: yet together they made the whole of the thing that was the last memory of Gideon Jackson, the thing indefinable and unconquerable.

I knew that my life would never be the same. I knew that the tragedy of the South would occupy the remainder of my days. It was a conversion experience comparable to none I had ever had, and I knew it would have to find expression.

But there were other letters which would continue to bother me. He talked of having visions, of his own impending death, of feeling that he was called to be a minister, and of how we could work together in a church somewhere. Often the very next letter would be filled with ribald reminiscence and the anticipation of good time sins when he got out of the hospital. Later there might be still another lengthy spiritual or supernatural rumination.

Knowing something of what lying for months in the isolation of an Army hospital bed could do to one, I did not take the letters too seriously. But now that we were both back home and the time had come to move on to other things, I began to be frightened at the sight of him lying day after day on the cot in our mamma's house. And during those days I began to have the lonely feeling that my leader was gone from me.

Hey, Brother. You little turd. Where the hell you been? Brother! God bless! Man, I been looking for you since seven o'clock this morning. I never been so glad to see your little scrawny ass in my life." With both hands pressed tightly around my waist he picked me up and threw me into the air, kissing me twice on the forehead as he did so.

"Damn it if it ain't good to see you, Brother. I ain't shittin' you. I been looking out that window since seven o'clock this morning. Myrtis said you might leave home last night and I really expected to get up this morning and find you beating on my door. Man you're looking good. Come'ear! Come'ear!" He jerked me between a tall hedge and the building. "I've got to examine you, Brother.

"Whence came ye?"

"From a lodge of the holy Saints John of Jerusalem."

"What came ye here to do?"

"To learn to subdue my passions and improve myself in Masonry."

"You got it! You got it! I knew you'd do it. I knew you'd follow your big ass brother. How did you like the traveling in the East? I bet they scared the shit out of you just like they did me. But I bet you learned faster than they could say it out loud. Man it took me six weeks to learn the first degree. I bet you passed all three in three days."

We had to go through it again.

"Whence came ye?"

"From a lodge of the holy Saints John of Jerusalem."

"What came ye here to do?"

"To learn to subdue my passions and improve myself in Masonry."

"That's it! You got it! Hell I knew you'd follow me. Now you know why I couldn't come right out and ask you, huh? Huh? Masons don't recruit. Nobody ever asked anybody to join the Masonic Lodge. They don't have to. They come asking *us*. Right, Brother? Right? Man it pissed me last summer when I couldn't ask you to join at the same time I was being initiated. Now you know why I didn't. Right? Right?

"But waitaminit! Wait . . . a . . . minute." He reached his right hand out for mine. As I extended it he slowly and ceremoniously crooked his thumb and pointed it in the direction of the appropriate knuckle that to be reciprocally touched would indicate that one had passed the first degree of Masonry. He waited for me to be the first to touch. As I did he returned the grip and stepped back, giggling and slapping his thighs. We went through the same thing for the second degree with him again laughing and applauding. Now he moved out from behind the hedge, turning around and approaching me as if we were meeting for the first time. His hand reached for mine and mine for his at once. At once we gave each other the secret grip of a Master Mason. He held the grip as if he would never let go, pressing his thumb harder and harder against the knuckle, crushing my fingers together until I thought they would break. As he held the grip his expression did not change. His gaze was one of admiration and adoration. Slowly he released the grip, moving his hand and body at the same time into the position which would be the final test of his brother in Masonry. Standing heel to heel, knee to knee, breast to breast, hand to back, cheek to cheek and mouth to ear he waited for me to whisper the first syllable of the secret and hallowed word. As I did so he pressed me closer and whispered the second syllable. I paused for a long time before I softly uttered the last and final phonetic sound which would certify, each to the other, that the one he stood holding was indeed a brother in Masonry. Still we stood, heel to heel, knee to knee, breast to breast, hand to back, cheek to cheek and mouth to ear, brothers. In blood, and now in an esoteric rite which in that moment had brought us into a bond closer than kin.

"Welcome, Brother."

"Welcome, Brother." My leader was back from the war.

"Well, shit. Where's Sug?" We stepped out from behind the hedge just in time to see Brenda pretending that it had just occurred to her that we had arrived and that it was time for her to get out of the car.

"Hi, Sug. Bless your heart. You'll have to excuse us. We had to tell one another some secrets." He had loved Brenda from the beginning and was as demonstrative toward her as he was to me.

"I hope you hit it off with my bride. She's a dandy. Not as good as Brother got, Sug. Not that good now. But you'll like her. She's show stock."

"Does that mean I'm breeding stock, Joe?"

"Get off my back, Sug. You know what I mean. She's pretty. Not as pretty as you are. But pretty. 'Course she's Presbyterian. (What do Presbyterians believe, Brother?)" He spoke in rapid bursts. "I know these mixed marriages are risky but maybe Brother will make a Baptist out of her in the ceremony tomorrow. Just slip something past her, Will. She'll say 'I do' to anything. Then as soon as she says it tell her she just agreed to be a Baptist." Brenda offered something to the effect that she had heard tell that Presbyterian girls were built almost the same as Baptist and that when you turned off the lights it was hard to tell the difference. Joe grabbed her and kissed her again.

"You're a mess, Sug. That was a good day's work, Brother, when you married this little Cajun filly. Show us the water marks on your legs, Sug."

He had very early given her the name Sug. Uncle Sug, an abbreviation for "Sugar," was our grandfather's only full brother. He was a good man but nothing ever seemed to turn out right for him. He and his wife, Aunt Orlea, lived in the two rooms which had once been the Woodmen Hall, and which had been our schoolhouse when the real one burned down. She had been totally paralyzed for twenty years, a condition she accepted with uncomplaining resignation, saying that it was for "her sin." Somehow we grew up equating "her sin" with her son. Oral tradition had it that Uncle Sug had been gelded as a yearling boy when the mumps "went down on him" and there was no other way to save his life. Put that with the fact that a bearded old man we knew only as "Stump John" had lived with them as long as we could remember and with his hunting, fishing and trapping was the only source of livelihood for all of them, and though it was never discussed in detail in the presence of children, we came to our own conclusion.

Uncle Sug, with no land of his own to farm, seldom worked and was often around with his never ending supply of yarns and stories. Joe was drawn to him and considered his demise one of the great tragedies of the community. Aunt Orlea had died some years earlier and Stump John had died or disappeared. Uncle Sug drifted from one place to another but as old age and illness overtook him he was left as literally a tramp in the road. During that period when Joe was convalescing and getting it together before moving on to Birmingham to study pharmacy at Howard College, he witnessed a scene which made a deep and lasting impression upon him. One cold and rainy February morning Uncle Sug was seen walking down the road with a paper bag containing all of his remaining possessions in his hands. His grey hair was dirty and wet and hung about his shoulders. He had been virtually smooth faced, like a little boy's face, for as long as we had known him. That day the few hairs on his chin and cheeks formed a thread-like and scraggly beard. His scanty clothing was dirty and unmended. His gait was the same as it had always been. When he walked it was always rapid and bouncy, starting on the heels and rolling forward to the toes in a rocking and optimistic fashion. That morning he presented himself at each house of his kin. He asked no one to take him in, simply presenting himself, letting his presence and person speak for his condition and circumstance. When no one made the offer he was seeking, but too proud to ask for, he made his way to Grandpa's house.

"Bunt, I know you would want me to stay here with you if you could. But you have Susie and her family here looking out after you and so you can't do it. I want you to get one of your boys to make arrangements for me to be sent to the Old Folks Home in Jackson." It was a euphemism for what we otherwise called the "po' house."

Joe had watched sadly and helplessly as the sheriff drove out of the Campbell community taking one of our own, sitting in the back seat clutching in his arms all he had to show for eighty years of living, taking him to his end in the same fashion as Mr. Hutchinson's pick-up truck had plowed through the early morning fog six years earlier taking Joe to his beginning. Within a month Uncle Sug was dead.

Joe had seen it as more than a human tragedy. He saw it as a family disgrace and vowed and promised over and over to me that no matter what the circumstance—family, children, sickness, poverty, whatever—as long as he had shelter, I had shelter. And I never doubted that he spoke the truth.

In a way it seemed an inappropriate pet name for his sister-in-law. Perhaps he wanted the name to go on living, in the form of something young, vibrant, beautiful and full of hope. We never talked about it. But she was always Sug.

"Damn. What time is it? It's almost six o'clock. I better call Carlyne. She can flat raise the devil when she doesn't know where her man is. You gonna love her, Sug. She's really something. 'Course, she's Presbyterian.

"You ever marry anybody in a Presbyterian church before, Brother?" I told him I hadn't. "No problem. But look. Now you're our preacher, understand? But as a courtesy we're asking Dr. Anderson to stand up there with you. You know, say a prayer or read the Bible or something. I don't know how you do those things. Just as a courtesy, you understand.

"We better get over there. Have to practice you know. Sug you come too. You can watch us practice marriage. How the hell do you practice marriage, Brother? And in a churchhouse?" Brenda allowed that the practice came later. She said it was all practice, being married. Like practicing law or practicing medicine. But Joe already had his next words ready. " 'Course, we been practicing a little bit already." Then he turned to both of us and grew calm and serious. "No. I was just kidding. She's a good girl. She's pure. Pure as Mary. You're going to love her. Believe me."

First he had to go and see that Mamma and Daddy were comfortably settled, knowing that Mamma was uncomfortable in a strange setting, depressed too at the thought of "losing my big ole boy." If she mentioned it, or said something like "Well, I guess you won't be coming home as often now," he would tease again, hug her close and say, "I'll be acoming back, Ma."

When the rehearsal was over and we were back in what was to be Joe and Carlyne's apartment, Joe said there had to be a party and no one was invited except him and me. Brenda retired to the bedroom and Joe rummaged through a dresser drawer and fished out a small paper bag. "Got something hid from the Missus." The bag contained a half pint bottle of Four Roses. He broke the seal, took a deep sniff in each nostril and addressed the germs as Uncle Coot used to do when inhaling camphor balm for a cold: "Run, you sons of bitches." "I know you don't drink, Brother, being a preacher and all. But hell, I won't tell anybody. This is a special occasion. Right? I don't see you every day and a fellow doesn't get married every day." He busied himself getting ice, finding glasses and pouring from the bottle in the fashion of a pharmacist, measuring it by the dram, being careful that both glasses contained precisely the same amount.

"Okay, Brother. Propose a toast to me. I'm getting married. Toast me."

I held my glass up and said that I wished for him and Carlyne many years of health and happiness together. A look of tentative inquiry came into his eyes and he slowly lowered his hand.

"Hell, Brother. That ain't no toast. Say something pretty. You know some pretty words. I'm getting *married!*"

He was obviously annoyed at the bland and routine toast I had proposed. "All right, goddammit. *I'll* propose a toast." He took three or four long pulls from the Four Roses bottle, almost emptying it. The drink he had fixed himself to match mine was untouched. He walked nervously across the room several times, saying nothing. The drawer he had taken the bottle from was still open. He walked over to it, reached in and pulled out another paper bag and another Four Roses bottle.

"I *had* us one apiece," he said, with an emphasis of resignation on the verb. I was beginning to feel uncomfortable. He replaced the new bottle on the floor, halfway between his chair and mine. The seal was unbroken.

Joe took the first bottle and finished it off, tossing it across the room. "Dead General!" He sat for a long time, looking at nothing, his hands folded in his lap. Suddenly he reached for my glass and passed it to me, taking at the same time his own and holding it high above us both.

> I have been half in love with easeful Death,
> Call'd him soft names in many a mused rhyme. . . .

"That's Keats. Ain't you going to drink to that?" His invitation was sardonic. The room had suddenly turned from gaiety and celebration to something else—I wasn't sure what. I remembered some of the letters Joe had written during the fourteen months he lay in the Camp Shelby hospital. I knew I was supposed to break the seal on the bottle standing on the carpet halfway between us. I knew it was my move, whatever was happening. But something stayed me. I twisted in my chair and several times started to reach for it. Joe observed every move. He began to speak again.

"Will, you know I'm proud of you. I'm so damn proud of you I could bust sometimes. I mean. You know. Well. The truth is we didn't have much of a chance. I don't mean Mamma and Daddy. They're giants on the earth. But we really didn't have it as well as most folks in the community, now did we? And here you are, little ole wormy Dave, given up for dead with pneumonia, almost through one of the best colleges in the country and heading for Yale." I tried to say that I hadn't yet been admitted to Yale and wasn't exactly burning the woods up in college, and that I thought he really deserved the greater credit because he was studying something difficult and I was just coasting along. But he wouldn't have it. The adulation continued.

He stalked about the room like a lion. "You know, Will, I really ain't much of a drinker. O, sure, I boozed a bit in the Army, mostly that three point two beer, you know. I really don't like to drink. I never could see any point in it." There was a long pause. "Except one. Do you know what that is?" I said I didn't. "The point of drinking is to get drunk as quickly and as painlessly as possible." He eyed the bottle on the floor but didn't pick it up. Nor did I. I just sat fingering and sipping the drink he had fixed me.

Suddenly he whirled his chair in the opposite direction from where I was sitting. He started to speak and I thought he was going to cry. "Will." There was a break in his voice before he continued. His speech was slow and just a little slurred. "Why didn't you come to my party?" The intonation was that of a child. I started to say that I *did* come to his party, that I was at his party at that very moment. But I knew what his answer would be, and I knew that it would be correct.

It would be a long time before I was to know what Joe knew.

"I'm here ain't I?" Those vapid words were not deserving of the enthusiastic response he gave them.

"Shit, yes, Brother! Damn right you're here! And at two o'clock tomorrow afternoon you're going to stand up there in that great big rich Presbyterian church and say the prettiest words that bunch of stuffed shirts have ever heard. You don't just read that crap that's in the book. I know you don't because I've seen you do it before. That's why I told Carlyne we had to have you do it. You know all those pretty words. You'll have 'em swooning. All them pretty words. You just make it up as you go along, don't you. I knew you did. I've watched you. I told Carlyne that you just make up them pretty words as you go along. I'm going to get some beer."

I insisted that I go. "Hell, no. I ain't drunk. I'll go. You're a preacher. You got no business buying beer. Anyway, it's my party. Come go with me."

He wanted to ride by the drug store where he was working part time as a pharmacist's helper. "You know what a pharmacist's helper is? That's a pharmacist who doesn't get paid. Hell, I fill as many prescriptions as anybody in there. They've already offered me a job and a chance to buy in when I graduate. I think I'm going back to Mississippi though." The store was closed when we got there. He stopped the car in front and sat for a long time telling me about pharmacy. "I love it, Will. I really like being a pill roller."

We stayed up far into the night, drinking beer and talking of random subjects which came to his mind—Masonic heroics, war stories, recollections of childhood—the Four Roses bottle still between us. When I had first gone off to college he enjoyed kidding me about how green and country I was. He had told the story of my packing ten pounds of slake lime to sprinkle in the john at college so many times that he appeared actually to believe it as he told it again. There was the time we had all gone to Liberty to see an ancient mummy on display for a nickel and some cynic had summoned Dr. Quin to authenticate it and Dr. Quin had come into the tent with his stethoscope hanging from his ears. "That damn thing was supposed to have been dead for four thousand years and Ole Doc was going to check it out with his stethoscope!" It provided us with a good excuse to laugh.

"Yea, and remember the time we saw the hairless calf in Mc-Comb? Soft and slick as a baby's bottom all over. And one of Charlie Delaughter's boys ran away from home when he heard about it and stayed gone until his brother wrote and told him to come on home, the calf didn't look like him."

I had to relate again everything that happened during my Masonic Lodge initiation. We traveled again with Grandma Bettye's clan from Georgia to Mississippi and heard the old patriarch whisper the secret word to a fellow Mason along the way when they needed cash to continue their journey. We watched a railroad engineer dive into the steam boiler to rescue a black fireman at a train wreck, despite the fact that the black Mason belonged to the clandestine Prince Hall Lodge. And stood with a firing squad in World War I and refused to shoot when the victim gave the grand hailing sign of a Master Mason.

Some of the earlier melancholy returned as the fragrance of the hops filled the room and what Joe referred to as the C_2H_5OH (he wouldn't refer to anything by name anymore if he knew the chemical symbols) did its work.

"Will, you don't know how I cried when I hit you in the eye with my nigger-shooter that time. Hell, I did it. We always pretended that we really didn't know who started it, who shot the first rock or whether it was Scott or me who shot the one that hit you. It was me. We both knew it. We just wouldn't say it. O shit, O Christ, how I suffered. Did you forgive me, Will? I mean, *really* forgive me."

I told him that it was nothing more than kid play and there was nothing to forgive.

"No, it was a hell of a thing to put you through. I was a mean bastard to you sometimes, wasn't I? But I guess that's all in the past now.

"Yea, Brother. I'm getting married. But listen to me. Let me tell you something."

With the melodrama of a schoolboy thespian, he held his beer can aloft and recited in sonorous and rhapsodic fashion:

> Whither thou goest, I will go; and where thou lodgest, I will lodge; thy people will be my people, and thy God my God; Where thou diest, will I die, and there will I be buried: the Lord do so to me, and more also, if aught but death part thee and me.

It was the toast Joe had wanted from me in the beginning, something pretty and something that would say nothing between us would change. Though he had said the words himself the party was over.

He picked up the unopened Four Roses bottle, placed it in the paper bag and put it back in the same drawer he had taken it from.

"That ought to teach you something, Brother. Yea, that just about says everything you need to know to work in Mississippi in 1954. I tell you, it isn't the same place we left. It's a lot tighter now. And you're so damned bullheaded you're going to get yourself killed. Or get somebody else killed."

I had just told him a story which I meant to be a joke on myself. But Joe had read a lot more into it than I had intended. I had been to visit a friend who was sympathetic to the cause of equal rights for Negroes. Outside his country store he had introduced me to a young black man. Looking to be about twenty years old he stood over six feet tall, was coal black, muscular, well dressed and his face was handsome but somehow sad. I had watched him through the window as my friend and I talked. I wondered why he stood alone, not a part of a nearby group of black youths who mingled under the trees, drinking soda water and eating candy. He just stood there, looking straight ahead. My host called his name and said that he was planning to study for the ministry. When we went outside as I was about to leave he called him over and introduced us. I was familiar with the local mores—knew that whites and blacks did not generally shake hands. But unless the setting was extremely volatile I violated that rule as often as I could. I extended my hand. He stood rigid, looking directly at me, calling my name, saying words of greeting but making no move. I thought that he did not see my hand and continued to hold it toward him. When he still did not move I stepped a little closer to him. By then I was taking it as a personal affront. After several awkward seconds my friend tapped me on the shoulder and said, "Will, Phillip doesn't have any arms." Later he explained that when Phillip was a small child he and his brothers were playing in the woods following an ice storm and he had picked up a fallen electric wire, burning his hands and arms so badly they had to be amputated at the socket of the shoulders.

"Yea, Brother. That ought to tell you something. They don't have any arms. None of them have any arms. It isn't their fault but it's a fact. Don't go around embarrassing them by trying to shake hands in public. For you to do it makes you a nigger-lover. And that's bad enough. But for them to respond makes them an uppity nigger. And that's worse. I'm telling you now, you're not in New Haven. Wise up, Brother. Rome wasn't built in a day."

When Joe came to Meridian from pharmacy school in 1951, he said that he had come to stay. And when I came to the University of Mississippi in 1954 as University Chaplain I, too, never intended to move again. Since the Army I had spent three years at Wake Forest College, one year at Tulane and three at the Yale Divinity School, and a little over two years as pastor of a little church in north Louisiana. Joe had spent four years at Howard College School of Pharmacy in Birmingham. We agreed that it was time for me to come home as he had done. It was a university community where, I assumed, there would be freedom to speak on issues as I pleased. It was but a few hours from Meridian, and Joe and I had already made many plans about his family and mine. And about being together as men who were brothers.

Race was not an issue when we were growing up. The prevailing system of racial relationships was never discussed. It was, I suppose, considered a permanent arrangement. There were, in reality, two parallel worlds, social, cultural and political, existing in one geographical location. There were schools for white children and schools for black children. It never occurred to anyone, except an occasional black person who kept it to himself, that it would ever be any other way.

And there were churches. Churches were for white people. And then there was niggerchurch. Niggerchurch was a social institution and in our minds had nothing to do with Christianity or any other religion. It was a place, just a place, where the blacks gathered about four times a year. Some of the older ones would sit inside and shout and wail, while the preacher, who often as not was unable to read the Bible in front of him but would bluff his way through in "Green Pastures" fashion, served as a kind of ringmaster for it all. Some whites, especially young people, would sometimes attend those functions for entertainment, but our family was never allowed to do so. Daddy said we didn't laugh at anybody's religion. Certainly it did not occur to us that within three decades it would be this institution which would challenge and overthrow the system we knew.

When I went to the University of Mississippi in 1954 as Director of Religious Life, the Supreme Court decision calling segregation in public education unconstitutional was exactly three months old. It was taken seriously by very few whites in Mississippi and not many more blacks. Many white people considered it a joke. "And how many nigger young'uns you going to have in your school, 'fessor?" a high school principal was asked at a meeting of the Lions Club. "Aw, 'bout twice what I had last year I guess." "Yea, twice nothing is nothing."

But there were others who took the decision more seriously. One of these, Tom P. Brady, a lawyer and circuit judge in Brookhaven, the town where Joe discovered the world in the Civilian Conservation Corps, the same town where I spent my first night as an itinerant preacher in a whorehouse. Tom Brady had attended prep school at Lawrenceville and was a graduate of Yale University. He had taught sociology at Ole Miss for a time and was a graduate of the law school.

I remember the day. My predecessor as Ole Miss Chaplain was a remarkable man named Malcolm Guess who continued to maintain an office on campus after he had retired and spent as much time there as he had for the past fifty years of his life. He had been Director of the Y.M.C.A., Dean of Men, Professor of Sociology, even Y.W.C.A. Secretary, and Master of the University Glee Club. Dean Guess had touched more student lives than any person in the state, and continued to do so as he strode about the campus in tennis shoes and freshman cap, never missing a Sigma Chi function. He had often told me he wanted me to meet Judge Tom Brady, one of his favorite protégés, a man so pristine that he had told Dean Guess on his wedding day that he would go to his nuptial bed as pure and undefiled as his little bride. That day he was coming to the campus en route to Greenwood to make a speech to the Sons of the American Revolution. He wanted Dean Guess to read and discuss the speech. We were introduced and spoke briefly. But he was in a solemn mood and soon closeted himself with Dean Guess where they talked in low tones for a long time.

When they emerged it was obvious that Dean Guess's mood had become as somber as the judge's had been before they entered the conversation. When he had gone Dean Guess shook his head in silence. When I asked him why all the solemnity he replied. "You'll know soon enough. That's a speech that will be heard for a long, long time."

And so it was. From the original presentation to the LeFlore County Sons of the American Revolution it was expanded into a small book called *Black Monday* and distributed widely throughout the South. I did learn soon enough why Dean Guess had reflected so long and so sadly on the visit of his protégé.

Speaking of Negroes the Judge wrote:

> You can dress a chimpanzee, house break him, and teach him to use a knife and fork, but it will take countless generations of evolutionary development, if ever, before you can convince him that a caterpillar or a cockroach is not a delicacy.

Later in the book, drawing upon his exposure to literature, sociology and law he said:

> Oh, High Priests of Washington, blow again and stronger upon the dying embers of racial hate, distrust and envy. Pour a little coal oil of political expediency and hope of racial amalgamation upon the flickering blaze which you have created, and you will start a conflagration in the South which all of Neptune's mighty ocean cannot quench. The decision which you handed down on Black Monday has arrested and retarded the economic and political and, yes, the social status of the negro in the South for at least one hundred years. . . . One rudimentary truth, which is apparently unknown and unappreciated by the high priests, is simply this: A law is never paramount to mores. Habits and customs produce folkways which in turn evolve into mores. Laws limp behind and reflect as a mirror the essence of the mores. . . . Sacred mores are invulnerable to the dagger of any Brutus. When a law transgresses the moral and ethical sanctions and standards of the mores, invariably strife, bloodshed and revolution follow in the wake of its attempted enforcement.

His teachers at Yale had been in the tradition of William Graham Sumner, who had first used those words—habits and customs producing folkways and mores, leading finally to law—and might have found the judge's application astounding. But they would have had to acknowledge that it was not inconsistent with their social theory and teaching. He reinforced his law and sociology with a touch of aesthetics:

> The loveliest and the purest of God's creatures, the nearest thing to an angelic being that treads this terrestrial ball is a well-bred, cultured Southern white woman or her blue-eyed, golden-haired little girl.

Some pages later he retreated briefly from his Southern Stoic thesis that the whites would rule justly and decently because the right to rule had inhered naturally in them and to do otherwise would be a defilement of their personhood. He took two paragraphs to move to a position reflecting some Christian values as well, values with which he was more than casually conversant:

> Men of the "Bible Belt" realize fully that the negro has not received the treatment which he should have received at our hands. We know, too, that no human being can mistreat another and escape paying a terrific price—that God's law of retribution is as fixed and immutable as God's law of gravity.
>
> We will give to the negro in good conscience all that he is justly entitled to, and what we in good conscience can afford. Let us leave our gift at the altar and go right the wrongs we have committed and then return and make our offering.
>
> It is not too late. In so far as the South is concerned, the Southern negro knows we are his friend.

It was Brady's book more than any other single factor which led to the formation and success of the White Citizen's Councils of Mississippi and the South. With his prose as a backdrop, a small group of Delta aristocrats met in Indianola that summer to discuss the possibility of an organization such as the judge had suggested. A Harvard-educated attorney, a prominent banker, and the manager of the well known Indianola Cotton Compress were among those present. Later the group was expanded to include fourteen of the most substantial civic and business leaders in the area, none of whom could be called ignorant rednecks or any of the other names which have so often been used to identify southern racists. They were not only leaders in business and commerce, they were leaders in culture and learning. Intelligentsia. Not just in Indianola, Mississippi. Intelligentsia in any circles. And their circle encompassed the world, no part of which would have considered them uncouth. The history of the movement they spawned is well known. They would spread from there to every part of the South and would develop a method and expertise of community organizing seldom rivaled in America.

There was something about 1956. Something about it for both of us. For Joe it was the year he would, for the first time, take his own medicine, take from his pharmacy shelf a clinical drug detailed by the pharmaceutical manufacturers as non-addictive and non-habit forming. One pill taken at three o'clock would get him through a long and busy afternoon. Just something to pick him up a bit. No more than Miss Fannye Nunnery's Coca-Colas used to do for her. We had heard, when we were children, that Miss Fannye was an addict, a dope fiend, that if you took her Coca-Colas away from her she would go wild and do crazy things. But that was a long time ago and we never paid much attention to it anyway.

For me it was the year I would take on the State of Mississippi and involve myself in the racial crisis in a fashion I had not intended, and really did not mean to do.

Each of us did what we did for good reasons. And for questionable reasons.

Joe had always hated pain of any kind. Grandma Bettye used to share her Bayer aspirin tablets with him. Sometimes he would save a few of them and take them all at once. Why hurt if you didn't have to. Why be tired if you didn't have to be tired. Aspirin would stop a headache. Amphetamine would stop fatigue. What's the difference. If you're tired you can't fill prescriptions. If you can't fill prescriptions someone else is going to hurt. Take an amphetamine and fill prescriptions.

An Army doctor doing some kind of research once told me that I had a high tolerance to physical pain. He said I could stand more physical pain than most people without hollering. I don't know if he was right or not. But he added something I never questioned. He said, "I'll bet you hate to be bored though. I'll bet you like excitement."

Joe took his pills so he could help other people. And so he would feel good.

I took on the University administration, the State Legislature, and the mores of the South to help other people. And to make me feel good.

Joe took his pills because he wanted to. And because he needed them.

And, even at the time, I suspected that my battle with bigotry might have to do with my glands as well as with my faith.

Religious Emphasis Week had always been a major campus affair at Ole Miss. Dean Guess had started it many years before and the list of speakers he had brought would be a credit to any university in the country. It was not as popular as Ole Miss football, but for religion on a state university campus it did all right. Fraternity boys made jokes about it, called it, "Be Good to God Week." But they made sure their chapter was represented in its activities. It meant five points toward election to O.D.K., the national leadership fraternity. The truth was, most Ole Miss fraternity boys *were* religious in their own way.

Everyone at the University understood that race was not to be discussed. There were a few who refused to teach mythology and call it sociology or history. But most simply avoided it altogether or engaged in some kind of deceptive honesty in which they knew what they were saying but the students didn't. It seemed to me the annual Religious Emphasis Week was a vehicle to fill the void. If racial justice could not be discussed in the classroom, then it would be proclaimed from the podium of the religious forum. I had a plan, a scheme. Through the sub-committee on speakers, I would manipulate the Committee of One Hundred, the sponsoring group of Religious Emphasis Week, so that the members would have to select people I knew to be sympathetic to racial justice.

Joe and I had discussed my plans and he had playfully scolded. "Next thing you'll be inviting a *knee-grow* to speak up there." Since there were no Negroes on the campus, and were to be none for another five years, there was never any thought that a black man or woman might have anything to say to us. There was, however, considerable pride that George Washington Carver had spoken there twenty-five years earlier and without incident. No one could accuse us of bigotry.

The team of speakers was selected in October but the program was not until February. One of the speakers, Alvin Kershaw, an Episcopal priest from Ohio, appeared as a contestant on the television show, "The Sixty-four Thousand Dollar Question." Kershaw's subject was jazz, and for a preacher to be an expert in that field had created a great deal of national interest. It would be easy to draw a crowd at Religious Emphasis Week with a T.V. celebrity. The University was pleased. To my delight, Kershaw decided to quit playing the game at thirty-two thousand dollars, announcing on the air that he wanted to give the money to certain favorite charities.

Next morning Joe called. "Have you seen the news?" "No, I haven't seen the news." "Well, did you see our man on the show last night?" "Yes, I saw our man on the show." "Well, you had better go look at the Jackson paper." He held the phone while I went and checked the front page. There in two parallel boxes were two stories. One was a news release I had sent out the day before stating that the candidate for $64,000.00 was to be a Religious Emphasis Week speaker at Ole Miss. Alongside it, also in a neatly bordered box, was a straight news story that Kershaw had announced that he intended to give some of his winnings to the NAACP.

"Now you've done it, Brother. The booger man goin' to get you for sure." "Well, the booger man won't get a cherry." "No, really, Brother. You're into something mean. Those folks mean business." Joe advised that I get the jump on the Citizen's Council and personally cancel the invitation. I told him things were going exactly as I had planned, that the REW team had been set up to get the issue talked about and, by damn, this would surely get it talked about. He assured me that he agreed with my motives, intentions and all that but he didn't want to see me get hurt. I was getting tired of the getting hurt bit. Not only did Joe abhor pain for himself he could not stand to anticipate pain for those he loved. When he went to visit our parents he always took a sack full of various and sundry medications. Joe could not stand pain and Mamma could not stand to be without it. So she seldom took the pills, capsules and elixirs he brought, for very long. But he brought them just the same, explaining in detail what each one was for. While the others of our family came to accept the fact that our mother would never be happy nor admit to good health, Joe refused to tolerate the thought, glossing over every instability, ignoring any offensive behavior, humoring every whim, attending to each new ache and complaint.

As for my connivance bringing me pain, I could see nothing but excitement in it. But Brother wasn't willing to dismiss it so lightly. "I'll be up this Sunday." "Okay, see you then."

When I outlined the plan to Joe on Sunday he was a mixture of pride and caution. I told him the whole thing was set up and well organized. The pressures to cancel the invitation had already started building up. (If I had known how intense these pressures would become I might have taken Joe's advice and backed away.) I knew that finally Kershaw would not be allowed to come. But I was determined that it would not be I who would withdraw the invitation. I would force the powers to admit publicly that *they* were the powers. And that we at the University were pawns.

I told Joe that whenever Kershaw's invitation was canceled the plan was for me to contact Joe Elmore, another speaker, in New York who would send a stinging telegram addressed to me, declining to come to the campus unless Kershaw was allowed to speak. Then he would contact the others and suggest that they do the same. If Kershaw couldn't come, then no one would come.

But Kershaw was being barraged with hundreds of letters and phone calls—most of them hostile. Many of them threatened bodily harm. I was afraid he would withdraw on his own, and Joe and I decided that I should go to Ohio to see him.

The meeting was to be in a big, downtown Episcopal church in Cincinnati. I assumed that there would be just the two of us. But when I was ushered into the room by the church secretary, I found five people waiting instead of one. Two men from the national staff of the College Y.M.C.A. were there from New York. With them was the Southern Regional Director of the "Y" from Atlanta. The Chairman of the Sociology Department of Miami University of Ohio was there. And George Mitchell, a colorful and crusading man, then Director of the Southern Regional Council, an old and well established race relations organization, who should have lived to see the Civil Rights Movement but didn't. I knew where he would stand, but since I had not shared my scheme with anyone except my brother and my friend in New York, I felt somewhat uneasy with the others. I was not sure that some at the meeting were not there at the behest of the University.

Kershaw gave a brief introduction and then asked George Mitchell to speak first. I was surprised and puzzled by the way he began.

"Every night I read my little girl an Uncle Remus story. Every child ought to have at least one Uncle Remus story read to her every day." One didn't mention Uncle Remus in sophisticated liberal company. Especially when one member of our group was black. Yet here was George Mitchell, alleged to be the most enlightened and progressive of Southern whites, opening our meeting with an Uncle Remus story. Only Kershaw and I knew Mitchell. The others looked as if they wished they could suddenly be somewhere else.

"Brer Fox heard Brer Tarrypin playin' a chune on some quills:
'I foolee, I foolee, I foolee po' Buzzud;
Po' Buzzud I foolee, I foolee, I foolee,'

"Brer Fox he wants them quills awful bad so's he can play on'em too. So one day he tole Brer Tarrypin he jus' wanted to look at them quills—said he had some goose fedders at the house, en if he kin des get a glimpse er Brer Tarrypin quills, he speck he kin make some mighty like 'um.

"Well, Brer Tarrypin he greed to that but when he showed em toem Brer Fox grabbed dem quills and run.

"But hol' on! You des wait a minnit. Nex' mawnin', Brer Tarrypin took hisse'f off en waller in a mudhole, en smear hisse'f wid mud twel he look des zackly lak a clod er dirt. Den he crawl off en lay down un'need a log whar he know Brer Fox come ever'y mawnin' fer ter freshen hisse'f.

"Brer Tarrypin lay dar, he did, en terreckly yer come Brer Fox. Time he git dar, Brer Fox'gun ter lip backerds en forerds 'cross de log, and Brer Tarrypin he crope nigher en nigher, twel bimeby he make a grab at Brer Fox en kotch him by de foot."

George began to rub his hands together and grin and chuckle and I could see Uncle Remus and Joel Chandler Harris and a terrapin and a fox all rolled into one body. But I had no idea what he was getting at, and I was sure the others didn't.

"Dey tells me dat w'en Brer Tarrypin ketch holt, hit got ter thunder 'fo' he let go. All I know, Brer Tarrypin git Brer Fox by de foot, en he hilt 'im dar. Brer Fox he jump en he r'ar, but Brer Tarrypin done got'im. Brer Fox, he holler out:
" 'Brer Tarrypin, please lemme go!'
"Brer Tarrypin talk way down in his th'oat:
" 'Gim' my quills!'
" 'Lemme go en fetch um.'

" 'Gim' my quills!'

" 'Do pray lemme go get um.'

" 'Gim' my quills!'

"En, bless gracious! Dis all Brer Fox kin git outer Brer Tarrypin. Las', Brer Fox foot hu't 'im so bad dat he pleeded ter do sump'n', en he sing out fer his ole 'oman fer ter fetch de quills, but he ole 'oman, she busy 'bout de house, en she don't year 'im. Den he call he son, which he named Tobe. He holler en bawl, en Tobe make answer:

" 'Tobe! O Tobe! You Tobe!'

" 'W'at you want, daddy?'

" 'Fetch Brer Tarrypin quills.'

" 'W'at you say, daddy? Fetch de big tray ter git de honey in?'

" 'No you crazy-head! Fetch Brer Tarrypin quills!'

" 'W'at you say, daddy? Fetch de dipper ter ketch de minners in?'

" 'No, you fool! Fetch Brer Tarrypin quills!'

" 'W'at you say, daddy? Water done been spill?'

"Hit went on dis a-way twel atter w'ile Ole Miss year de racket, en den she listen, en she know dat 'er ole man holler'n' fer de quills, en she fotch um out en gun um ter Brer Tarrypin, he let go he holt. He let go he holt."

George placed both his hands on the long, well polished mahogany table and pushed himself up. Grinning all around he said, "Okay boys. That's what I came up here to say to you. Now unless somebody has something to say to *me*, I'm fixing to go down to the bakery next to the Gibson Hotel, get my wife a cheesecake, get back on that train and go to Atlanta, Georgia."

We sat there in silence, George standing, grinning down at us with an occasional chuckle from the top part of his throat, sounding like Brer Terrapin must have sounded. He just stood there grinning for the longest time.

Kershaw broke the silence. "That's a nice little story, George. But it doesn't tell me much. I won a lot of money on that television show and gave some of it to the Southern Regional Council. Gave some of it to the NAACP Legal Education and Defense Fund too. That got some of us in a lot of trouble. I'm in trouble. Campbell's in trouble and we don't know what to do. We want to do the right thing but we aren't sure what that is. Now you'll have to tell us what you just told us. What does the terrapin and the fox have to do with it?"

George snapped his head sideways and began to scowl, obviously offended that he had to ruin a good story by explaining it.

"It's got *everything* to do with it!" He banged both fists down on the table.

"Listen boys. They got our quills. Whether we're talking about our freedom to speak or freedom for Negroes to get educated. They got'um. And they stole'um. They stole freedom from the Negroes and they stole the First Amendment from us. Just like Brer Fox did. Now the terrapin here . . ." He reached over and placed his hand on my shoulder. "The terrapin here, he done wallered in some dirt. Subterfuge. Maybe even a little deceit. But he got'um by the toe. I say hold on 'til it thunders. Or until they give us our quills."

Now there were some questions.

The black man from New York spoke. "But what if they refuse to let him come?"

"Dey got'ta let'im come. Bilbo done ruined them once over First Amendment rights. They know that. It would ruin them again."

"What if he gets hurt? There have been an awful lot of threats. What if he gets killed?"

"They don't kill white folks in Mississippi. Not yet anyway."

The Director of the Southern Y.M.C.A. was not convinced. "Mr. Mitchell, some of us have a concern for what this will do to the University. Aren't we running the risk of hurting the University, tearing it all to pieces?"

"Nope. Not *us*. *They*. All we want is our quills. And, then again, *yes* too." He began to finish his Uncle Remus story.

". . . but long time atter dat, w'en Brer Fox go ter pay he calls, he hatter go hoppity-fetchity, hoppity-fetchity."

He reached for his coat. "Now. I'm going to get my cheesecake and get back on the train and go to Atlanta, Georgia." With that he left the meeting, not more than twenty minutes from the time it began.

I relaxed because I knew that no matter what else was said the decision was made. I still didn't have to play my hand, though George Mitchell obviously knew that it hadn't all happened by a sequence of accidents. We talked another four hours but the real meeting ended with Uncle Remus.

Back in Mississippi Joe had to know every word that was spoken. I began the way George Mitchell began. I told him the Uncle Remus story. He made me tell it again while he tried to figure it out.

"Yea, Brother. I get it. They got your quills and you got their toe. And a terrapin won't let go 'til it thunders. Only one thing wrong with that though. They ain't going to give you your quills. So you got to wait 'til it thunders to turn him loose, 'til the explosion next month. And when it thunders there ain't one damn thing to keep the fox from turning around and stomping your ass. Naw, Will, I'll tell you the truth. I was hoping he would back out. I know how you felt but I was hoping he would back out."

On Monday night, one week prior to the scheduled beginning of the program, I was sitting in James Silver's house sipping bourbon and talking with him and John Popham, then Southern correspondent for *The New York Times*. Silver, chairman of the history department, was considered the most liberal man on campus. Well past midnight the doorbell rang and when Jim answered it, a campus policeman asked, "Is Will Campbell here?" He came inside and said the Chancellor wanted to see me at his house.

When the policeman escorted me into the room I saw a circle of about a dozen men, quiet and solemn faces. The chancellor tried to put me at ease. The Ole Miss Rebels had recently won the Cotton Bowl. "Will, we've been sitting here talking about the Cotton Bowl. And about Religious Emphasis Week. We decided that if you can handle the Committee of One Hundred as well as Johnny Vaught handled the football team you're a powerful man." I was the only one who chuckled. Then he grew serious as I went to the only vacant chair in the circle, wondering how long the group had been talking here about the Cotton Bowl and the Committee of One Hundred. And wondering too why neither Johnny Vaught nor I had been invited.

Mr. Clegg spoke first. Mr. Hugh Clegg looked like an F.B.I. agent. And that was what he had been for many years, assistant to J. Edgar Hoover in charge of agent training, until he retired and came to Ole Miss as Director of Development.

"Will, we've talked to the Governor about this thing. He says it's the Willie Magee case all over again." (Willie Magee was a young black man tried for the rape of a white woman in south Mississippi in the forties. The trial became a celebrated case for the Communist cause and the execution was aired on a statewide radio broadcast which Joe had heard. The Governor, J. P. Coleman, was Attorney General at the time.)

I said nothing, hiding behind the gales of smoke I was blowing from my pipe. It was the Dean's time to speak. "Will, the way we have always done things here, when the chairman of a department hires a new faculty man . . . if he doesn't work out . . . if he isn't what he thought he was when he brought him here, we see it as the chairman's responsibility to get rid of him. . . . We feel like it is your responsibility to ask him not to come, to withdraw voluntarily." I continued to sit in silence, tension mounting with every new speaker. My predecessor, Dean Malcolm Guess, was there. He, too, sat in silence, staring at the portrait of Chancellor Hume, chased from office by Theodore G. Bilbo, hanging on the wall, remembering, no doubt, another time when his beloved Ole Miss was threatened with destruction.

Finally the Chancellor spoke. "Will. The man can't come. Whatever it takes, he can't come to the campus. We just can't afford it. Let's word a telegram. Will, we'd like for you to stay if you like."

I went home and called Joe. He was still awake. He sounded his usual warnings but added his usual support. Mostly he cautioned me in subtle code not to say too much for he was convinced by then that my telephone was tapped. Looking back, I expect that he was right.

By Wednesday night the wheels were in motion. Elmore, my friend in New York, had read the cancellation in *The New York Times* and sent a long telegram to me as we had planned. With no prompting Joseph Fichter, a well-known Jesuit sociologist, wired that he could not appear on a program in such an atmosphere of blatant suppression of free speech, adding that he, too, was a longtime member of the NAACP and supporter of its goals. One by one the telegrams came. By Friday evening the last speaker had withdrawn.

The Chancellor had one last move. His plan was to invite the local ministers to take the places of those who refused to come. "We don't need them. We have fine homegrown talent who can speak as well as anyone. We'll have one of the best Religious Emphasis

Weeks the campus has ever known." He said he had already discussed it with his own Methodist pastor and thought he would accept.

I left his office and drove to the home of Emile Joffrion, a close friend and the local Episcopal rector. And for the first time I told him the whole story, adding that if the local ministers agreed to pull the University's chestnuts out of the fire none of it would accomplish anything. The White Citizen's Council would win and that would be the end of it. He needed no further coaching. I was never sure how he worked it out; not one local minister agreed to come.

I issued my first, and only, public statement, saying that I would go to Fulton Chapel at the scheduled hour of each day and sit in silence, meditating upon the things that had brought us to such a sad day. Each morning prior to the session I slipped into the chapel, really not a chapel at all but the main auditorium for the campus, and pulled the curtain shut upon the stage, leaving two vacant chairs exposed, a spotlight shining on each one. And each morning several hundred students, faculty, and townspeople joined me in the silent hour.

The last day Joe and his wife came to Oxford. He wanted to tell me that he had never been more proud of anyone in his life. He hugged me close and kissed me on the head. He had to have me replay the drama over and over and far into the night. Every detail about the night at the Chancellor's house had to be heard. And after each step he would tell me how proud he was, usually with a pat, a slap on the back, and we would both repeat some childhood sayings to one another, like "How's your mamma-an-nem?" "Ain't it a bitch, Brother?" and things like that.

Some of Joe's earlier fears and misgivings returned when I told him that the Governor had said it was the Willie Magee case all over again.

"Willie Magee! Willie Magee! Do you know who that was? My god, is that what they're saying?"

I replied that I did know who Willie Magee was.

"Willie Magee! Good Lord, Will, they're calling you Willie Magee!"

"No, Joe, they're not calling me Willie Magee. They're suggesting that the communists are using us for their own propaganda purposes. Nobody's talking about putting your brother in the electric chair for inviting the wrong speaker to town. We haven't come to that yet."

"Yet. Yet. That's right. Not *yet*. But we will. You'll see. Willie Magee! Goddam!" His voice became calm and he shook his head in a manner of resignation.

"I'm telling you, Brother, get the hell out of this thing. You stayed up North too long. You really remember Willie Magee? By god, I damn well remember it. It took the National Guard to keep him safe. You know. Safe. 'Til we could kill him ourselves. You remember that? You were still in the Army when it happened. Or off at Wake Forest, or somewhere. And up at Yale when they killed him. Or somewhere. You know what they did, Will?" He was almost shouting again.

"They had the electrocution on statewide radio. Damned if they didn't. I heard it on the radio. We heard it, didn't we, Carlyne?" Carlyne said they did. "You know, they have this portable electric chair they keep up at the penitentiary at Parchman. And when they're going to electrocute somebody they send the chair and a great big generator on a truck to supply the power . . . send it to the county where the crime was committed. The radio announcers called it like a football game. You know, here's the lineup. Described what the kid looked like when the troopers brought him in from Jackson . . . yea, they had him up in Jackson. For safe keeping. Yea. Safe keeping. The radio shits used words they learned in broadcasting school on the G.I. Bill of Rights. 'Willie Magee glanced furtively from side to side as they brought him from the trooper's car to the courthouse.' *Furtively!* That's a bitch of a word to use about a human being about to be fried to death, huh? Furtive! Jesus Christ!"

He began to speak in the manner of Mel Allen, a popular sportscaster, forming one hand into a megaphone, holding the other fist up like a studio mike.

It's a beautiful night here in Laurel, Mississippi. This crowd began gathering by late afternoon and grew into the several thousand you can hear in the background. But it's a well mannered crowd . . . none of the unruliness so feared and anticipated by the Laurel police has occurred. The glare of the floodlights are overwhelming the stars from the open sky above, but as we drove in from Hattiesburg the stars and the moon were a peaceful and lovely sight. We noted State Police cars at each intersection, just sitting there, facing the highway, turning their headlights on as each car passed. We believe that means that Willie Magee was brought from Jackson by way of Hattiesburg instead of directly to Laurel. Every precaution has been taken, security measures have been exceptional, everything humanly possible has been done by the courts and law enforcement agents to prevent the threats against Willie Magee from being carried out. We do not, of course, know the exact time when the switch will be pushed which will send the surge of electricity through Willie Magee's body . . . the surge which will finally end his life as payment for the crime he committed. But since he was sentenced to die on Tuesday, Willie Magee cannot legally die until at least one minute past midnight for it will be Monday until that time. Our estimate here in the remote broadcast unit of WFOR is that it will not be more than one to three minutes past the midnight hour. You can hear the roar of the powerful generator in the background which was started up about thirty minutes ago to be in readiness for this event. The most accurate way we can describe the scene is to put this microphone out the window, up over our WFOR mobile unit here in Laurel so that you can get some idea of just how strong and how powerful the generator is which was brought in here this afternoon to supply the juice for the execution of Willie Magee.

Joe stuck his fist up over his head as if holding a mike boom through a vehicle window. As he did he imitated the protracted hum, grinding and roar of the generator. After half a minute or so he lowered his fist and continued with his simulated broadcast:

Those of you who know anything at all about electricity know that a heavy surge of current will cause a groaning and straining from the generator . . . much as your room light will dim when something more powerful is turned on. And that is how you will know . . . know that the life of Willie Magee has indeed come to an end . . . when you hear the groaning and straining of the generator outside our WFOR mobile and remote unit. When that occurs we will again place the microphone outside the window so that you can experience, with us, the actual end for Willie Magee. There will probably be an initial long strain, followed, we are told, by two shorter and less distinct groans of the generator as the final surge of juice flows through the body of Willie Magee.

Again Joe held his fist aloft and imitated the sounds of the straining and groaning of the generator. Then he sat down.

"And you know what happened next, Brother? Do you know what came on the air then? They switched us 'back to your respective local studios' and it was Arthur Fiedler and the Boston Pops playing *Gypsy Suite*. I swear to God above me and Him being my witness, Brother, they went from the groaning of a goddam electric generator snuffing out the life of a human being to Arthur Fiedler and *Carmen* without even a station break. All that separated the two sounds was some guy telling us about the tonal qualities of the new RCA Victor automatic phonograph, the golden throat system, providing beautiful 'true to life' music. That's how fast they can go from lunacy to reality and nobody knows which is which. I'm telling you, Brother. Get the hell out of this thing. They'll gobble you up and in two weeks nobody'll know if you got struck by Arthur Fiedler's baton or three surges from a portable generator. What the hell kind of a Christian witness is that and there's three things you need to remember. One, you don't go to Jerusalem but once. Two, even Jesus was older than you are when he decided to go. And three, you ain't Jesus." Brenda returned us to the earlier mood of the evening by injecting that she didn't know much about the first two points but considered herself an expert on the third.

"Aw, Sug. Get off my back. I'm just trying to scare some sense into your crazy husband."

For the most part it was a relaxing and happy occasion for us both. Next morning he told me again what a great job I had done. The disproportionate praise was beginning to wear thin. But I accepted it as graciously as possible. Before he left he handed me two envelopes and said, "Now, Brother, get the hell out of town for a week or so." In one envelope were two crisp hundred dollar bills. In the other was a tiny red pill.

"What is this man? I ain't sick or nothing."

"I know. I know, Brother. But it won't hurt you. I'm a scientist, Brother. You think I'd give you anything that would hurt you. The scientific name for it is 'Amphedroxyn' and it's made by Eli Lilly Pharmaceutical Company of Indianapolis, one of the most reputable houses in the country. Take it. You have been under a lot of pressure and this'll help you relax. Just knocks a little of the rough edge off. Makes things look just a little more like they ought to be."

We sat alone in a small, all-night cafe in Eupora, Mississippi, halfway between Oxford and Meridian. I had called Joe that afternoon and told him I needed to talk with him. Without any query as to the purpose and without the slightest hesitation he said he would leave as soon as he closed the pharmacy and each of us would drive halfway, to Eupora. Joe had moved from his seat opposite where I was sitting in the booth when he finished his meal and was sitting as close to me as he could get. His right arm stretched over the back of the red plastic seat, his hand almost hugging my shoulder. It was past midnight and the shift workers on coffee break, overnight truck drivers and teen-agers moving on home from the drive-in movie glanced at us curiously, obviously not accustomed to seeing two grown men seated so close together in public.

We had sat for more than an hour in casual conversation, through whatever the cafe had for supper, dessert and coffee. Now Joe was ready to talk, and as was becoming more usual lately, assuming a more dramatic accent than was called for. "You want to get a cigar and ride around, Brother?" I agreed. He paid the check, got several of the most expensive cigars they had and we got into his car and left.

"Okay, Brother. Lay it on me."

"Well, Joe, no big deal, but I'm afraid I've about had it at Ole Miss."

"No surprise," he said. "Tell me about it."

I began to tell him things that had been going on and he would respond to each incident with embellished outrage.

I told him first of going to visit a young black minister in town and talking with him about applying to the University for a correspondence course from the School of Continuing Education. We both meant it more as a joke we could play on the State and University administration than anything else. But the more we talked the more serious we both became. There had never been a Negro student enrolled at Ole Miss in 1956 and our reasoning was that if we could slip him through a correspondence course we could at least say that the ice on the frozen pond of racial segregation had been slightly cracked. Because there were black janitors, workmen, and service personnel of all types on the campus at all times I thought it no danger at all in inviting him to accompany me back to my office to check the catalog to see what he might be interested in and get an application. When we finished talking in my office I started to drive him home, and as we passed through the lobby in the Y.M.C.A. building where my office was located, he spotted the ping-pong table.

"Hey, Brother Campbell. Man, I played ping-pong all the way through seminary. How about a game?" Before we had even established who would serve first I saw a staff member of the student personnel department and a senior law school student enter the front door. Both were well known and rabid segregationists. They said nothing, simply stopping just inside the building, standing with their arms folded and observing the game.

I don't recall who won. But when I returned from driving him back to his church, taking side streets and twice circling the entire town for fear of being followed and there being reprisals against my friend, I found the two men waiting in the shadows outside the building.

The staff person spoke first. "Okay, Campbell. Was he a nigger?" I assumed that because there were Central and South American, and other dark-skinned students on campus they really were not sure.

"Well, friend, if you can't tell the difference, what difference does it make?" The staff man was a big fellow who had played football at Ole Miss and had never been the star he apparently thought he should have been. I was afraid of the man. He moved several steps toward me. "Goddammit, I said was he a nigger?" I kept moving in the direction of the administration building where, I reasoned, if he beat me it would at least be in the presence of the Chancellor. And I kept talking. "If you can't tell the difference, what difference is there?" Other words were spoken and by the time we reached the building all three of us were almost running.

There was, of course, a session with the Dean of Student Personnel that night.

"Okay, what else?" Joe asked.

There was the time Carl Rowan came through town a few

months earlier writing a series of articles for the Minneapolis *Tribune*, later to become the book, *Go South to Sorrow*. He had written to me in advance and I had invited him to have dinner and spend the night with us, there being no hotel in town which would then give lodging to a black person.

Joe exploded. "Dammit, Will. That was stupid. It was dangerous for both of you. To say nothing of Brenda and the kids. You know I don't give a damn how many Negroes you have in your home. But man, you just don't do that in Mississippi right now. Both of you could have been lynched. What happened? What happened?"

"Well, Joe, a bunch of stuff happened. The ship hit the sand. But we weathered it okay."

"All right! All right! What happened about the ping-pong game? Is that silly bastard still there?"

"Well, not much happened. I mean, not really. Brenda went out one morning to get the paper and there were a couple of dozen ping-pong balls on the lawn, all very neatly painted. Half-white. Half-black."

"Them bastards! Them dirty, rotten bastards! Will, you going to get yourself killed!"

"Aw, man, they don't kill white folks in Mississippi."

"Well, the hell they won't. And they will. Before this thing is over they will. And you'll see. Okay. What else. Tell me all of it."

"Well," I said, "I tried to quiet the Dean when he called me in about the ping-pong game by telling him that it was really quite within the Southern pattern. We had used separate but equal paddles, the ball was white, and there was a net drawn tightly between us." Joe didn't think any of it was funny.

I told him of an incident which had happened the week before. Our staff was having a party for new students in the Y building, a large, ante-bellum structure which had been used as a hospital for Union troops. There were games and dancing inside the lobby and on the back gallery we had a large punch bowl and snacks on a long table. One of the denominational chaplains called me aside and said he thought I should go out and take a look at the punch, that it appeared someone had added some foreign substance to the original concoction. And they had. Floating in the sweetened fruit beverage, supported from sinking by crushed ice, was about a cup of human feces, sprinkled lightly with what appeared to be powdered sugar.

Joe was so mad when I finished that story I thought he was going to faint. He jerked the car to the side of the road and jumped out, pawing the shoulder gravel like an infuriated bull, pounding the hood of the car with his fist. "Dammit, Will, they can't get away with it! They could have killed three dozen people if they had drunk that punch!" "No," I said, "the Dean said they checked with the Med School folks and unless the feces came from a diseased person there would have been no danger. He did acknowledge that there was the minor matter of the aesthetics of it all."

"Goddamn. Unless! Unless! What's he going to do about it? Doesn't he know who did it?"

"Well, the Assistant Chancellor used to be first assistant to J. Edgar Hoover but he said there was no way to find out who did it. Of course, I'm pretty sure I could have told them who did it if they had asked me. But they didn't."

"Well, why didn't you blow the lid off the damn place? Why didn't you call a press conference and announce that the highest center of education and culture in the State of Mississippi puts shit in their student's punchbowls? Why didn't you call that guy on the *New York Times*, you know, the one who wrote all the stories about the Religious Emphasis Week stuff? He would have loved it. Man, you're crazy. I'd blow that thing sky high. I'd embarrass the living hell out of them. I'd make that the most celebrated crock of shit ever to be flushed through their schoolhouse."

"Well, Joe. Enough of all that. That really isn't what I wanted to talk to you about."

"My god! You mean there's more?" Well, what is it? Will, you've got to get the hell out of there. I don't know what we'll do but just get out before you get hurt. You and Sug and the kids can move in with us. Yea, that's what we'll do. Y'all can just move in with us. Hell, I make enough money to support us all. You'd do the same thing for me. Just go back and tell them you're leaving, that you can't deal with a fecal mentality. That you won't work for anybody who puts shit in your punch. Yea, yea. That's what we'll do. So it's settled. Right?"

"No, Joe. It isn't that easy. But I do have an offer to get out. And that's what I want to talk to you about."

The National Council of Churches had voted in executive session to put a man in the South to work in the general area of race relations. He would be a sort of trouble-shooter, fighting the brush fires, visiting folks in jail and in trouble, almost anything he wanted to do. And he could locate his headquarters in any city in the South.

Joe became very calm and thought about it for a long time. "No, Will. That's not it. That's not getting out. That's getting deeper in. You know how unpopular the National Council of Churches is in the South? That's just like saying you're going to work for the Communist Party. Man, they'd kill you. No. That isn't it. That's jumping from the frying pan into the fire. No. Y'all can just move in with us. Hell, I make enough money. What's wrong with that?"

And I think he really didn't know what was wrong with it. He really didn't understand why a grown man and woman with two children couldn't just move in and let the working brother support them all. He was willing to do it, wanted to do it, loved us enough to do it. So why not?

We rode and talked for a long time. "I'm just a preacher, Joe. That's all I ever wanted to be and that's all I am and that's all I ever will be."

We talked of the day I was ordained, when Joe had come down from the CCC Camp, observing in silent pride and approval. We remembered the Friday night when a council composed of our uncle, our cousin, our father, and a country preacher asked me a lot of questions about verbal inspiration of the Scripture, the Virgin Birth, a literal hell, and the Plan of Salvation, and then declared and decreed that on the following Sunday afternoon they would join with the others of the faithful of East Fork Baptist Church in a ritual setting me apart to the Gospel ministry.

Joe said he remembered what the preacher said that afternoon. He talked of how moved he was as he watched that little band of kinfolk file by, each placing his hands upon my head, how he knew that I knew as I knelt there when it was Grandpa Bunt's hands on my head. And I remembered it too, how I wondered how long he would stand with those bony, calloused, arthritic fingers pressing down hard, like he was waiting until all the spirit had drained from his own body into mine, how he finally leaned down and touched my head with his lips, puffing with exhaustion and whimpering with deep emotion at the thought that he was progenitor to this awesome initiation.

"Will, you were just a child, just a little boy. But I knew you meant it. Yes, I know you are a preacher, Brother. But what do you do when they won't let you be what you are? You've already tried it all. You tried being a pastor and they cut you down. You've tried being a university chaplain and they have cut you down because you don't want to send all the Negroes back to Africa. And these people will cut you down too. You'll see. You aren't one of them, Will. That's not your people. These are your people. Why can't you be a preacher from behind a drug store counter?"

It was a good question. But, of course, my mind was already set. I was going to work for the National Council of Churches. And in a program the purpose of which was in opposition to the roots and culture Joe and I had sprung from. And Joe knew it.

"But you have to do what you have to do, Brother. You know I'm for you."

I replied with another memory from the past. "You remember the time when we were little tykes and Grandpa Bunt called us all around him when we called John Walker a nigger and told us all the niggers were dead? Well, they're not. There are still a lot of niggers left in the world. Before we can get on with talking about Good News we've got to get rid of the niggers."

"You're still ahead of me, Brother. But as near as I can follow you, you're wrong and Grandpa Bunt was right. As near as I can figure it, all the niggers *are* dead. The white folks just don't know it. The *knee-grows* know it but we don't. If that's what you see as your job, then go to it. I understand. I wish you wouldn't but I do understand. You have to do what you have to do."

"Yea, I guess you have to do what you have to do. I appreciate it, Brother."

In two months, Brenda, Penny, Bonnie and I would move to Nashville and set up the Southern Office of the Department of Racial and Cultural Relations for the National Council of Churches of Christ in the U.S.A.

We would remember that evening several years later as we sat in his living room discussing and writing a letter of resignation to the National Council. The anticipated freedom just wasn't there. The drama, the romance and the tragedy of seven years at the hub of the Civil Rights Movement was worth it all. But the channel one was expected to swim in was really no wider than Taylor, Louisiana where I had been a pastor for two years. Or Oxford, Mississippi.

But right then only Joe knew that. I didn't. I had to find it out. And he would let me. You have to do what you have to do.

Not long after he was elected President, John Kennedy asked Ralph McGill to bring a small delegation of white Southerners to Washington to talk with his brother Robert who was to be appointed Attorney General. Civil rights had not yet gained the political popularity it was to enjoy for a brief period later on, so the meeting was to be completely "off the record." So "off the record" that it would not be listed on the Attorney General's log for the day. We were told to enter the building through separate doors and at different times and we were requested not to discuss the purpose of our journey to Washington with anyone, not even family. Despite the fact that McGill was publisher of the Atlanta *Constitution*, and Claud Sitton, another member of the party, was covering the South and civil rights for *The New York Times*, we had been assured that our visit would be in complete secrecy.

The day after the meeting, David Halberstam called me. I had met him during the Religious Emphasis Week fracas when he was working for a newspaper in West Point, Mississippi, but had not known him well because in those days I was not talking to the press. I got to know him better when I went to work in Nashville for the National Council of Churches and Dave was with the Nashville *Tennessean*.

"What were you doing in Washington yesterday, Preacher Will?"

"Well, David, who said I was in Washington yesterday?"

"I did. And I also said Ralph McGill, Harold Fleming, and Claud Sitton were there too. I further said you were talking to Robert Kennedy about the civil rights crisis. What I don't know is why there were no Negroes in the group." I knew he was fishing, but he was a good friend and a source of information for me and I wasn't going to lie to him.

"Just tell me how you knew we were there and I'll tell you what you want to know. Provided you don't file a story on it." He said he didn't intend to do a story on it, was into something else at the time, but was just curious.

"So how did you know it?"

"I glanced at the register at the National Press Club and saw where McGill had signed in. And alongside his name there was a list of his guests. I knew you guys weren't up here to repeal the Fifteenth Amendment."

One thing that had developed from the meeting was a request from Kennedy for me to recruit a comparable group from within Mississippi to come up and talk with him and members of his staff assigned to civil rights. So I was sitting in Joe's living room late at night, drinking iced tea and sharing with him my cloak and dagger mission. They had told me in Washington that I should make the trip by car, seeing each person individually, not calling anyone by telephone in advance of my visit. I was consulting with Joe as to who could be trusted among the small and still dwindling number of white liberals within the state. But Joe wanted to talk more about the previous meeting than about who should attend the next one.

"Will, I never trusted that little bastard. I voted for his brother because I couldn't vote for a Republican but, hell, they would be the first ones to march you off to the gas chamber."

I admitted that I had not liked some of the things in the original meeting. After asking McGill if there was "anyone from the clergy" present, and I had said grace over the apple and cottage cheese he was eating and the broasted chicken we were being served in his private dining room, Mr. Kennedy suggested that we go around the room, letting each person state his concerns. "What would you do if you were the Attorney General?" he asked us. He admitted that he did not know the South very well and had brought us there so that he might learn from us. Of course, all of us had some stories to narrate.

I told him I had recently been in Canton, Mississippi to visit a black minister who had written the National Council of Churches that he was in physical danger and needed some help. I found the address he had given me, a shotgun type frame house on the edge of town. He came to the door but when I told him who I was he didn't utter a word. Instead he came down the steps, walked down the driveway and sat in my car. I got in beside him but he still would not speak. I had a small portable dictaphone on the seat and he kept pointing to it. Realizing that he was afraid to talk to a white stranger I explained what it was, opened it and took the plastic disc from it and unplugged the microphone.

His first words were, "Can I see your credentials?" I had some calling cards in my wallet and this seemed to convince him that I was in fact a staff member of the National Council of Churches. He began to tell me his story. He had lived and worked on a plantation all of his life and had been a part-time preacher. When he got too old to work in the fields he had moved to town, and was pastor of a small rural church. In addition he did odd jobs. He reached into his shirt pocket and pulled out a rumpled and faded wallet-size picture of Reverend Joseph Jackson, President of the National Baptist Convention, Inc., a man of tremendous power and influence who had used his prestige to oppose much of the Civil Rights Movement.

"That's my leader," the old man said. Had I not known just how little it took in Mississippi in those days to be considered a radical, had I not been considered radical for so little myself, I would have been suspicious of anyone, black or white, talking to me about race relations and holding up to me such a well known reactionary as his "leader." But the calloused hands, the wrinkled face, the tired, sad eyes of this man told me that there was no way he could be anything but honest.

"Reverend Campbell. I don't mind telling you. I'm scared. I ain't scared for myself. I'm an old man and my life is done with. But I'm scared for my people. They gonna kill every last one of us it looks like."

He spoke of "the law." "They the worst ones." He told me of an incident which had happened just the day before, in sight of his house. A thirteen-year-old black child was walking down the road when two policemen stopped their patrol car and ordered her to get in. They said they needed to talk to her about some stealing. Instead of getting in the car she jumped through the fence and ran into the woods and made her way home.

"That little child already knew. She knew they was gonna ravish her. And that's what they woulda done too. Ravished her."

He told one story after another, reasons why he was afraid. A member of his church had been arrested, handcuffed and put in the back of a patrol car. They had searched his house and found a bottle of whiskey and had accused him of bootlegging. In the confusion, and perhaps thinking he would destroy this "evidence," the man had grabbed the bottle and smashed it on the floor. The officer threw the door open and filled his body with bullets.

The preacher had taken the widow to another preacher, a white man who had come down from Indiana as a missionary from one of the smaller sects to conduct training sessions for black Sunday School teachers in the area. Because his work was with black people he was suspect, no matter what his mission. The white preacher had suggested that they go to the F.B.I. in Jackson. After they went an agent from that office had come to the Canton police and told them of the complaint. The local police, in turn, had come to the woman with an ultimatum to be out of town within twenty-four hours. She and her children had moved to another town to live with her mother.

I asked if it would be possible for me to meet the other minister while I was in town. He said that it would but that he couldn't drive me over there because they couldn't be seen together.

When we finished talking I promised to "do what I could," wondering as I was saying it what in the world it would be. He said he could call the other preacher and let him know that I was coming.

He was waiting for me when I arrived and took me quickly inside. With hardly a greeting he began to speak of a more urgent matter than proper salutations.

"Brother Campbell, it's up to you, how long you want to stay. But within five minutes there will be a police car drive by. He won't stop but will drive to the end of the street and turn around. That will take him about two minutes. He will do that twice. On the third trip, if you're still here he will probably stop and want to talk to you. He may not, but my guess is that he will. You're driving a car with an out-of-state plate. That's enough to question you on. It's up to you. If you want to stay we'll fix some lunch. If you don't we have about fifteen minutes."

I had some copies of correspondence between James Meredith—whose eventual admission to Ole Miss caused a riot and the occupation of the campus by Federal troops—and the University which had been given to me, not by Meredith, but by a friend at Ole Miss. I was not anxious to be asked by the Canton police to explain how those letters happened to be in my possession. I indicated that I thought it best to be on my way.

"Okay. Just to be safe. When we see him pass the second time, your car is headed in the right direction, you jump in and you'll be on your way before he gets to the end of the street and turns around."

He suggested that I try to make it to the Natchez Trace and head north instead of taking the main highway toward Memphis.

I told all of this to Mr. Kennedy and he, obviously annoyed that I had taken more time than the others, asked me what I was suggesting. I said that I was trying to indicate the cloud of fear that hovered over the state, and that I was further suggesting that F.B.I. agents, native to a particular area not be assigned there, and that they be more careful in sharing information with local officials.

He asked one of his assistants to go and see if such a report had come in from the Jackson office. When the aide did not understand which of the stories was to be checked Mr. Kennedy snapped, "the alleged killing!"

When the aide returned and reported that no such incident had been reported, the conclusion seemed to be that it had not happened. When I timidly suggested that perhaps an agent so involved would be reluctant to put it on his report, Mr. Kennedy appeared even more agitated, saying that Mr. Hoover had more control over his agents than that, that Mr. Hoover briefed him almost every day on such matters, and inserted—though I had not asked for such assurance—that he and Mr. Hoover had a fine working relationship.

Otherwise the meeting was cordial, and the Attorney General assured us that he was on the side of justice and law, and would do everything possible to protect all citizens, black and white. One method he indicated the government was beginning to use was electronic listening devices. This crisis, he said, had become a matter of national defense. "If law officials are involved in breaking the law, that is subversion. It will be discovered and they will be prosecuted."

Most of us in the room were thinking the same thing. But none of us said it: Doesn't this man know that *our* telephones are already being tapped, and for the precise reasons he was suggesting—national defense, subversion? Doesn't he understand that we are suspected by our neighbors because they think *we* are subversive and are a threat to national security? Doesn't he know that the policeman in Canton knew that I was where I was because the preacher's telephone was bugged? But we only *thought* it.

When I reported the meeting to Joe his first words were, "Well, there you are." He asked me if I had learned anything at the meeting. "Not much, I guess." "Well, you should have learned who the

Attorney General is, and it isn't Robert Kennedy. And you should have learned to be careful, Will. You're going to mess around and get your head blown off." But I didn't really believe either of those things. Not then.

Joe fixed some more iced tea and wanted to hear everything I had been involved in since our last visit. He was especially upset about the Canton incident and begged, cajoled, warned, and made me promise over and over that I would be careful. "Man, you've been gone from Mississippi too long. This is dangerous stuff."

Eventually he wearied of the war stories and started telling jokes.

"Now here's something that'll preach, Brother. Now don't make me hush before I get started. It starts off like a nigger joke but it winds up like a *knee-grow* joke." He touched his knee with his hand, motioning upward with a growing sign.

"There was this old colored—okay, Negro—man out plowing in the field. He had on old, ragged overalls, plowing a mule that looked like it was left over from the Spanish-American War Cavalry. Had a shredded pair of cotton plowlines tied together and hanging around his neck.

"Well, along comes this white cat in a brand new coupe-de-ville convertible, top down and the radio turned up real loud. He sees the old man out there plowing and slams on his brakes and stops and hollers at the old man. 'Hey, boy. Is this the way to Jackson?' The old man just kept on plowing. Didn't say a word. The cat screamed at him again, 'I said, Hey, boy. Is this the way to Jackson?' The old man got to the end of the row, turned his mule around and started back down the row. Didn't say a thing. The guy reached in the back seat of his convertible, pulled out a brand spanking new aught-thirty deer rifle with a telescope sight, aimed in the direction of the old man, knocked a clod of dirt right out from under his foot. 'Hey boy. Can't you hear. I said is this the way to Jackson?' The old man kept going, never said a word. Got to the end of the row and turned around. Started back. Didn't even look in that direction. The guy cut down on him again. Whizzed a bullet right past his ear, cut one of the plowlines right in two. By now the old man was about up even with him. 'Whoa.' He stopped his mule, walked slowly over to the fence right beside the guy in the Cadillac. The old man, quick as a flash, jerked a rusty little single shot twenty-two pistol out of his overalls pocket and stuck it right up to the guy's head and said, 'Hey, boy. You ever kissed a mule's ass?' The white guy dropped his aught-thirty and started to climb through the fence toward the back end of the mule. 'No, sir, Mister. But I've always wanted to.' "

I thought it was a funny story so he had to repeat most of it again, making sure that I had not missed any of the nuances. "Now won't that preach, Brother?" The next time I heard the story it was told at a civil rights rally in Alabama by Ralph Abernathy. And though the non-violent movement *was* non-violent, it was always the stories with overtones of force and violence that brought the biggest applause and laughter.

I knew a rabbi in Dallas, Gus Faulk, who worked for the American Jewish Committee and had taken a strong stand on integration. The press he had received had been less than favorable and after a speech he had given he went home, knowing that he was going to get more of the threatening and harassing phone calls he had been receiving. I had seen him a few weeks later and he told me that for years when the phone rang and someone, always friendly up until that time, asked to speak to Rabbi Faulk he had a habit of saying simply, "That's me." That night the phone rang and someone on the other end of the line said. "Is this that nigger-loving, communist Jew son of a bitch?" "That's me!" With such a spontaneous admission from the rabbi the caller hung up.

I told Joe about him. And about Mrs. Tilly, a little Methodist woman from Atlanta who never weighed more than a hundred pounds in her life, who looked about eight years younger than God, who joined forces with a group of forty thousand women in the thirties and forties in what they called the Association of Southern Woman for the Prevention of Lynching. She was then active in advocating the desegregation of public schools and got a lot of obscene phone calls, calling her everything but the gentle woman she was. She had an engineer hook her telephone to a phonograph and when someone called her late at night the answer they heard was some deep-throated baritone singing the Lord's Prayer. The calls soon stopped.

There had been a conference at Highlander Folk School in 1957 which had been infiltrated by a photographer from the Georgia Education Commission, a segregationist agency. He did not have to come under false pretenses because Myles Horton, founder of that adult education center in Tennessee, made no secret of his policy of admitting anyone to the sessions, no matter what their political ideology or orientation. Pictures which circulated among segregationist groups for a long time were taken at that particular conference, including the one which became a prominent billboard seen on hundreds of highways throughout the South purporting to show "Martin Luther King attending a communist training conference."

Another friend, Fred Routh, worked for the Southern Regional Council in Atlanta. Fred had also been at the Highlander meeting and his picture had been circulated in most of the quarters where hate callers gathered. He came in late one night, and the phone was ringing. An elderly woman was on the other end of the line. Her voice, though creaking, was polished, polite and cultivated, "Is this Mr. Fred Routh?" "Yes, m'am." "Is this Mr. Fred Routh who attended the communist meeting at the Highlander Folk School with Martin Luther King?" Fred tried to explain in his usual calm fashion, that he had attended a meeting there but that it was not a communist meeting but a democratic meeting. But the lady continued. "Well, Mr. Routh, I have something to say to you." "Yes m'am." "You're a son of a bitch." Fred snapped back, "Oh, Mother, I didn't recognize your voice." There was a long pause, and then a gentle, but still polite, click on the phone.

Joe began to fret again about the danger he felt I was in and about all the traveling I did. "What do the kiddies make of all this?" I told him of how Penny begged her mother to build a big iron cage, like the one she had her hamster in, and keep me in the garage so I couldn't leave home. Joe, always kind and gentle with the children, said that was about the saddest thing he had ever heard. "That ought to tell you enough." I softened it up a bit with the account of overhearing Penny, in kindergarten by then, lecturing to three-year-old Bonnie as they played school. "Now today, boys and girls, we're going to talk about George Washington and Abraham Lincoln. George Washington and Abraham Lincoln were both born in February. They both worked for the National Council of Churches. They were both gone from home *most* of the time." Joe didn't think that was very funny.

"Do you get a lot of hate calls and nasty letters?" He was so frightened and so protective of me I didn't tell him the truth. "Well, I get a few. But not many. Anyway, you don't have to worry about people who call you on the telephone and tell you they're going to kill you. They won't hurt you."

Sometimes when I'm missing Joe I miss those nasty calls and letters from the Right. He would be surprised that they come now from the Left.

EVENING

I f blue skies, lenient summer temperature, and an unruffling
breeze moving in rhythmic and welcome spurts off the Louisiana
Gulf make for beauty, then the day after my thirty-fifth birthday
was a beautiful Sunday. All of us, including Webb—still in the
womb—had checked into the Holiday Inn in Baton Rouge. Baton
Rouge is just seventy miles from Liberty and we would drive up
there on Monday. The folks were getting old and living alone and I
felt both duty and desire to see them as often as I could. But for
five years there had been increasing reasons why I should be somewhat discreet about visiting. Though no one was even talking at
that point about integrating schools or churches anywhere in the
state of Mississippi, everyone sensed the imminent storm. And everyone knew that I worked in "race relations." Therefore, if integration came and I was in the county it would be perfect logic to
assume that I had brought it. Until six months earlier, the urgency
to visit outweighed the pressure to stay away.

Joe had bought out Uncle Luther's old homeplace just down the
road from our parents' house. He, who could ill afford it, had
purchased it so that the folks would not be so alone and so that our
sister and her family would have a decent place to live. He was also
feeling some of the agony of wanting to visit the home folks but,
since he had so clearly identified with what he had begun to call
"Will's cause," he sometimes felt it best to stay away. Since he had
bought the place and Sister was next door, I did not feel uncomfortable in being so close and yet not there. Brenda and the children wanted to swim in the Holiday Inn pool and visit her sister,
and I needed to see some people in Baton Rouge who were active in
civil rights. It started out to be a day of work, fun and relaxation.

Less than an hour after we had checked in Joe was on the phone.
We were traveling by car from Houston to Nashville and how he

found us from his pharmacy in Meridian I never got around to asking.

"Brother, I have some bad news." His voice broke slightly as he rambled on about unrelated trivia, seeming never to get to the news which I somehow knew was bad as soon as the phone rang in a motel room no one except the room clerk knew we were in. He assured me that Daddy and Mamma were all right. So was he, Joey and Julie. It was almost by elimination that he got around to who was not all right.

"Sister's folks were going to church and some of the kids wanted to go early to Sunday School. They sent Will Edward up the highway to tell Daddy to pick up the rest of them when he passed going to the meetin." Then there was silence except for a faint sobbing. (The "meetin" was an expression our Father had always used for the main church service.) I had to pry the story out. Will Edward, fourth of our sister's seven children, was riding an English bicycle I had given them a year before—because they had never had one and I had never had one as a child. As he was crossing the road in front of Sister's house a car had hit him. No, he didn't know how badly he was hurt but since I was so close he felt it important that I go on up there as quickly as I could.

Further questions brought no more information. That was all he knew. I called the McComb Infirmary and Sister was able to talk. "The doctor just gives him a fifty-fifty chance of living. We sure do need you, Will. I hate to bother you but come as soon as you can."

It was a traitorous Sunday. The beauty of the early morning had turned to forenoon tragedy. I did not get the details until I reached the hospital. The car had thrown the bike and Will Edward onto the hood and his head had gone through the windshield. The jugular had been severed as with a knife. During the half-hour period from the moment of the collision to the moment transfusion needles could be inserted into his veins most of his own blood had been lost. O. B. Honea, the father, and Britt, elder brother, had raced as fast as the four-year-old station wagon would go, O. B. driving, thirteen-year-old Britt in back holding his twelve-year-old brother in his arms, thinking, each of them, what thought no one will ever know.

Britt was to Will Edward as Joe had been to me. He was older brother, ever ready to defend and protect against any threat. And best friend. Now he was befriending and protecting him the only way he knew how—holding him cradled in his arms, pressing his body and clothing against the lacerated neck and absorbing as much of the hurt as he could stand. But there was no defense, no protection against the rapid emptying of the vital fluid from the young and strong, but human, body.

He was rushed through everything the country hospital and its staff had skill and equipment to offer. Blood had been replaced, X-rays had been made and the neck wound, eight inches or so, had been closed. And that was all. He remained conscious until they reached the hospital. No words were spoken but as they placed him on the stretcher he looked at his daddy and smiled. It was a way he had of doing when he was caught in mischief.

But the smile was not enough. When I arrived I found him unconscious and struggling to free his arms and legs from the restraining ties. The room was filled with relatives and neighbors, some being helpful, some simply satisfying their own morbidity. Sister had not gone into the room, and never did. "I can't stand it. I can't stand to look at him with his head cut off." Some insisted that she do so, saying that she would be sorry later if she didn't. And both she and they knew what "later" meant. She preferred to wait until she could see him in his pretty sport coat, bow tie and white shirt he had saved his money to buy a month earlier. And she knew what the circumstances would be. In her mind the consignment was already made. I refused to let it happen. But my efforts to reverse the consignment took only the form of standing by and begging him not to die. There was too much at stake. Too much that was unfair, too much suffering, too much that was cruel, too much agony inflicted over the years on these more innocent than most people.

Lee Campbell. A man called good. Declining years filled with boredom, head held high yet bowed and shoulders stooped from so many defeats, so much worry over the years about his only daughter and her children and the welfare of them all. For six months— since their move to live in the house Joe had bought—there had been joy for him bordering on ecstasy. Every morning two little boys ran eagerly up the road. "What we gonna do today, Granddaddy?" It turned the pages back thirty years. And the return was better than the original for then it had been a matter of survival— making the crops, feeding the pigs, milking the cows. Now it could be fun. Plant a garden with those two boys. Make a little crop with them. Teach them to plow a straight furrow, to make a mule go right or left, gee from haw, giddup, whoa, tie a hame string, what a clevis is, seven-inch oliver chill, trace chain, when to plant butterbeans, which land is best for peanuts—all the things a farmer is proud to see his sons learning. And more fun to see grandsons learning it for it is an extension of mortality few experience anymore. Now his reprieve was a sand castle on a drill field, trampled and washed away by the tide.

Lorraine Honea. Firstborn and only daughter. God how much! What's it all about? Seven children in not many more years. Maybe that's too many but it is far from enough if you're talking about giving one of them up. Every offspring is an only child. Even identical twins are born one at a time. And what of all her other suffering? Doesn't that even count? The misery, the violence, the unhappiness, the poverty, the loneliness, the . . . god . . . dammit . . . all of it! Just all of it! She didn't have it coming. And I knew it. And I wasn't going to have it.

And Joe. Four times a day he would call from his pharmacy in Meridian. Sometimes more. "Any change?" "How you're holding up, Brother?" Things like that. He could no longer ask about Sister. He had said before he bought the house for her that he simply refused to think of her situation. And each time he called, there was the obvious he would state. "If I had left them down there in those damn woods this wouldn't have happened." I could counter with, "Yes, Joe, but something worse could have happened and we both know what that could have been." But that which could have happened was a part of what he refused to think about.

And he could articulate his greater tragedy. "This is the most decent thing I ever tried to do. Everything I've ever done in my life has been somehow mixed up with my own self. I swear, Will, there was absolutely nothing selfish in this. I didn't want that land. I just wanted Mamma and Daddy to have somebody close and Sister and her folks to have a nice place to stay." "I know, Joe. I know." And that was all there was to say.

Now his act of selflessness, his act of purity, of nobility had boldly, arrogantly set out to bring us all more suffering than we had yet known.

And Will Edward. Half of his name was mine. The other half belonged to our other brother, Paul Edward. Put together it belonged to him. And he wore it proudly. A good kid. Pleasant.

Always a little browbeaten, yet with a countenance of openness and stability. "Don't die, pal. You're gonna make it little buddy. Come on, man. We're gonna help you, and you're gonna make it."

It lasted three days. Who knows what—shock, kidney failure, rejection of that much new blood. The doctor had been most concerned with kidney failure. I had told him that we would bring in a college friend who was a successful urologist in New Orleans. He said that we would wait another day and see if there were any change. "Why another day?" "Well, let's see if there is any change in the morning."

There was. He was dead.

Even when it came I would not have it. I pumped his adolescent chest with frantic and defiant motions. There had to be something left to do. His breathing had stopped the night before and the pumping motions I had done restored it. Why didn't it again?

It was about five o'clock in the morning. The sun was inching its way down the dreary hospital corridor. I knew that any minute Sister would be calling to check. The telephone was in the lounge far down the hallway but I could hear it when it rang. At just about the time the doctor had arrived, answering the nurse's call to him, the ringing began. My feeble and futile efforts to resurrect a corpse must have been both comic and tragic to one trained in the science of doing the practical thing. He motioned me away and ceremoniously placed the stethoscope upon his chest. He shook his head and walked away. The nurse said she was sorry, that he was so young. One other person was in the room, a young truck driver and neighbor named Maxie Whittington. I embraced him and he returned the embrace with equal emotion. The phone at the end of the hall was still ringing. And I knew I had to answer it.

"How is he Uncle Will?" It was Carolyn Sue's voice, Sister's oldest child, now in her second year in college. "Not too well, Sugar. I'll be home in a little while." "Okay, Uncle Will." That was it. She knew. And I knew that she would say nothing until I arrived.

An aunt, and a good woman, lives a quarter of a mile down the road and, since the coming of Southern Bell to the East Fork community, she has felt it her Christian duty to listen in on all phone calls on her party line in any time of crisis. She meant no more harm by that practice than others would mean by stopping on the street where two or more people stand talking. If the occasion is right she will join in the conversation, answering questions one or the other party is not able to answer or offering information they do not have. To her, telephones are a means of visiting with one's neighbors or responding to news of tragedy. As I drove in she was walking into the house with eggs for breakfast and homemade biscuits ready for baking. Somehow in rural, Southern culture, food is always the first thought of neighbors when there is trouble. That is something they can do and not feel uncomfortable. It is something they do not have to explain or discuss or feel self-conscious about. "Here, I brought you some fresh eggs for your breakfast. And here's a cake. And some potato salad." It means, "I love you. And I am sorry for what you are going through and I will share as much of your burden as I can." And maybe potato salad is a better way of saying it.

Sister was standing in the middle of the front room floor when I arrived. She had not heard but she knew. I had pondered what words to use. I tried to recall some of the things they told us in "Care of the Parish," or "Pastoral Counseling." But when I saw her standing there, the helpless, hopeless, pleading look on her face, I raced far back into my earliest beginning for a resource.

"He just went to sleep." I had mumbled the only words I could think of. I was the only one crying. The others stood around, moving here and there and nowhere, looking at me in stunned silence. After a minute or so Sister turned and moved into the room where the boys slept. Everyone followed. As placid as I had ever seen her she reached under the bed and pulled out a plain little box. Inside was a sack with draw strings which she unloosened. One by one she began to remove tiny, very personal articles. A pretty rock. A well shined bolt. A glass marble. Dozens of things that were dear to a little boy who did not have access to what the world would consider much, but which had never occurred to him were not much, for no one had ever told him that his precious possessions were less than much. One by one she looked at them, held them up for all to see and put them back. Then into every room gathering pictures. There were faded school pictures of as many different years as she could find and a few snapshots. The most recent one was placed on the mantle in the parlor. She had not whimpered.

"Sister, you have to cry. Will Edward is dead, and you have to cry."

"I'll cry, Will. I'll cry. It was just so sweet the way you told us."

But the crying was slow in coming. News of death seems to

carry a sort of built-in mercy. It produces various degrees of shock which act as some kind of sieve, letting just the amount of consciousness seep through that one can bear at the moment. She busied herself with the pictures and a few other personal belongings. When crop time had come after the move, Daddy had looked all over two nearby towns for the type of straw hat he used to buy for us when we were small and working in the fields. That was a sombrero type, round crown with a crease down the front. Not succeeding in the search he found some more in the western style. Since the boys had never known the type Daddy's nostalgia sent him out looking for, they were just as pleased, and wore them every waking hour. Will Edward's hat was carefully wrapped in a piece of cellophane and hung in the hall where it remains to this day. His few clothes—pants, shirts, socks, underwear, everything—were as carefully folded and put in a drawer. Everything he owned was sought out. "He mowed Daddy's lawn on Saturday and Daddy gave him a dollar. Does anybody know where it is?" No one did, so a new search was begun.

At two o'clock the body would be in the parlor at the funeral home. The child who had lived in simplicity would be buried in splendor. The insurance company of the driver had hastily assured us that they were taking care of all expenses. He lay in a bronze casket and upon the finest satin. I had preceded the others to town, though I do not know why. By then I was beginning to go through motions without reason. When Sister, her husband and six remaining children arrived, I walked inside with them and ever so slowly we approached the front, each one making certain no one got there either before or behind the others. Sister was not crying. She stood in a silence of reverence and a silence approaching awe. Then there were her voluble, yet subdued words: "Now ain't that the prettiest thing you've ever seen!"

And then the crying began.

I had walked back down the hall and had not heard Daddy and Mamma come in. Suddenly everyone in the room was startled by loud and hysterical words: "What we gonna do today, Granddaddy?" Then a hush spread into every corner and crevice and sideroom of the building. Daddy was repeating words he had heard every morning for six months by two wide-eyed and anxious little boys. Now he was saying them one more time for a little boy who would say them no more. It had been a glorious reprieve. And now it was over. The sounds of grief which followed were totally out of character for this giant of a man who had learned to live with hurt. They were sounds I could not bear. I was no longer priest, son, brother or comforter. I was a defeated, bewildered, and worn out human being, feeling nothing except that I had been abandoned by whatever I had always leaned on. I moved outside the door just as Joe and Carlyne were arriving from Meridian.

Joe stepped quickly to me and held me in a long embrace. He began to speak to me in quiet composure—he who had always been first to cry. "The actual presence in it all has been too much for you, Brother. You are emotionally and physically exhausted." He told me not to be afraid to cry and mildly denounced the world for being too far gone to weep. I recall his words. "When the goddam world is so callous that it can't cry at anything it is awful late in the day of history." It was a time I was seeing a lot of pain and injustice and suffering in the Civil Rights Movement. I did not know then that it was just beginning—in 1959. And I did not know as I heard his words that the country we had each given three years to defend was already moving into a war that would fulfill his prophecy— "can't cry at anything . . . awful late in the day of history."

He moved effectively into the void I had left, running errands, meeting callers, relatives and old friends with poise and quiet charm.

As the long evening began to wind down Sister came with one last request. "Will, I know you're tired. Except for a few hours you've been with him for three days and nights. But will you stay with him tonight. I hate to ask but I'm asking." I said that I would.

Now the wake was over. Everyone had gone to their houses. I sat in the funeral room with the glow of one remaining light casting a huge silhouette of the bank of flowers upon the wall. Summer moths bumped the windows or dived with instinctive purpose into the fluorescent light over the door, dropping forever to the pavement below. The mixture of gardenias, roses and gladiolas blended into an indescribable and unforgettable smell.

"Believe it's cooled off a bit." "Yea, I believe it has." Slowly the realization encompassed me that someone from out of the darkness, six or eight rows behind, had spoken to me. And I had answered. I did not need to turn around to ask the identity of the speaker. I had not heard that voice for a long time. But I knew it was that of a favorite uncle of our childhood days. In recent years he had been one of the most critical and vocal ones concerning my activities in the civil rights and desegregation controversy, expressing bitter disappointment and displeasure that his own nephew had turned out to be a nigger lover and renegade preacher. I had ceased to visit him when I came because I loved him too much to risk rejection. He was the one uncle who would never, and did never, *join the church.* At revival time he was always the prime subject for conversion teams. While lesser men would offer excuses of how they knew there were hypocrites in church they were just as good as, or allow that they could worship God in their own back yard, he always listened politely to the evangelistic pitch, thanked the caller but offered no explanation or promise regarding his recalcitrance. It was considered strange behavior.

He moved quietly out of the darkness and sat down beside me. I glanced at my watch. "It's three o'clock," he said. I assumed that he knew of the promise I had made my sister, and had been sitting in the shadows since the last mourner had left, deciding in his own time and in his own mind when I had been alone—though not alone—long enough.

He poured coffee from a lunch box thermos and handed it to me. Until the dawn I sat in the redemptive company of a racist Jesus.

Joe's composure was the same with the morning. I was at once grateful and baffled. For the remainder of the time until the service he limited his ministry to me, never leaving my side. His speech was fatherly and logical. He could discuss the tragedy in all its many aspects and components and unrelated parts, but it was philosophical and rational. The hurt was obviously there but something was containing it, pushing it down, masking it, so that he could go on.

It was to be two years before I was to discover, or at least have to accept, that what I had interpreted as grace or strength was in fact—at least in part—a dangerous killer, a combination of drugs, pills, all accessible from the shelves of his pharmacy, dozens and finally hundreds, whatever it took to keep on going and to live with the hurt of living.

Time takes time—sometimes too long—but it is all we have. The healing was slow in beginning. I tried to tell myself that now was two years hence but each morning awakening brought a new awareness that it was still now. The hurt seems always greater in the early morning. Consciousness provides the resources for protest but the wearying of the day numbs one finally into silent submission. Each new day brought a return of the fifty pounds of melted babbit in my chest and a renewal of the fight with God and doctors and automobile drivers. But every setting sun meant a little chip of it had spun off into eternity.

The healing really began six weeks after the accident. At least for me. I was lying across the bed in mid-afternoon, neither asleep nor awake, staring at the ceiling, speaking to no one. Brenda, wife, woman and friend, came into the room, bellowing as she strode.

"Get up! Now I just mean, get up!"

So I got up.

But for Joe the getting up would not be the same.

H ealing for Joe had to be different. It would not be as simple as wife and friend screaming, "Get up!" It is difficult to treat a wound if you don't acknowledge its existence.

We continued to visit Meridian as often as possible but we realized that our visits were now out of duty. There was little joy left in them. Joe was always cordial, rational, and calm. But there was something new in the air. The house was dark and depressing. The shades were always drawn. The rooms were too hot in the winter and too cold in the summer. Everything seemed exaggerated. A steak had to be thick as a roast. Iced tea was served in immense glasses. Peanut butter was in gallons. And lots of money had to be spent. Joe would not come home in the evenings without bringing presents for everyone, sometimes simple but often elaborate. If I passed through while traveling somewhere else he would give me a hundred dollars. Always in one bill which he had tucked away in the safe.

And he became a collector of guns. But they were never collector's guns, just guns—shotguns, rifles, pistols and cases of ammunition. Billy clubs, blackjacks and various "instruments of interrogation," obviously tools of torture, given to him by police friends, hung on walls and decorated desks and tables. The guns were generally new and of the type to be found in any hardware store. While I did not consider Joe's new hobby (he had never had one before) a healthy development, I didn't try to analyze him on the basis of this. Maybe he just liked guns.

Nearly a year after Will Edward's death we were all forced to admit that things were not well. Previously Carlyne would "leak" hints and bits of information to Brenda and me in conversation. But with Joe everything was always rosy. No problems. Everything's fine. We were spending the weekend in Meridian on our way to Louisiana. I had heard some commotion in the hallway after we had gone to bed but paid no attention to it. Next morning a big hole could be seen in the hallway wall, facing the room where Penny, Bonnie and Julie were sleeping. Carlyne tried to tell us what had happened but in such a subtle manner that I didn't try to put the pieces together. To Joe it was just a joke. His version was that Carlyne had gone in the room to lie beside the children until they went to sleep and had gone to sleep herself. Finding the door locked when he started to go in to kiss her good-night, he had placed his foot against the wall as leverage and the pressure had crushed the flimsy wall board. It was not a very good story but we let it pass. Later in the morning Penny got her mother alone and said that she was scared and wanted to go home. Uncle Joe, she said, had broken in their room and when they awoke he was choking Aunt Carlyne. And Julie had confided to her little cousins bits of information concerning other altercations.

During the day further subtle jibes between Joe and Carlyne indicated that the household was not simply unpleasant, it was sick.

I could not remain brother and pal any longer. I had put it off too long. Somebody had to become practitioner, counselor. I brought the subject up at lunch on Sunday. "Let's quit trying to kid one another. Something bad is going on. I love both of you and don't want to see you hurt one another. I can't stand to see you unhappy. Let's talk about it and see where it takes us and try to get some help before it is too late."

To Joe it was still a joke. "Aw, Brother, get off my back. There's nothing to talk about. We have our little spats but who doesn't." He turned to playing with the children. Joey was a big boy at ten and was beginning to resent being lumped in with Julie, Penny, and Bonnie in games. But either from fear or respect he never questioned his father, going along with whatever he said. A favorite teasing was the daily "foot inspection."

"Okay," he would yell. "Everybody line up. We're going to have foot inspection." They would run, squealing and giggling, to see who could be first in line, knowing that everyone would get a prize, no matter how dirty their feet were. He would make each one put a foot in his lap. It could be either foot they chose. Unless it was "double inspection," in which case he looked at both feet. Sometimes he would send one or the other to the bathroom, explaining that they had failed the inspection, but he would give them another chance. That one would have to go back to the end of the line and if they were taking it in particularly good humor he might send them to the bathroom two or three more times before finally "passing" them, giving them the same quarter or fifty cent piece he had secretly given the others, always telling each one not to tell the others that they had won the highest honor in foot inspection.

Or if one of them was crying he had a big ceremony of "planting cry seeds." The one crying would be asked to hold their eyes over the palm of his hand and let a teardrop fall into it. He would pretend to put it in his pocket and everyone had to go outside and watch him dig a hole in the yard where he would very carefully plant the teardrop from his pocket. Long before the final homily about cry seeds growing into laugh trees the eyes would be dry and the playing resumed.

But Carlyne was ready to play it straight. There was an outpouring of incidents, not just quarrels but violence, threats upon her life and his threats to his own life. Still it was funny to Joe. He handled it as if he were humoring a paranoid situation. "Aw, Babe. Now you know I didn't hit you. Everybody who knows Joe Campbell knows he wouldn't harm a fly." And because I wanted to believe that was the case I suppose I did believe it.

But not quite. That afternoon the two of us went to one of his shooting places, an abandoned farm house in the middle of a field. He shot at nothing in particular, no target, tin can or bottle, just some distant spot on the ground. He was holding a western-type sixgun, forty-five caliber, in his right hand. I spoke to him from his left side and as he turned to look at me it fired. The pressure from his finger as he turned had been enough to cause the hammer to come all the way back and then snap on the cartridge cap. It blew a two inch hole in the ground at my feet as the bullet exploded. Bits of rock and dirt flew in every direction. I asked him to give me the gun, that I thought he couldn't handle it, but he did not intend to get serious. And all of my counseling techniques didn't help. Finally he did admit that things were not too pleasant. "But you know how Carlyne is. You can't pay any attention to what she says." I reminded him of the backlog of evidence but he masterfully parried it off. I insisted that the two of them go for marriage counseling. His answer was that he had been for that for two years but that Carlyne would not agree. As a humoring gesture I said that maybe Carlyne did stretch the truth at times, may even be a chronic liar, but that the marriage was certainly worth saving. He promised to try to get her to seek help.

It took only a few hours for my counseling to come back to haunt me. Again, after all of us were in bed, I heard a scream coming from the living room. I ran down the hall just in time to see Carlyne retreating in the opposite direction with Joe following close behind, cursing and threatening as he went. Standing like a midget before a giant, I heard myself saying words which were not my own: "Goddammit, sit down or I'll knock the hell out of you." It stunned him as it did me. He slumped into a chair and I realized that I was standing in the middle of the floor with both fists clenched into hard-knuckled balls. He could have picked me up with one hand. But he made no sign of defiance toward me.

"No, Joe, nothing's wrong. Everything's fine!"

I turned to follow Carlyne and found her in the basement crying. She refused to let me comfort her. "No, you don't want to talk to me. I'm just a chronic liar." My clinical words of the afternoon had become one more weapon which Joe could use to cut her down— "Would you believe something if Will said it? Well, he says you are a chronic liar."

There continued to be brotherhood after that but somehow the buddyhood seemed to wane. I had taken a clinical posture, and I could tell already that turning professional was a mistake. Clinical postures are hard to shake.

Thirty minutes after the fracas Joe wanted to take me for a ride in his little Karmann Ghia, laughing, telling a joke a neighbor had played on him. When he first got the car he kept careful records on the gasoline mileage. The first week he got about thirty miles per gallon, just what the salesman had promised for local driving. But the second week it was over forty. He began boasting at the pharmacy and wherever he went about his good motor. Each week it was a little better. When it got to almost seventy miles per gallon he took it to the service department where he had bought the car to tell them about it. The service manager said he would keep it a day or two and try to adjust the carburetor. Joe thought that was about the funniest response he had ever heard from a mechanic. "Like changing a patient's prescription if he feels too good." A few weeks later, when his figures showed that he was getting over a hundred miles on a gallon of gasoline, he sat beside the carport one night and waited. What he suspected was the case. His neighbor had been sneaking over every night and adding a little gasoline to the tank. Joe watched as the prankster started to open the can. When he did Joe threw a miniature penlight at his feet. "Want a light, Buddy?" The joke was over.

We rode for an hour or more. But if I tried to discuss the earlier happenings Joe would parry me off with another story, another joke.

A few months later Carlyne called. Could I just happen to be in the Meridian area and talk to Joe. He was taking some kind of pills, passing out in front of the children, some nights sleeping not at all and some nights sleeping so soundly that nothing could rouse him. She didn't know what to do.

It happened that I had a good reason to go to Meridian and did not have to make up an excuse. I called Joe that night and asked him if he knew anything about a Church of God preacher named Horace Germany. I had read that he had been badly beaten because of his racial views. He lived in Neshoba County, near Meridian, and I wanted to see him.

"Been expecting your call, Brother. Yes. I know about him. I don't know him but I know some of his church members. Fill prescriptions for them. You coming down?"

I told him that I thought I would.

"He was in the hospital here until yesterday. They say he won't talk to anybody. Guess he'll talk to you though. But be careful, dammit. They almost killed that poor guy. Maybe I'd better go with you. There're some mean white folks in that county."

I explained that I felt it best that I go alone but that I would see him when I got through with my business.

"No. Hell no! You come here first. I'll check with Chief Booker (the daughter of the Chief of Police in Meridian was Joe's secretary). He might have a guy off duty who'll follow you over there. I'm telling you now, they're tough and you're hot, Brother."

I knew a Church of God preacher near Nashville and after Joe's warning that Horace Germany wouldn't talk to me I went to see him and asked if there was some way he might introduce us. He had known him for a long time and spoke sadly of his great concern for his friend's safety. He was encouraged that I was going and wrote a letter explaining to Mr. Germany that it would be safe for him to talk to me. After reading the letter aloud to me he folded it in one of his church bulletins, saying that Brother Germany would know for sure by that that it had come from him. He handed it to me and walked with me to the car to bid me Godspeed.

When I found Horace Germany he was lying on his side on a couch in his living room. He was a white man but had been beaten so badly that it was hard to tell. His wife had met me at the door and I had handed her the letter. He read it and invited me in.

He told me that he had lived on that same farm all his life, that the house had been built by his grandmother. He made his living farming, as his people had done on that same land for three generations. He was also a Church of God preacher. For many years he had wanted to build a school for Church of God young people who wanted to preach. He would teach them about farming, and they would study the Bible. He had let it be known within the community and around the country that the school would operate with no regard for color. "The Gospel," he said "is a universal Gospel to all men, as given by Christ in the Great Commission. All men are made one in Jesus Christ." Because of that his first three students were black. They lived, worked and studied in the house where we were sitting.

To reach him I had traveled down a country dirt road which took me very near the scene where, a few years later, three civil rights workers, Mickey Schwerner, James Chaney and Andy Goodman, were killed, setting off a massive wave of sentiment against white resistance to desegregation. About three miles down the recently graded, winding and sloping dirt road, hardly wide enough for two cars to pass, there was an open gate at the top of the slope. Through the wooded area there was a clearing and a large pond, the kind the U. S. Department of Agriculture builds for farmers to water cattle. And the kind that the three civil rights workers had been buried in until their bodies were unearthed by a bulldozer six weeks later. Beside the pond was a long shed with lumber stacked almost to the tin roof. Outside the shed was more lumber and concrete blocks, some with black mildew and spider webs, indicating that this building material had been gradually accumulated as time and finances permitted. In the center of the clearing there was the foundation and part of the first story of a large building. This was the beginning of what was to have been his school, the Bay Ridge Christian College.

For two or three hours Horace Germany talked. This had been his dream. He had preached all over America trying to raise enough money to begin. But the beginning had been the end. A few weeks earlier a large crowd had gathered at one of the main-line churches in the area. The building was small and could not hold more than two hundred people. But another five hundred gathered on the dry, dusty lawn and pressed as closely as possible to open doors and windows in order not to miss what was going on inside.

He talked of how he understood that they had opened the meeting with prayer. And added, "But I guess you're supposed to open a church meeting with prayer." A resolution was presented asserting that the school going up down the road was seeking to destroy harmony between the white and colored races of the area. He handed me a copy of the resolution. "The college is purportedly a Christian educational institution," the resolution stated, "but we are convinced that the purpose of this college is to promote, foster, and encourage violence and to disrupt the good will between the races."

"After they met, a committee came here to see me. I walked out in the yard and met them. I say 'committee.' There were about two hundred of them." The spokesman told him of the meeting at the New Ireland Church, read him the resolution and added some words of his own. "Preacher, this is it! We mean, this is it! You get your family and them imported niggers away from here within forty-eight hours, or we will not be responsible for what happens."

"Brother Campbell, you wouldn't believe it. They was supposed to have just come from a church meeting. But liquor and tobacco smelled strong. And some of them talked rough."

"But," he said, "I wasn't scared of them. I told them I was going to finish building the school."

A few days later Horace, one of his associates and the three black students were in town loading material onto a truck from an abandoned school building they had bought. A mob of five or six carloads of men drove up, ran the black students off and then with fists, clubs and blackjacks beat Horace Germany into unconsciousness.

He was a big man, muscular all over from hard work. He said that they took turns beating him and that if he had wanted to he could have killed any one of them. "But I don't believe in violence. I don't want to hurt anybody."

He talked sadly of his shattered dream. I asked him what he planned to do. He said that he wasn't afraid. "Jesus died for me, and I will die for Him. I could finish the school all right. People from all over the country have said they would bring their mobile homes and tents and stand guard until the school is finished. But all I would prove is that I am not afraid. I could build the buildings. But it wouldn't be a school. There wouldn't be any students. A school is not a school without students."

"And what will you do with what you have built?"

He turned away and gazed at the wall. A plaster of paris plaque, like those won at county fair carnivals or made by children at vacation Bible schools, hung on the wall with the inscription: "In all thy ways acknowledge Him, and He will direct thy path."

He spoke again. "Yesterday morning one of the biggest bootleggers in the county sent word that he wanted to buy the property. I know what he wants with it. He wants to make a dance hall out of my school. And sell whiskey."

"And will you sell it to him?"

"Yes," he said. "Yes, I'm going to sell it to him. I told these people that if they won't let God do His work in this county, the Devil will sure move in and do his." And then he added, "You know, there's a lot more to this race thing than just segregation."

His words seemed a fitting epitaph for the Bay Ridge Christian College.

I drove the thirty miles back to Meridian and went to Joe and Carlyne's house. Joe was still at work. Carlyne unfolded an unbelievable story of Joe's behavior. His violent outbursts had become more frequent and he sometimes went for days without sleeping. At other times she and Joey would have to drag him from his chair to bed. She said she was afraid of him. He had guns in every room and a trunk filled with ammunition.

I knew Joe as a kind, considerate and gentle person. I knew that he did not drink excessively. I found the things she was saying unbelievable. Yet I found them convincing. When he came home that night, again with gifts for everyone, he was jovial and alert, making jokes, teasing the children, telling stories, complaining good naturedly because there had been steaks for supper when Carlyne's folks visited but hamburgers for his. Not long before we sat down to eat he darted into the bathroom.

"You'll see, now," Carlyne said. "He's taking something."

Ten minutes later he was having trouble holding his fork and his words were so slurred that it was difficult to understand him. One sweeping glance told Carlyne that I believed.

But not more than an hour later Joe was turned around, sitting in the basement den urging everybody to hurry with dishes, school-work, and chores so we could all go bowling. It was the one thing, she told me, in which he still had any interest at all, except guns.

While the others were dressing, I asked him bluntly, "Joe, what are you on?"

"Now, for Christ's sake, Brother, don't start that again."

"What are you on, Joe? You sat there and couldn't even get the fork to your mouth." Eventually he sighed and said that just as he had seen me have a highball before supper he sometimes took *one* Seconal to knock a little of the edge off at the end of the day. Nothing serious, nothing to worry about. It wasn't a narcotic and I shouldn't fret about it. But I badgered him into a brief but serious discussion of their marital problem. He stated again his willingness to go to a counselor or even a psychiatrist. But I should understand that it was only because he knew that Carlyne was in bad need of therapy.

Next morning Carlyne and I would have the same kind of conversation. She was willing to go to a counselor or psychiatrist because she realized Joe's need for professional help.

Then she said something that I wasn't expecting.

"It may get so unbearable that I will have to leave. I am afraid of him and I don't know how much longer I can stand it." I knew that she was going to leave.

And in less than two weeks she did.

At about nine in the evening she called. Calmly she reminded me that I had made her promise that if she had to leave she would call me. "And when are you leaving?" "I left at three this afternoon. I'm at Daddy's. In Birmingham."

And then bedlam, confusion, pandemonium. Children screaming, grown-ups yelling. I could hear it on the phone. "He's at the door. He's trying to break the door down. What'll I do? I'm hanging up the phone and calling the police!"

Joe had come home from the pharmacy and found his world collapsed. Carlyne had packed her Volkswagen bus with clothes, books and toys and they were gone. He had wasted no time in driving to Birmingham to bring them back. But they were not coming back.

I waited ten minutes and called her. The police were there but Joe had gone. I asked the officer to try to pick him up and hold him until I could get there, that I feared he was sick or had a serious drug problem. He said he had no authority to do it but would try to talk him into staying until I arrived. A few minutes later he called back to say they had found Joe and charged him with carrying a concealed weapon. "But," he said, "if he makes cash bond he will be free to go." I explained again the reasons I felt for detaining him, and added that it would take me four to five hours to make the drive. He said he would hold him.

In less than four hours I was there. One of the officers at the desk was visibly angry. "Nothing wrong with your brother. He's as sane as you are. And he's been asleep ever since we locked him up. If he was taking narcotics he would be climbing the walls for a fix by now." Joe told me later that he had identified himself as a fellow member of the Masonic Lodge and that the officer had told him he would get him out of there.

Joe was casual, even jovial about it all. Just a little misunderstanding. He really could recall no single incident since I was there that would have made Carlyne do such a thing. When he found them gone he had driven over to bring some presents to the children and when he went to the door Mr. Bowen had met him with a gun. It was as likely a story as breaking down the wall to kiss his wife good-night. But Joe expected me to believe it. And I did believe that he believed it.

When I was ready to leave the cell I called out and someone, a trustee I suppose, came to the door. "I'm ready to leave." "Yea, I know, buddy. We're all ready to leave." "But I'm not a prisoner.

I'm not supposed to be in here." "Yea, I know. None of us is supposed to be in here. You can see the sergeant at eight o'clock in the morning." And then he disappeared.

Joe could still be funny. "Well, Brother, here we are. Both of us in jail. It's a long way from East Fork, isn't it?"

Though there were six steel bunks in the cell there was but one mattress and it was on the floor, caked with dried vomit and smelling of urine. Joe, using his shoes for a pillow, stretched out on one of the top bunks. With a sweeping, circular gesture he addressed me. "Well, pick you out a good bed, Brother. There are plenty of clean sheets, pillows, towels, soap and talcum in the bureau. Shall I call the maid for you? Ah, Brother, *The wrong of unshapely things is a wrong too great to be told.*"

I remembered some other lines he had quoted me on the eve of his marriage, only a few blocks from our jail cell. And the vows which had been taken and the promises made. And East Fork, Lee Campbell's family altar, and the dragonfly in the aspirin box which Joe had declared alive on Wednesday. I remembered a lot of things, and feared there would be much more to remember.

Carlyne would not see either of us and would not allow Joe to see the children. Her father, a kind and gentle man who had worked himself into a responsible position with the Southern Bell Telephone Company—and into a near fatal heart attack a few years earlier—came to the phone when I called and softly advised me to get Joe out of town. Our conversation was cordial and understanding on both sides until I said that I thought both of them needed help and that I would do whatever I could. His voice became curt and impatient. "Well, you're right about one of them but we have done all that we can do!" The graveness of the situation struck me as it had not before. I knew that the road back would be long and hard. And I had serious doubts as to my brother's ability to cope with the reality of it all.

It was a grim ride back to Meridian. I deliberately made the wrong turn three or four times as we made our way out of Birmingham, delaying as I sought vainly to persuade Joe to check into a psychiatric hospital there, where he could be away from the social pressures of his community and where he could prove to his family that he was seeking to shift from what he had become to the man he had once been.

Bessemer, Tuscaloosa, Cuba, Eutaw, Livingston. Alabama towns on the road from Birmingham to Meridian, Mississippi. For the first hour Joe didn't speak at all. Finally he broke the silence. "Did they give you my gun back?" I told him that they didn't. "Why the hell not? It's mine. I bought it and I have a permit to carry it because I am a pharmacist. I work in a hazardous profession." I had related all that to the sergeant when we were being released but he said that Joe had been detained and arrested in the first place because he was carrying a concealed weapon, a crime in Alabama, and having a Mississippi permit is not valid in Alabama. Although they were not going to prosecute—no doubt because of the intervention of the arresting officer who proved to be a brother Mason—they could not return the gun because if the charge had not been dropped the gun would have been used as evidence. Joe said that didn't make any sense. And I agreed.

"Will, I'm not mad at you, but you shouldn't have had me locked up. That was a hell of an experience. Have you ever been in jail before?" He spoke as if we had both been locked up on the same charge.

And maybe we had.

I told him I had been in prisons but only to visit with other people.

"Will, you know I'm not mad at you. You know I couldn't get mad at you, no matter what you did. Do you believe that? You know that, don't you?" I said that I believed him. "I mean do you really, honestly believe that I could never be mad at you?" I assured him that I really did believe that he could not be angry with me. "Could you ever be angry with me? You're mad at me right now, ain't you?" I started to respond but he interrupted, like he didn't want to hear it. "Man, it's getting hot. Shit, it's hot."

He tilted the seat of the little Karmann Ghia backward and closed his eyes. "Brother, tell me a story." I really felt in no mood to tell bedtime stories to a forty-two-year-old man.

"What kind of story?"

"Any kind. Just tell me a story. Tell me about some of the folks you visited in prison."

I called several names. Martin Luther King, Jr., Ralph Abernathy, James Lawson, John Lewis, James Bevel, Diane Nash and dozens of others.

"Name one," I said.

"No, you just pick one out and tell me about it."

I began a verbal journey around the South to where various people had been locked up for their involvement in civil rights demonstrations, settling finally on the occasion when fifty rabbis, preachers and priests from up North had been jailed in Albany, Georgia.

"Yea, Brother, I'll tell you a dandy story. I'll tell you a story about seventy-five folks locked up in jail. All on the same charge."

"Okay, Brother. Lay it on me."

"Well, you remember the big Albany campaign. That's where it happened." He pulled his seat up a bit and opened his eyes. "It's 'All-benny,' Brother. You know we don't call it Albany down here. You spent too much time in Yankee Land."

"Okay, Brother. All-benny." I launched into the story.

"Well, put them in jail," the chief said. Seventy-five men, mostly white, mostly preachers, standing in front of City Hall in Albany, Georgia. Then they marched by me and I looked at their faces.

The Chief of Police in Albany was a handsome, heavy set man named Laurie Pritchett. The seventy-five men had come there from New York, New Haven and Hartford. From Chicago. And God love him, one had come from Texas. They had come in response to a special appeal from Dr. Martin Luther King, Jr., who was then on the verge of losing one of the most crucial civil rights battles of his career. I had gone down as an observer and to help if I could. I felt a little sorry for them as I saw them climbing out of the chartered Greyhound buses which had brought them to Albany from the Atlanta and Columbus airports. They came out of those buses the way I had seen nineteen- and twenty-year-old soldiers coming down the gangplanks in the South Pacific on their way into jungle combat. They were Protestants, Catholics, and Jews. Just as the soldiers had been. Some of them could have been the same folks for this was twenty years later. But unlike their counterparts of two decades earlier each brought with him the sum of his release from captivity. They had been given a copy of the scenario. It read that they would march from the Big Bethel Baptist Church to the Al-

bany City Hall, line up in front of the building where by city ordi-
nance civil rights demonstrators had been forbidden to congregate,
stand in prayer and protestation until they were arrested. They
would then be marched off to jail where for the sum of fifty dollars
each of them would be bailed out. They would be free and could
get the next flight home.

By then I had observed so many such events I felt quite at ease.
But these men left the buses and entered the Big Bethel Baptist
Church clutching breviaries, Union Prayerbooks, and Revised
Standard Versions of the Bible in a fashion that made it, at this
stage where civil rights demonstrations were so commonplace, at
once pathetic and comical.

They entered the Big Bethel Baptist Church and attended the
mass meeting, nightly gatherings scheduled during civil rights cam-
paigns where black people sang freedom songs, clapped their
hands, shouted, listened to a rousing speech or sermon by Dr.
King, Reverend Abernathy or one of the other leaders, finally joining hands in giant circles within circles, bodies swinging and sway-
ing back and forth like so many palm trees by the seashore, voices
blending in close harmony, raising the rafters with:

> *We shall overcome. We shall overcome.*
> *We shall overcome someday.*
> *Ooooooooooooo, Deep in my heart,*
> *I do believe*
> *We shall overcome someday.*

At the conclusion of the meeting one of their number, an elderly
rabbi from somewhere far away, arose and said, "All those who
have come here with our group to be arrested tomorrow reconvene
here at the Big Beth *El* Baptist Church at ten o'clock sharp tomorrow morning." His pronunciation of Bethel brought a few chuck-
les. One of the blacks called out playfully, "Is that C.P. time,
Brother?" There was confusion within the visiting group because
most of them were not familiar with C.P. time, Colored People's
Time, meaning that the meeting began when the meeting began,
not by the white man's clock, but when the field hands had been
released from their duties, the farmers had milked their cows, fed
their hogs, gathered their eggs, and dressed the children. The

rabbi, finally understanding, stammered something about gathering at ten o'clock "our time I guess."

Next morning they came with their fifty dollars and one by one walked forward to sign their name and deposit with the treasurer, seated at the communion table, bail money for their release.

When they marched the few blocks to the courthouse that afternoon they lined up on the sidewalk in military formation. One of them said a prayer but they remained in place. Chief Pritchett stood behind them, saying nothing, even bowing his own head as their prayer was being said. When the prayer was over the chief stepped to the front of the rank and, looking up and down the line at each one, asked them to disperse. They remained in place. Laurie Pritchett, in a different context and upon another occasion, would have been deemed a good man. He was a deeply religious man, a Southern Baptist then taking instruction in the Roman Catholic Church—a big jump in Albany, Georgia. The men stood in place and the chief spoke to them again, gently. "Go back and preach to your own congregations. Convert your own cities before you come here to convert us." The morning paper that day had used as its scripture text for that issue the passage: "And when you pray, you must not be as the hypocrites, for they love to stand and pray in the synagogues and at the street corners that they may be praised by men."

They continued to stand and the spokesman recited the prayer again, the chief once more removing his hat and bowing his head. And again he addressed them: "I ask you again in the name of decency, in the name of justice, to disperse. You have stated your case, you have said your prayers, not once but twice, and I ask you to return to your usual places of livelihood."

But again they did not disperse, standing there in two straight rows, seventy-five men, Jews, Catholics and Protestants, skull caps, turned-around collars, dark suits in the summertime.

That was when the Chief said, "Well, put them in jail." And the people gathered on the front porch of the New Albany Hotel across the street applauded when they heard his words.

Who were those several hundred who applauded? Those who had come to watch their chief in action as they had done every day now for several weeks? Were they Baptists under instruction in a new religion? No, just Baptists, and Methodists and a few Presbyterians and Episcopalians. No Pentecostals, for they would have been out of place on the veranda of the New Albany Hotel. Just good churchgoers, good people.

They had heard the chief say, "Convert your own cities before you come here to convert us." And they had read editor Gray's paper that said to pray "not as the hypocrites on the street corner." And they cheered their chief as the strange looking group of clergy were marched through the alley and into the jail to be fingerprinted and booked.

That's when I really saw their faces. I had seen at least a hundred groups marched off to jail by then, maybe two hundred. Generally they were cheerful, even frivolous. For they knew they were winning. Their time had come and they knew it and there would be evidence of it in their faces.

But these men were sad. Some had been preaching three, five decades. Some were crying—old men crying. Not at all as if their time had come; more as if their time had gone by and all of a sudden they knew we had all waited too late to stand on the streets for simple justice—as if each were saying, "I'm scared lest I, after having preached to others, have missed the way myself." As if for the first time they understood, and were expressing for us all, the sadness of human existence, the depth and complexity of human sin, the nature of humanity in microcosm. For they had heard the cheers across the street, and they had heard the chief, and they perhaps remembered the other reasons why they had come, and they had been to the mass meeting, and they had been under instruction from the Albany Movement. How could they not understand? How could they not be sad?

"Well, put them in jail!"

The plan was that as soon as they were arrested the representatives of the Movement would begin the process of bailing them out. I crossed the street and met Reverend Andrew Young, then administrative assistant for Dr. King and the Southern Christian Leadership Conference. I had known him since he was a student. "Well, Andy, I guess we'd better start getting them out." "Ah, Will. Man it's been a long day. Let's go get some coffee." We got in my Hertz car and drove back to the Big Bethel Baptist Church. I was beginning to get nervous as Andy seemed to be taking more than the usual amount of time to drink his coffee. When he finally did finish I tugged at his belt and reminded him again that our friends would be looking for us to come get them out. "Now

Brother Will, I'll tell you. I'm just about worn out. Let's drive over to Cedar Street and I'm going to stretch out for a little while." I was beginning to understand.

It was almost sundown when Andrew came from his nap. He looked at me and grinned. "Will, those folks came a long way. They want to make a contribution to the Movement. They want to be part of us. They are our *Brothers*. Now it would seem rather a shame if they didn't get to spend at least *one* little night in one of our fine jails. Now wouldn't it?" "Well, Brother Andy, it's your show." "Yea, and it'll probably be my tail come the morning. But it's too late to get them out now. Let's go to the mass meeting."

Because the Albany City Jail was already filled to capacity the men had to be separated and farmed out to jails, rural work camps and penal farms all over southwest Georgia. It was difficult to find them all. It was late the next afternoon before we got the last ones out. We located them in a quonset hut near Plains. Most were still cordial. But some were sullen and mad. A few months later I was attending a sophisticated conference on civil rights in Detroit and one of the group was reporting to his friends during the happy hour all the things he had said to "that redneck sheriff" who held him prisoner overnight. He had really laid him low. Made him look like a real ass in front of his own deputies. I had appreciated the group coming down. I guess. I had agreed with the Movement leadership that it was a factor in getting further national publicity on the prevailing conditions at the time. But I had not remembered anyone getting sassy with the local law.

Joe said he guessed not.

I figured that was enough about jails. But not for Brother. "No, I didn't want to hear about that. I'm sick of all that civil rights stuff. Tell me about someone like me in jail."

I wasn't sure what he meant but I remembered a young man, nineteen or so, who was the first person I had ever visited in jail, other than soldiers in stockades, and Joe had said that didn't count. I began to ramble on.

The boy's mother had called and asked if I would go to see him. I would. The jailer brought him into a little room set aside for ministers and lawyers. "You want to talk secrets with him?" I said that I didn't. "Then you can just sit right here and talk. But if you want to talk secrets we have another room." I began the usual palaver of trivia preachers learn to engage in. "Hey, man. How we doing? Good to see you, pal. What we doing in here, man? We got to get us out of this place." Things like that.

He answered only one bit of the chatter. "Not too good, preacher." I responded with something to the effect that he didn't look any worse for wear and he came back with some words I wasn't quite ready for.

"Preacher, my ass hurts." I saw a trace of a smile on Joe's lips so I went on. He had heard my sarcasm about theological education before so he knew where I was going.

"Now you understand, Brother, that I knew how to field that one. I knew because I had just graduated from a first-rate divinity school where they taught me to be a skilled and non-directive counselor. And, Brother, maybe you didn't know it but what a non-directive counselor does is just repeat everything the counselee says. So I repeated. 'Your ass hurts.' Not putting it in the form of a question but a simple declaration as he had done."

"Yea. My ass hurts."

Then I explained to Joe that the only problem with a non-directive counselor is that he sometimes meets a non-directive counselee and the interview can go on all day—"My ass hurts." "Your ass hurts." "Yea, my ass hurts." "Yea, your ass hurts." And so on ad infinitum. Joe was starting to show some interest in what I was saying for the first time since we left Birmingham. So I began to embellish the story to get us as far down the road as possible.

"But, you know, Brother, in those first-rate divinity schools they teach you how to break out of such an impasse." Joe was beginning to chuckle way down in his throat. Not anything like a belly laugh. Just a steady sound of intermittent gurgling.

"So I said to this young fellow, 'And why does your ass hurt?' "

"Because," he said, "they locked me up last night with four guys who have been in here eight months and they took turns half the night fucking me in the ass!"

Joe bolted upright, pulled the seat up with him and grabbed me by the arm, almost jerking the little car off the narrow Alabama road. "Are you shittin' me, Brother?" I said, no, that it had really happened that way.

"Have you ever told that story in a church-type meeting?" he wanted to know.

"Yea. A few times I guess."

"And I'll bet they get pissed at you for telling it, don't they? Yea, it's all right for the world to let things like that happen but if you say the words out loud it's poor taste. Ain't that about the way it is, Brother?" He was never more pleased than when he took a point I was trying to make and advanced it to a higher and clearer stage.

Having done that, he wanted to compare the young man to himself. "Yea. He was like me all right. That's right where I am—getting screwed in the ass." I tried to talk about whether he was the young boy or whether he could, in part, be compared to one of the four who was doing the screwing. But he wouldn't have it. "Will, you know I didn't hurt my family. You know I couldn't do it if I wanted to. They are all I have in the world and they've got to come back home. I wouldn't hurt my own wife. My own children. Hell!" And he really believed that he had not and could not and would not hurt them, and I saw no point in dealing with specifics.

For several miles we talked seriously about where the real tragedy in the jail scene was, whether it was the young man who had been sexually abused through the night while locked up by the state or the four men who had somehow been turned into something less than human. We talked about ministry. Joe said that since I had been to seminary and he hadn't, he would take the kid for his ministry and he would give me the four. Obviously I was supposed to ask him what he would do for the lad. So I did. "I would take him some Preparation H. I'm a druggist! Now. How are you going to minister to the four who did it?" Of course, that was not quite so easy. I talked more of their plight and the evil of the prison system than I did of remedy. "You noticed I said, 'less than human' and not 'made animals of them' because you can't do that to animals. No matter how long you keep them locked up you could never force them to do that."

Joe did not choose to be serious for very long at a time. He began to laugh and talk frivolously about something out of our childhood. "Yea, you can, Brother. Remember that sweet-ass steer?" A neighbor had once rented our pasture and barnlot to feed a herd of steers in preparation for slaughter and one of the steers had been singled out by all the others who would ride and hunch on him all day as if he were a cow in heat. Joe had called him "sweet-ass." "Yea, I remember that but they didn't actually accomplish anything. They were just aggravating him." "Hell yes they did too accomplish it.

Right in his rear end. That sweet-ass steer got it from every one of them. Don't ask me to explain it. I reckon when they castrated him it caused some hormone imbalance or something and he gave off some sort of cow smell. But they sure as god did it to him."

It gave me an opening to try to make my point in a different way. "Well, you say you're like that kid locked up in the jail? Maybe so. Maybe you're the sweet-ass steer." "Yea, maybe so, Brother. Maybe I'm a sweet-ass steer."

There was a long period of silence. "Okay. Tell me another story, Brother. That was a good one. Tell me a story about someone like you." I hedged. "Well, tell me a preacher story, any preacher. Tell me about that guy over in Louisiana. You know, the one we went to see that time."

As often as I could I would stop at a service station and call Dr. Med Scott Brown, his doctor, to see if she had succeeded in getting him an appointment with a Jackson psychiatrist we had discussed. She cared so much for Joe that she also wanted an hourly report on how he was doing. As soon as we made the stop Joe asked for the story again, saying nothing about whom I had called or why.

He had heard me speak so often of Thad Garner that he already knew most of what I would say. But I began as if he had never heard his name, embellishing and distorting to suit my own fancy and what I knew would suit his. Anything to eat up time and get us on down the road. He sat with his eyes closed for the miles it took to tell the story, sometimes smiling, sometimes frowning, occasionally grunting, but not once interrupting. I just drove and told the story.

Thad Garner was, I suppose, the most profane man I have ever met. And, I suppose, in a way he was also the most profound. Whatever he was, he made a deep impression on me at the time. He was a preacher in Louisiana, down the road from where I was a preacher. He had been there for a long time when I got to Taylor and he sort of took me under his wing.

Both of us were Southern Baptist preachers. When we first met it seemed easy for me to think of him as a Southern Baptist preacher. He was older than I, had a much larger church, held lots of revival or protracted meetings, was popular with the young people, played a small harmonica in his nose while playing a larger one in his mouth at the same time, played golf and was an ardent hunter, was Chaplain of the Volunteer Fire Department, had been a professional boxer, had been to the Holy Land, attended the Baptist Seminary in Louisville as well as two years at Yale, and had recently hosted the state annual meeting of the WCTU.

I did not do any of those things and was just out of a liberal Yankee divinity school. Not only was I younger than Thad, I wore white buck shoes and a tweed cap—even in hot Louisiana summers—smoked a calabash pipe, committed sermons to manuscript, had never held a revival meeting, conducted a building campaign, spoken to a Sweetheart banquet. I had not been to the seminary in Louisville, a sort of union card in those days, and did not even have a map of the Holy Land.

Then I discovered that Thad had once worn white bucks and a tweed cap, still smoked a pipe, conducted revival meetings for money, had gone to the Holy Land only because his congregation had lifted a surprise love offering for that purpose, and had bought the set of color slides he showed to youth groups in the Tel Aviv Airport, really disliked teenagers, drank a lot of wine—though he had but one kidney and couldn't handle it very well—and cussed a lot.

Learning those things made it easy for me to think of myself as a Southern Baptist preacher and increasingly difficult to think of Thad as one. I believed some rather definite things about the Faith while Thad would not admit to believing anything. Yet somehow you did not get the feeling that you were in the presence of a fraudulent or deceitful person. You didn't think of Elmer Gantry. Marjoe was barely born at the time and he wouldn't have come to mind anyway. There was just a fascination that you had not met anyone quite like this before.

Sometimes I would go hunting or fishing with him. I was not really a hunter but he taught me how to shoot and how to avoid copperheads and quicksand, and he would compare both those enemies to various aspects of the pastorate.

On one occasion we were about to conclude an all day and totally unproductive bird hunt. The dogs had pointed at everything from rabbits to starlings but not one quail had been flushed. Thad had excused them by saying the weather was too dry, and he had maligned them as stupid, useless mutts. He had pampered and cajoled them, and he had dragged one of them across a barbed wire fence by the tail as punishment for pointing a brown thrasher. Now the three of them were frozen in a hard point position at what was sure to be the biggest covey of quail in the parish. At least that was what Thad allowed. And when the flush signal was given, that proved to be the case. Even when I am expecting it, even when I have seen the movement of the little critters through the underbrush, I am always startled by the sudden fluttering of quail wings, lifting their fat bellies like giant bumble bees from the earth and away from their pursuer. Consequently I seldom got a shot before they were well out of range. This time Thad got off three quick shots, each BOOM! blending with and echoing the last. As his last shot was dying away I jerked the trigger and waited for the jolt against my shoulder and the ringing in my ears. But nothing happened. The thing was not even loaded. Despite the three volleys in such rapid succession nothing lay dead for the dogs to retrieve. Thad had missed as surely as I had with an empty gun (or piece, as he liked to call any weapon). Though I had not led what one would call a sheltered existence during my life, and my own language did not always measure up to garden party standards, I was not familiar with some of Thad's words. For a full sixty seconds the big Louisiana field was filled with his expletives. At the dogs, at the birds, at me, at the gun, at the manufacturer of the shells, at the Almighty—all were profaned and reviled because of this misfortune. When he had quieted down he sank backward onto an eroded levee. I sat on the ground not far away. It was an occasion for a question I had wanted to ask him for some time.

"Thad, why did you ever decide to be a Baptist preacher?" He looked puzzled and not just a little hurt. He pondered my question for a long time, sighting and squinting down the barrel of his shotgun. Finally he looked me straight in the eye and answered my question: "Cause I was *called*, you goddam fool!"

I have met a lot of preachers since then. But none of them could preach with such assuring certainty, claimed to believe so little, or was as convinced that he was indeed *called* to do exactly what Thad was doing.

Thad had a lot of notches on his Bible. He called it "drawing the net," or "gettin'em ready for the waters." He made fun of every auxiliary and every organization in the church but promoted and organized as if his very life depended upon their success. (And maybe it did.) When I called him a hypocrite for making the rounds of country churches, preaching his fundamentalist brand of religion because he knew what would sell, he countered that I was the real hypocrite because if I really believed all that I said I believed about Jesus and the Gospel I would not be working for one of those rich edifices masquerading as the House of the Lord.

Joe shifted his weight in the seat but said nothing.

I am not so sure now that I was right about Thad. But I am very sure now that he was right about me. When I castigated him for taking money to preach something he didn't believe, his answer was that a man had to make a living for his family.

But he always added something else. "Don't watch me in the church house, boy. Watch me on the street." I guess that he was telling me that his Sunday antics were a tent-making operation, and had nothing to do with his vocation, his call. And I guess he was telling me that if we really believed in grace then the chief sinner might well be the preacher. And apparently St. Paul would have concurred. And whether he was telling me or not, I was learning from him that the Gospel does not depend for its efficacy upon the personal habits of the preacher.

Privately Thad called himself his congregation's mascot. "They feed me well. They even love me. They pat me on the head and brag about me. They show me off before the other teams. There's only one thing wrong with being a mascot. Just one little inconvenience. They keep you on a leash. Otherwise, it's a great life."

There was one term that always sent him into a rage quicker than any other. A pet name for the minister who was liked and approved was the "little preacher." "We just love our little preacher," he would say mockingly. "We have the cutest little preacher." He had a comic routine about the term which began with a guy who was six feet four, weighed nearly three hundred pounds, was a weight lifter in the Olympics, and still his congregation called him "our little preacher." The routine ended with Mary Magdalene running up to old man Zebedee after the crucifixion exclaiming, "Did Jimmy tell you what they've done to our little preacher?" And sometimes Thad would launch into a discourse about a college somewhere that had a fine registered dog for a mascot. A neighboring school stole him one night, bred him to a mongrel bitch, kept him until the puppies were born and then returned him to the campus with his mate and whelps. He never explained his story but the way he would shrug and wink his eye the listener was led to believe that it meant that even a mascot can't be controlled absolutely, that once in a while the Lord will steal him away, get him involved with what the world calls common and use him to mess up their pretty system.

Anyway, after a time I learned to watch him on the streets and not in the pulpit.

Once it was a bond issue before the voters of Granny White to build a swimming pool for the children. Since this was long before civil rights days, the matter of whose children would get to use the pool and whose would not never came up. Nor would Thad bring it up. At least not directly. "I operate like a rubber band," he liked to say. "I stretch things just so far and when it's about to break I let it snap back in place. Only every time I stretch it, it's a little weaker." Thad was, of course, very active in the Lion's Club International, the most influential civic club in Granny White. Clown that he was, it was only natural that he should hold the office of Tailtwister. That's the one who cuts off ten-dollar neckties of a member who comes in late, makes a shy guy sing a solo for not joining in club sing-songs, and little things like that.

On this day the club was discussing whether or not to make an all-out effort on behalf of the bond issue for the swimming pool. The sentiment was strongly in favor of it. Most everybody had said his piece. Then Brother Thad took the floor, told a few stories—like the one about the airline stewardess on a transoceanic flight who kept *insisting* that he have a drink, not knowing that he was of the cloth. "In complete disgust and annoyance I said, 'Lady, I'm a dry alcoholic. If I had one little drink I would rip this whole airplane apart and send it diving into the sea if you wouldn't give me every drop you have on board.' " (This was very funny to the club because just the thought of anyone pulling a social error like offering a Baptist preacher a drink was hilarious.) And I believe that was the occasion when he told about the "Ole colored preacher" who went to a church for a trial sermon and at the dinner table of the head deacon passed his glass instead of his plate when the good sister asked if he wanted more corn. And things like that.

Then the last throat was cleared and the last chortle faded because everyone knew that Brother Garner had some little something serious he wanted to say. "Brethren," he said, "I want us to have a swimming pool. I have two little boys as all of you know and they want a swimming pool. And they asked me at the breakfast table just this morning if I was going to vote to have one. And I told them what I'm fixing to tell you. 'I just can't vote for water for my own children to swim in when there are children in this town who don't have water to drink.' " And he sat down.

Now there were a few more throats cleared and the president fondled his gavel. But no one wanted to get into a discussion of that. Everybody present knew that two years earlier a bond issue had been defeated which would have extended water lines into a part of the black community where dozens of families still got water from a single hand-dug well.

Going back to the house I chided him about the propriety of telling "ole colored preacher" jokes. "That's the trouble with you shithook liberals, Willie. You had rather see a hundred children die of dehydration than have the sound of 'nigger' heard from your lips. Whether I say 'nigger' don't matter a damn. If one of those young'uns die of thirst he ain't nothing. Just one more dead nigger, whether I say the word or not, or whether I go to Hell for saying it or not. But if he lives to get grown maybe he can lead his people out of this godawful Egypt and there won't be no more niggers."

Joe chortled quietly to himself at this, but still didn't open his eyes; so I continued.

On another occasion it was a papermill strike in a small town more than a hundred miles away. The president of the company who lived in Jacksonville, Florida, said that weekends was the only time he could be present for negotiation sessions. When the union said they would be glad to go to the table on weekends the president said he couldn't come on Sunday either because he had to teach his Sunday School class. This had made the local press and for me it seemed a perfect springboard for a Labor Day sermon—straining at a gnat and swallowing a camel, whited sepulchres. But Thad took another approach. There had been a lot of violence accompanying the lengthy strike. Almost every night a gasline leading to the plant would be dynamited far out in the swamps. The union version was that armadillos were stealing dynamite in the mill, burrowing under the fence and storing it under the gaspipes and accidentally igniting it with their teeth. Management did not quite buy that explanation. On the same Sunday I was preaching my social action sermon, Thad mounted his pulpit and delivered a stinging indictment against violence. And it was against every form of violence—war (we weren't in one at the time), racial floggings, fist fights between children (always throw something in for the kids), cock fights (there hadn't been one within a hundred miles of

Granny White for thirty years), and, of course, destruction of private property. All the rest was lagniappe, a redundancy heard by no one. Everyone knew that the sermon was directed at union violence. And everyone approved.

Next morning he called to compare notes. After I accused him again of hypocrisy, dishonesty and moral inconsistency, he asked me if I wanted to go down to Oakville with him that night, the scene of the strike. Of course I did.

There was a giant Labor Day rally of all the strikers and their families. The country high school auditorium was filled beyond capacity. Thad was introduced as a courageous prophet, long known as a fearless friend of organized labor, his body bearing the scars of battle. As I wondered about the scars he proceeded to preach a sermon the delivery of which would have made Billy Sunday blush with envy. He spoke with power and authority. Taking his text from Exodus 14, over and over again he pounded home his point, comparing Moses looking back to see the Egyptians lying dead on the seashore to contemporary labor leaders looking back at the sinister mill owners, lying rotting on a sea of decadence and injustice. Pharaoh became Robert Taft, the Israelites were the rank and file of working people and Moses was the president of the State Labor Council. He was so convincing that it was reported by one of the organizers that two company "spies" sent from the scab ranks expressed an interest in joining the union. At the end of his homiletical excursion he exorcised the demons from the ranks of management, then lapsed into a long and pious prayer that God forgive them all for they did not know what they did.

When we left he insisted that I drive while he sat on the back seat of his Chrysler automobile blowing gales of smoke over my shoulder from a cigar he had fished from a glass container looking like a test tube. From the first day we met he called me "Willie." He bellowed above the noise of the motor, "Do you know what the Church of Jesus Christ is?" I said I sort of thought I did. "Well, I'm going to tell you anyway. The Church is one cat in one ditch and one nobody of a son of a bitch trying to pull him out." When I acknowledged that I had no serious disagreement with that, he continued.

"Yesterday was to pay the rent for tonight. If your integrity was giving you trouble, well then maybe your sermon did something for it. But I don't have any trouble with my integrity 'cause I ain't got none. And yours is probably an idol. I didn't push anyone in the ditch with my little sermonette yesterday. And I didn't pull anybody out. Everybody broke even. But tonight!"

He slapped the back of the seat with one hand and knocked my cap into the windshield with the other. "But tonight! Man, the ditch was full." By now he was screaming to the top of his voice. "The ditch was full! And I sat 'em on *my* ass and took them to town!" He waited for me to respond. When I didn't he started again, this time in a much lower and slower tone. "And if you don't believe it was *my* ass, then just wait till my people find out I was down there and you'll see whose ass it's going to be." He began to laugh and make funny noises in his throat, beating both knees with both his fists until it seemed one or the other would break. Stopping this he reached in his pocket and dug out a little bottle of pills, swallowed two of them dry. Then he pulled a bottle of Mogen David wine from under the seat, took several long and noisy gulps, finally gargling his throat with the last swallow. Feigning drunkenness he slurred, "Man, if I didn't have Milltowns and Mogen David to prop up Jesus Christ I never would make it."

Neither of us spoke for a long time. Then Thad started again, leaning over my shoulder, whispering a mockery of piety. "Brother Campbell, my language bothers you, doesn't it." I just shrugged, watching for armadillos, wild hogs, and stray cattle in the darkness of the Louisiana road.

"Yea, Willie, it bothers you. I'm not asking you. That was a period, not a question mark. I don't use many question marks. Mostly periods. Yea, my language bothers you. That's because you don't understand about language."

"I don't?"

"No. You really don't. Now I'm gonna give you a little lesson in language. Ready or not . . . here I come."

I said, "Come on."

"Now. You're hosting the Lion's Club at your church and I'm the speaker. All your best paying members are there and the ladies have drifted out of the kitchen to hear the speaker. You introduce me and I stand up and say, 'Granny White, Louisiana, is the asshole of the world.' How would you respond?"

"I guess I would just about faint."

"Right! Okay now. Suppose when you introduce me I get up and say, 'My Christian brothers and sisters, if you wanted to give the universe an enema you would have to insert the tube in Granny White, Louisiana.' How would that grab you?"

"I guess a lot better."

"Whadda thought. See. You just don't understand about language."

Again there were miles of silence. He was down from his high. Finally he reached over the seat into the glove compartment for his harmonicas, the tiny one for his nostril and the larger chromatic one to be played in the usual way. Beginning with *Amazing Grace*, sometimes playing just the little one with his nose, singing the words of a verse in harmony with the melody of the harp, he played and sang us on into Granny White, stopping only once to say, "Yea, Wee Willie, the Church is one cat in one ditch, and one nobody of a son of a bitch to pull him out."

I suggested to Joe that the ride from Oakville to Granny White with Thad reminded me a little of the ride he and I were taking then. He nodded but said nothing. I went on with the story.

Despite his seemingly simplistic definition of the Church, the study of church history was almost an obsession with Thad. He knew the dates and outcome of every council from the beginning, the issues of every controversy, the reasons for every split, the ground of every new denomination. And sometimes he would speak nostalgically and even sympathetically of "the old whore." And on occasion he would vow to restore her to some imagined day of purity and glory. But generally his ambivalence tilted in the direction of hostility and revenge.

He came one day with a grandiose scheme for church renewal. It was complete with charts, budget, timetables, and a written foundation proposal.

"Willie, what's the biggest wasted manpower resource in the world?" I said I didn't know.

"Well, I'm going to tell you. The greatest wasted manpower resource in the world is preachers." He explained at some length that as a professional group we were better educated, more sensitive to human needs, had more insights into what the world is all about, were better organizers, and a lot of other things I don't remember that we were supposed to be.

"And the world thinks we are a bunch of eunuchs. They tried to make us eunuchs. But they didn't pull it off. At least not with most of us. We have something to offer this world, but we'll never be able to do it as long as we're in this box. Now here's what I'm gonna do."

He outlined the most detailed scheme of how he was going to renew the Church and at the same time make it possible for preachers to be ministers to the world. First, he would hire a staff which for two years would go to industry, agencies, businesses, everyone who employed people. He would convince them that this wasted manpower resource was waiting at their doorsteps. Then he would get a commitment from them as to how many they would hire and in what capacity and at what starting salary. All this would be filed away until he had seventy-five thousand jobs available for preachers in his files. All this would be done in secret.

When that job was complete a press conference would be held with the announcement that he had the biggest religious story since Wittenberg. "It'll get the coverage. Don't worry about that. Religion is big news in this country. Christianity ain't! But religion is. And as soon as the news hits, that any preacher who wants out of the cage has a job waiting for him, security for his family, and a chance to really *be* the Church, man! They'll fly like martins to their gourds. I'll empty two-thirds of the pulpits in a month."

"And then what, Thad?"

"And then what? You stupid fool! Then we'll have some ministers abroad in the land. Folks making a living because they have to and doing what they are called to do because they want to. And then those dead souls who have been sitting in those rich pews for fifty years with their mascots minding their altar fires and tea parties will have to start asking some questions. Then you'll see some church renewal. Then you'll hear some folks singing the Psalms for the first time in their lives. Then you'll see some idiot church bureaucrats from Nashville and Chicago and Atlanta and New York and wherever they hang their fat hats beating their ecclesiastical swords into plowshares if they have any degree of humanity left in their bones—which most of them don't—and then you'll see Jesus Christ get a fair shake in this world for the first time in a long while. That's 'and then what.' "

There was the usual long silence when one of us came out with something the other thought too far out to merit discussion. And, as usual, it was he who broke it.

"Man, it's got the Armageddon idea beat all to hell." And then another long period with only the sound of his foot and mine tapping out a brotherly cadence upon the ground.

"Naw, Wee Willie, you're right. Yea, you're right. It wouldn't work. As long as they're rich, they'll get the technicians. It's just too good a deal for a fellow to give up. Aw, we'd empty some pulpits. But they would see it as the providence of God, getting rid of the uncommitted riff-raff. They would turn the whole damn thing right around on us and rip out our emerods. Yeah, *they* would call it church renewal—getting rid of all the false prophets in their midst. Man, ain't it a bitch!" I allowed as how it was and we went on to something else. But after a while, he came back to it. But not for long. "You know, Wee Willie, I don't hate anybody. 'Cause the Bible says it's a sin to hate. But there are some folks I hope dies of cancer of the tonsils." Thad always had a way of putting things.

I glanced at Joe and saw the whiteness of his knuckles as he opened and clinched his fists. That meant he was awake, listening or not, so I continued with the chronicles of Thad Garner. We needed the miles.

It wasn't long after that he showed up at the door one morning too early for anybody to be stirring. In fact it wasn't even four o'clock. Sometimes he would do that if he wanted to harangue me into going hunting with him. But it was clear that he wasn't dressed for hunting. It was Monday morning and he still had on his preaching suit, a garment of which he always divested himself as soon as he reached the parsonage. There was a sort of confused look in his eyes. When I beckoned him inside he didn't move. Usually he walked in without even a knock. He was whimpering softly, like a small baby coming off a long crying trip. I was so baffled and frightened that I joined him outside in my underwear, not even noticing the cold. As I did he turned and buried his face in the crook of his arm, leaning forward into a giant sweet gum tree. His whimpering became loud, uncontrollable sobs. I had never seen him cry before and didn't know what to do. (Women can cry together but few men have yet attained that freedom.) I slipped my arm around his waist and he turned quickly around, my shoulder replacing the tree. He kept muttering something I couldn't understand and his tears were not quick in stopping. His body shook and trembled. But then suddenly he stopped, placed one thumb and then the other against each nostril and blew his nose, kicked the ground lightly over the droppings and came inside.

Now he was well composed, steady and seemingly calm. "Willie, I'm quitting." "Quitting what?" "Quitting it all. I'm tired. I'm tired of lying. I'm tired of running. I'm tired of being patted on the head. I'm tired of being a whore. I just want to be a human being. I'm tired, Brother. And I'm sick."

The courses in pastoral psychology, counseling and all that had not been among my best or favorites. But it took no Menninger to know that he was for a fact, sick. He slumped down in a big arm chair and began to roll out a self-analysis—the things one new to the couch might think it necessary to blurt out in his first session. Conversion at an early age, growing up in a round of revival meetings, church camps, "surrendering to preach." (He always said that was an apt description and term for when one *decided* to preach under a modern-day steeple he was for a fact surrendering.) At the age of twelve under the urging of a fast-talking, high-powered returned missionary, life with father, life with mother, life with brother and no sisters—all the things I suppose one talks about to his therapist. But I was not a therapist. I had no way of evaluating what he was saying, only the good sense to bring him coffee.

It was a long day. There was the secret call to a good mutual friend, a parishioner of his who was a doctor in Granny White. There was the doctor's visit to Thad's wife and their secret call to an analyst in New Orleans and finally their arrival to take my friend and mentor away.

But there was no problem. He was more than willing to go. He helped with the quick decisions which had to be made. He agreed that he was having what they call a real, old-fashioned nervous breakdown. And he knew that it would take some time and a lot of money to get over it.

Guns, camping equipment, insurance policies, a piece of retirement land, furniture, the big Chrysler—all of it would be turned into enough money to make the move and begin paying the doctor. (A bit of the old Thad returned as he grinned with devilish delight when he was told that the analyst was a woman.) The doctor friend would resign for him on Wednesday night at the church's business meeting, with dignity and in good taste. He would ask for six months' full salary for Thad.

At six that evening they drove away, Thad crying softly in the back seat as he said good-bye, the strong wife at the wheel, the doctor at his professional best.

I paused, not looking at Joe but somehow feeling what he was thinking. "That damn little brother of mine. He's told me this whole tale just to suggest to me that people he loves and respects sometime need to see a shrink. That damn little brother of mine."

Knowing, I went on.

It was a long time before I saw Thad again. I heard that he and his family moved in with his mother, that he was in a hospital for three weeks, and had then settled in for two years of unemployment and complete analysis.

When he surfaced again it was as chaplain of a large metropolitan hospital. I saw him by accident while visiting a relative. It was as if we had been together the day before. "This is it, Willie. Yea, man, this is where it's at. I've found it and I've found myself. Ain't it a bitch. I'm a counselor, a natural born counselor. That's what I am and always was. Tell the boys old Thad is back on the yard." And there was no doubt that he was back, and higher than ever.

Not only was he back on the yard, he was back in the fields, the swamps, the forest, wherever there was game to be stalked and killed. Nothing got him as excited as hunting or just talking about hunting. "Yeah, Wee Willie, I'm a killer. A born killer. 'Course, everybody is a killer. Me, I just kill animals. Not people."

On one occasion one of our friends was in his office when he was about to leave on one of his island treks with two of his rich planter friends. Everyone was dressed in camouflaged denims, rubber boots, wide gunbelts around their shoulders and waists, each one trying to look the most like Hemingway or like Bogart in *African Queen*. Thad was in complete charge, telling the funniest jokes, the biggest lies, and getting all the laughs. Going down in the elevator Thad was still talking, still entertaining in anxious preparation and anticipation of the hunt. An elderly black man was sitting in a wheelchair. A young, well-dressed, collegiate-looking black man was standing behind the chair. Thad noticed the pair and looked down at the old man. "Well, Uncle, so you're going home today. I know you'll be mighty proud to get home."

The old man grunted and nodded in the affirmative. The young man pounced as if he had been waiting since May 17, 1954 for this moment. Feigning a dialect which obviously came hard for him he moved a bit closer to Thad in the elevator.

"He yo uncle? Why, he my uncle too. That done make me and you cuzzins." Then looking around the elevator he addressed everyone there. "Hey, everybody. I wants y'all to meet my cuzzin, Chaplain Garner. What you know 'bout dat! Me an' the Chaplain cuzzins. Ain't dat sumpin'!"

The warts and moles on Thad's nose and face seemed almost to disappear against the redness of his skin. The laughter of his two friends was uncontrollable. Thad made a feeble comeback by patting the old man's shoulder and telling him he hoped he wouldn't get sick again for a long time. The old man had not changed expressions and again nodded in the affirmative. As they left the elevator the young man was guffawing like Amos and Andy's Kingfish, slapping his thigh in hambone fashion, stomping a light buck and wing before rolling his own uncle down the hall.

Out of sight Thad was even more humiliated. He knew better than to call the old man "uncle" but he knew better still than to try to explain it in the presence of his rich planter friends. As they left for cigarettes his clergy friend said, "Looks like somebody in one family or the other has been messing around." "That smart aleck son of a bitch. After all I've done for the Negroes. He knows who I am and what I stand for. What did he have to do that for?" "Because you called a black man 'Uncle,' Thad." "Well, hell. I call *all* old men, 'Uncle.'" "Naw, Thad, you call all old *black* men 'Uncle' in the presence of rich white folks who take you on all-expense-paid hunting trips." "Well, he's still a smark aleck son of a bitch."

Then, never to be outdone, he started to laugh and turned the whole incident into one more funny and entertaining story, kidding the friend about his knee-jerk liberal embarrassment, adding it to his vast repertoire.

He stayed four years as a counselor. He was too active politically for the hospital board, plus the fact that serious disillusionment had set in quite early in this phase of his institutional journey.

The next time I saw him he was some kind of a college administrator. He had just received a letter from his seminary informing him that his Bachelor of Divinity degree could be traded in for a Master of Divinity degree with no additional work. He was highly indignant. "Now that's their contribution to the social crisis. A stupid war going on in Vietnam, prisons running over with our brothers and sisters, millions of people starving to death, black people no better off than they ever were, a nut in the White House and their response to the Gospel is to rename a crock-of-shit diploma." Suddenly all institutions of theological learning were a giant punching bag and he danced and sparred around, jabbing away like he used to do as a boxer. He held the letter in his hand, all crumpled up in a tiny wad. Students stole quick glances at us as they went to and from classes.

He began to laugh. "Willie, we got took. You know what! They never should have called our degree Bachelor of Divinity. It should have been Bachelor of Sophistication. They took our country asses up there and filled us up with New England culture, sent us back playing Bach fugues on hundred-thousand-dollar pipe organs, smoking calabash pipes, wearing tweed caps and white bucks. Man they did it to us. They gave us the treatment." He began to make jokes about the way you could tell where a professor had done his graduate studies by his campus manner. "Now if he went to Edinburgh he always wore a tweed jacket, complete with coat of arms. And smoked a big pipe and had a yachting cap or braided tam. If he rode a three-speed Raleigh bicycle to school you could bet he was an Oxford or Cambridge man. He generally wore a tweed cap too. And carried his books around in a sack with a neck strap on it. If he studied in Germany he had returned with a Volkswagen. That was before *everybody* drove Volkswagens. And they all, no matter where they went, would eat with the fork in the left hand, pushing their food onto the upsidedown fork with the knife. And sometimes they would forget and drive on the left side of the road. I had a prof who would give half the class 77 on exams just so he could write it 7̶7̶. Man, what a crock."

He began to rave again. "Willie, the whole screwed up world is going to hell in a bucket and this is their commentary. Jesus Christ! Willie, where's your nervous breakdown?"

I said I was just waiting around.

Then there was some minor position with a labor organization, another period of unemployment, and finally what appeared to be an important assignment with the Peace Corps. But his letters indicated that he might as well be back with First Steeple by the First National. I didn't see him again for a long time.

I was about to miss a plane at Dulles Airport and he was there to meet some dignitary in connection with his work. I told him I was sorry I didn't have time to visit. He said he was too, said he had something important to tell me. As I hurried toward the gate he kept dancing backward just ahead of me trying to convince me to catch the next plane. As we reached the gate he was loudly explaining what it was he wanted to tell me. "You know, Willie, I've figured out two things." By then we were both outside the terminal, the airline official protesting vehemently that Thad didn't have a boarding pass and hadn't put his pipe out at the gate, the change of voice for each offense indicating that he did not know which was the more serious. Ignoring him, Thad continued. "I've figured out what the two most evil influences in America are and I've figured out the difference between me and you." He was talking now in machine-gun-like bursts and jogging around me in circles, screaming above the sound of the jet engines. "The two most evil influences in America are Billy Graham and Marcus Welby! And the difference between me and you is that I never took the goddam church seriously enough to hate it and you never took humanity seriously enough to hate the goddam A.M.A."

The airline guy grabbed him from behind by both arms, obviously more angry now at his iconoclasm than at his violation of Eastern Airline rules. Thad broke the hold in some quick, judo-type manner, looking nonchalantly at those gathered around with a "poor chap, he's lost his marbles" glance, slapped his hands back and forth across his thighs in a cleansing sort of gesture, and strode slowly back inside.

I had hoped to make Joe laugh out loud but I had failed. Maybe he had laughed a little inside. I didn't know. I told him I didn't know what Thad was doing for a living then. And I still don't. I guess it doesn't matter. I hope it is something easy and well paying. The last time I saw him I didn't bother to ask. The setting of our meeting made it seem unimportant. He was sitting in a small lounge near the Greyhound bus station in a large Southern city. He had a crew cut and was wearing what might have been a J. C. Penney suit. At the table with him was a middle-aged woman who had on a striped shirt with French cuffs and what I took to be a roach clip for a necktie clasp. They were drinking coffee and engaged in subdued conversation. I would have guessed that the woman's former professional means had been somewhat hampered by the years. I also guessed that she was in some kind of trouble. I walked over and casually put my hand on Thad's shoulder. The woman was obviously startled and her hand shook as she pretended to sip her coffee, spilling it onto the oilcloth which covered the table. Thad was equally surprised. He glanced quickly at her and then back at me. He was friendly but far from effusive. His words were pleasant and cordial enough but it was not the loquacious Thad Garner I had met in Granny White twenty years ago. We engaged in low-toned introductions, some meaningless small talk, everybody laughing at nothing.

I soon excused myself. He followed me to the street. I felt disappointed that after all these years he found it necessary to explain, for I did not know if his explanation said something about him or something about me.

"Willie, the Church is one cat in one ditch and one nobody of a son of a bitch trying to pull her out." I said that I remembered. Glancing back into the restaurant he winked and the old grin stretched his lined, warty face. "Cause I was *called*, you goddam fool!"

Opening his eyes, Joe, for the first time, began to speak, indicating that he had been listening all the while.

"You jumped a lot of rabbits with that one, Brother."

"Did you recognize any of them?" I asked.

"Yea, one or two I guess. You ought to write that story down. That'll preach."

There was another period of silence and a few more miles behind us. Now suddenly we were turning the curve and passing the hospital and pharmacy where Joe worked. As we did he quickly snapped his seat back again, securely tightening the seat belt as if he were seeking some kind of assurance that all would be well and closed his eyes again.

When we reached his house he sat there for a moment with his eyes still closed. "Yea, Brother. There's a lot of folks in this world getting screwed in the ass. And you know what? I'm one of them."

He sat there for what seemed an hour but which, I am sure, was not more than a minute. He threw the door open and jumped out. "I've got to get to the pharmacy. All my prescription addicts will be beating my doors down."

As we were walking in the house, Mrs. Temple, wife of a circuit court judge, friend and next-door neighbor, was sweeping her carport. "Hi, Joe! Where's Carlyne? I haven't seen her all morning." He flashed a big smile, waved and calmly replied, "We all went to

Birmingham last night and they decided to visit with Mr. Bowen for a few days." They really were good friends. Close neighbors. Yet neither knew any more of what went on behind the closed doors of the other than if they had been strangers living in different countries.

At the pharmacy he explained that Carlyne was having some emotional problems, made up one convincing story after another, whatever was indicated at the moment in defense of what was left of his world.

But by the next night he admitted to me that he couldn't function. I had been afraid for him even to go to the bathroom alone. My fears that he was suicidal proved not to be the case but I had had a friend in deep depression who was left alone for five minutes and shot himself. I even slept in the big bed with him.

At two o'clock I awoke with Joe crying. "I can't stand it. I've got to see my babies. I've worked my head off day and night for them and now I can't even see them. I've got to see my babies. I can't stand it." He said it over and over for at least ten minutes. There was nothing I could do but listen.

Next morning he was back at work. But by now the word was out. I talked to Dr. Med Scott Brown, his physician and good friend. She tried to reassure me. She insisted that Joe was not going to harm himself. He just isn't the type. "Why, Joe Campbell is the kind of guy who thinks suicide is a sin." She did agree that he couldn't handle the situation by himself and ought to seek professional help and said she was still trying to get him an appointment. But she also insisted that he was not mentally ill. "He's just a little boy. He kept on growing but the little boy stayed inside him and what's wrong with that?" His bosses, also longtime friends, got me aside and talked. They were fearful of an accident in filling prescriptions.

At one point it was I who cracked. His bosses had told him to take some time off to think things through. That left us all day and all night to sit around the house and agonize. It was late afternoon and the tension of being away from my own family, staying awake most of the time, the frustration of getting nowhere with Joe in seeking professional help had got to me. I began to cry like a kid hurt in a game of puppy love. "Joe, I just can't stand it. I can't bear to see you like this. I've got to go home and I can't go with you in this shape and sitting here in the middle of a damn arsenal." And a lot more but that is what I remember.

It was a cue in the script. Joe became counselor. "You're the one who needs help. You've always told me I ought to have a hobby and then when I have one you call it an arsenal. You're the one about to have a nervous breakdown. Maybe I'd better get *you* to a shrink." And things like that.

The next morning the development I had hoped for came. He called every day to Birmingham. Generally Mr. Bowen answered the phone and generally he would not let him talk to Carlyne. Apparently on that occasion Mr. Bowen succeeded in convincing him that the only possible hope for the family to return was for him to get some help. I could sort of feel the presence as the conversation was taking place.

Joe gently placed the phone on the hook and spoke to me as if the subject had never been brought up. "Brother, do you think I should see a psychiatrist?" "Yes, Brother, I do." "Okay, I will."

I went immediately and talked to Med Scott Brown. (With a name like that each time I saw her I wondered if her parents had any vocational notions in mind when they named her.) She couldn't get an appointment with the only psychiatrist she really trusted in Jackson without a long waiting period. So, we decided to take a chance on another one. He was available the next afternoon.

He gave Joe the battery of tests and went through an hour long interview. He came with Joe to the waiting room and gave his report. He told me that my brother was sick, that he was not recommending that his wife come back and may *never* recommend it, that Joe had a serious paranoid condition and could hurt himself or someone else at the slightest provocation. He wanted to admit him to the hospital that very day. Joe protested that he would not be stampeded into doing something that serious, that the report was a matter of one man's opinion, based on the most superficial evidence. The doctor did not like being crossed or questioned. "Then, by god, I'm recommending that you be committed to Whitfield." "Man, that's a place for crazy people. I'm not crazy. I work every day. I pay my bills and I've never hurt anybody in my life. Maybe *you* belong in Whitfield." I was later to conclude that Joe was right about the psychiatrist.

We started the ninety miles back to Meridian and his first bit of frivolity was, "Okay. You told me if I went to see a psychiatrist my family would come back. Let's stop and call them so they can be on their way." But I was in no mood for his jokes. Nor was I done with my godplaying. I badgered him into seriousness by reminding him that it was quite within my power to have him committed and that we should be done with the nonsense.

And then he told me. "I don't need some quack like that guy to tell me what's wrong with me. I know what's wrong with me." I was anxious to hear his diagnosis but did not expect what he said.

"What?"

"Too many pills."

I think he meant to tell it all but he stopped short. I knew nothing of pills. It was before the "speed" fad had hit the streets and I was completely ignorant of what he was talking about. He told me that he had started years ago taking one amphetamine in the middle of the afternoon to get him through the day. He explained how they would give him pep and improve his outlook. But the number increased and had to keep on increasing into the dozens. I later learned that when one confesses to dozens it really means hundreds. And then, matter of factly, he made the only true diagnosis ever given on his case.

"They dumped me."

We talked about it for awhile and he explained what he knew already but which medical science was to take several more years to prove with extensive research. He said that when they dump you, it is not just that they don't do anything for you any longer. It is that they do the reverse of what they used to do. Where they once kept you calm and optimistic, they come to make you irritable and paranoid. So you turn to something else to bring you "down." In his case it was Seconals, a rather heavy sedative when taken in sufficient quantities.

It was a good diagnosis. But it was one carefully designed to make the point that there was no point in going to a hospital.

I naively asked him why he didn't quit. And he gave the answer that such a question deserved. "I have." He said after going through what he had been through with the loss of his family that nothing in the whole world could ever again make him take one of the things. I believed him and I am sure he believed it. He said over and over that if Carlyne came back nothing in the whole world could ever again push him to strike her, lift his voice against her or cross her in any way. "All I want," he said, "is the chance."

My dim view of psychiatry as a science and his convincing affirmations of reform caused me to abandon any thought of committing him to a hospital against his will. But I continued to harangue him about it.

Despite the fact that he kidded about "now I've been to a psychiatrist so when is my wife coming back," I think he really believed that would be the case. He continued to try to reach her at least twice a day. Though never religious he now insisted on saying a verbal grace at each meal. And he would lie in bed for hours reading the Bible, though always pointing out to me that he was aware that such behavior was considered a bad symptom by some but that he knew what he was doing and why.

I continued to stay with him every minute of the day and when he would wake up crying in the middle of the night I would often cry with him. I was so concerned I even followed him to the bathroom.

It was nearly a week later that he called Birmingham but succeeded only in talking to Mr. Bowen. He did little talking and it was apparent that he was getting another fatherly lecture. Just as he had done before when the conversation was over, he turned and said, "Maybe I ought to go to a hospital."

Then he collapsed in the middle of the bed, crying. "I'm a nut. I'm a self-admitted and self-committed nut. I'm a nut." He said it over and over. I at least had the good sense to know that I should not rush him, that the time for consolation was at hand. "No, you're not a nut. You're my great big beautiful brother with a problem."

We sat in the darkened room for a long time. He tried to analyze himself, but it was not like the clever, though true, diagnosis he had made of himself in the car. He was no longer seeking ways to manipulate me. He was, at least for the moment, looking for answers.

I do not remember a lot about the conversation. But I do recall his saying that his real problem had something to do with the way we were raised. He pitifully recalled that he never had any friends or buddies when we were growing up. He mentioned one or two, cousins, but said that we never played with other boys like most people, that we were always working in the field, and added with a touch of bitterness that it seemed as if Daddy was always sick. I remembered that it was for a fact always Joe who had to carry the load, from making a crop almost single-handedly to joining the CCC Camps to bring us out of poverty when youngsters his age usually had other things on their mind. But I knew that we could not escape now by engaging in mutual self-pity.

I called Med Scott and she advised admitting him under her care until arrangements could be made to transfer him to Jackson.

We parked his car and walked down the hall he had walked so many times in his capacity as hospital pharmacist. He knew where his room was and we didn't stop at the desk. Nurses, orderlies and interns smiled and called him by name as we passed each station. No one had been more respected or more loved. And no one believed that Joe Campbell had been violent or mean to anybody. We entered his room and he got into one of the funny little bobtailed hospital gowns. Dr. Brown had told me she was placing him under heavy sedation.

I could see the nurse hasten by the door, back and forth, quickly glancing in as she passed. Joe took a stand by the window, saying nothing. He stood gazing in the direction of the hospital pharmacy and softly called the name of each customer as they entered or departed. I went and stood beside him. He continued to study the pharmacy entrance, still announcing each person by name as they came and went, visualizing, no doubt, precisely what went on inside—what their prescription called for, how much of their particular medication was in stock, how much longer it took the pharmacist substituting for him to decipher each doctor's signs and symbols than it would have taken him, hearing again each one describe his or her illness in the details he had so often heard before, wondering perhaps if the new man had taken the time to listen and show sufficient sympathy as he had always done, no matter how busy.

Eventually three Meridian executives from a near-by building jogged by. He said nothing to indicate that he had seen them. After they passed the window three or four times, faces redder each time, perspiration pouring down their necks in the late afternoon Mississippi sun, the spell was broken.

"Something about jogging always depressed me," he said. I responded with something about good health being a desirable quality and good physical health keeping the head clear. He turned and stretched his long body upon the bed and began to speak with the sagacity I had so admired in earlier years. "No, Brother. Jogging is like a Brownie camera. They are both reaching out, staking a claim on infinity." Then he reminded me of a conversation we had had years before outside the Grand Ole Opry in Nashville. We had watched a group of tourists in the Opry Souvenir Shop next door buying trinkets to take back home, little ceramic ash trays that said PUT YOUR BUTT HERE, or coffee cups cut square on the back saying, YOU ASKED FOR HALF A CUP. Inside we watched them race to the edge of the stage with their cheap little cameras popping flashbulbs when Roy Acuff, Minnie Pearl or another of their folk heroes came on stage.

"They thought they would go back to Lima, Ohio, and keep it forever. Well, they won't. And those running fools out there are trying to outrun death. They won't pull it off. Probably drop dead on the jogging trail." I tried to counter with some inane bit of trivia. But he continued.

"When you're somewhere you're somewhere and when you're gone you aren't there anymore and pictures and souvenirs don't make it so. And when you're old you're old and jogging won't roll back time and when it's over, old or not, it's over. And for me it's over."

I was by then bored with my own vacuity and was glad to see the nurse enter the room.

"Okay, Joe. Where you want it, baby?"

"Anywhere you say, Nursie." The mask he had continued to wear in public was back in place. He revealed no more concern or anxiety to her than if he was getting some periodic inoculation.

"What about in the left arm?"

He held out his left hand toward her and extended his right to me.

"Bye, Brother."

I stood holding his hand in mine. He winced slightly and registered a playful complaint at the pierce of the needle. The nurse pulled the cotton sheet up around his broad shoulders, kissed him on the cheek and pretended to tuck him in. He continued to hold my hand, repeating twice, "I'll be acoming back, Ma." Within five minutes he was asleep.

The sound of "Bye, Brother" was lodged in my head and would not go away. I sat beholding my friend and buddy with all the uncertainty of a corporal leading an army. There was the tortuous gnawing in my bowel that this was not what he needed.

And I recalled and thought again about the 'skeeterhawk he had buried on Sunday and vowed that if it were alive on Wednesday I would come back and we would be together the way we had always been. I wished that I could become as a little child and thus receive the Kingdom, that I could make such wager, have that trust and certainty on his behalf. But now we were grown up. The world had given us different ways of doing things, of looking out for each other. Now we had science and technology, learning and technicians and therapists and institutions to bring and hold brothers and families together. And progress among the nations.

The dragonfly would not go away. Quintessence of speed and motion and restlessness. Sometimes flying a mile a minute. And sometimes not stopping for rest from dawn to dusk, speeding through time and space, dreading the awkward cessation. Work and play and mating and mealtime. All of it in flight. And only in flight. Not only swift and agile but skilled in dodging. Close in upon him with an argumentative net and he will hover in faked submission. Fold the net around him and he is gone. Like a bullet ricochets off a tilted armor, he is gone. Perfectly attuned to life on the wing. Maybe it is his vision that keeps him forever in motion; those eyes, occupying more than half the surface of the head, made up of more than a thousand separate cameras. What they see is a cosmic mosaic. Their reality is not our reality. Maybe they see so much that they simply cannot stand it, cannot bear the awful weight of stillness. And thanks. For some say we would not have survived, not in near tropical Mississippi, without the dragonfly to control the mosquito. Low flying aircraft, hissing spirals of Malathion onto marshes and swamps and shore lines do it better **now,** though the dragon goes down with the anopheles, the blue **and the** gray lie together. How strong and how frail is this carnivorous creature, without whom Joe, the joggers, the nurse and the prescription addicts going and coming might not have been. Endowed with six feet and legs he cannot walk. With all his consciousness and accomplishment he cannot stand upright. Even with such abundance of appendages he can only cling, hold onto something external and stationary when he is not speeding through the air.

"I can't walk, Major Rollins, I tell you I can't walk."

"I can't stand up, Cousin Vernon. I can't stand up." And those four transparent, gauze-like wings could hardly be expected to withstand the jetstream they create. But still he flies, dodging and darting, controlling and patroling land and water. Until one day, with the same swiftness and suddenness and sureness of flight, he drops to the earth. Finished. Roll on, civilization!

I dropped his hand and left the room, went to fetch my belongings and close up his lonely nest which had once been so filled with laughter and play, comfort and security, and began the long drive back to Nashville.

Three days after Joe was admitted to the psychiatric section of the Jackson Baptist Hospital, he called to demonstrate that he was in complete control of the situation.

"Brother?"

"Yea, Joe."

"This is the lunatic."

I was a bit nervous. "You're not a lunatic, Joe. You just have a problem you can't handle by yourself."

"No, Brother. I'm a nut. I'm crazy, man. You said I was." Then, to exhibit his continuing Joeness, he reminded me that he was behind bars, that the door was operated electrically and that only a nurse, doctor or orderly could open it. Then he called a nurse over and began talking with her. I could not hear all the words but it was something to the effect that he wanted to walk halfway down the hall and assured her that he would return with no resistance. I was not surprised when she agreed, after a slight protest that it was against the rules and she could be fired for it.

"Okay, Brother. I'm going to walk down the hall, past the locked door. You talk to the nurse while I'm gone." We engaged in small chitchat and in less than two minutes he was back on the phone.

"That's how crazy *they* think I am. Now. When are you coming to get me out of here?"

He knew he could sign himself out anytime he chose. But I did not remind him of that. I still thought that I was going to choreograph, direct and produce a miracle. I told him that I would be down in two days and we would talk about it and that he should take it up with the doctor.

By the time I got there he was not so sure. For almost a year I had waited for him to hit bottom and recognize that he had hit it and begin the long, painful trip back up. But he always bounced back. Now I found him half asleep on his bed. He did not get up to embrace me as he had always done. There was barely the acknowledgment that I had entered the room. I tried the pastoral cheerfulness. "Hey, Brother. How we doing?" "Not too good, Brother. You've got to get me out of this place. I'm not crazy but I will be if I stay in here much longer." He explained that they were giving him shock therapy with insulin. He pointed out what I already knew—that when a doctor does that it is because he doesn't know how to do anything else. "I'm about as much in need of insulin shock as Bertrand Russell." He pleaded with me to take him home. Again I did not ask him why he didn't simply go to the desk and sign himself out. And again I talked him into giving it a whirl with that hospital and that doctor.

In another week he was out. He called me to come and together we went back to Meridian. The doctor assured me that he could function on his own with out-patient care, and that he could stay alone at home. But now Joe was quiet and withdrawn and frightened. The closer we got to Meridian the more pronounced the symptoms became. He wanted to go to the Holiday Inn where he, Carlyne, Joey and Julie used to check in on Friday evening, spend a hundred dollars or so before Sunday afternoon just for the privilege of swimming in the pool and sleeping in the motel rooms. He ordered a big meal but as soon as they brought it he was ready to leave. I paid the check and followed him outside. "What's the matter, Joe?" "I don't know, Will [he seldom called me anything but "Brother"]. I'm scared." "Of what?" "I don't know. I guess I'm afraid I'll have to go back to the hospital." He said it almost as if he wanted to go back. I asked if he wanted to go home with me and he said he did. We went by his house and he rushed through every room, grabbing little items to take with him, refusing to fix his eyes on anything in particular. He wrote a short note and put it on what was once Carlyne's pillow. I knew that it was too personal to read so I left the room.

He called Dr. Anderson, his boss and colleague, who invited us over. Dr. Anderson took his hand and gave him a half-bear hug. Having twice been in Lexington, Kentucky for drug addiction, he spoke to Joe with a tone of authority and sympathy, advising him to "stick with your brother and let him help you." We soon left and Joe exaggerated the visit and interpreted every word and gesture as evidence of confidence and good will. "Did you see the Masonic hug he gave me? Did you hear him give me the password?" It wasn't a Masonic hug and I had heard no password. It was the first time I realized that Joe was broken. Though I had wanted him to hit bottom I realized that I had only thought I wanted it. I wanted my brother back. I wanted things to be what they used to be. We drove the three hundred miles back to Nashville with few words.

Brenda treated him like the infant he had become. She cooked his meals, washed his clothes, and took over all his business affairs. She found unbelievable bills and threatening letters from creditors. For an eight-hundred-dollar ring he had given Carlyne weeks before she left, a sixteen-hundred-dollar bedroom suite not three months old, all kinds of credit cards with enormous billings, utility bills, house notes, insurance, everything. Nothing had been minded since the family went away. And Joe made it clear that he had no interest in any of it. By accident Brenda discovered that he had a disability insurance policy which would pay him almost his entire salary. She made him sign the claim and with his salary from the pharmacy which was continuing and the insurance she began to pacify the wolves. But not for long.

Twice each week I would drive Joe from Nashville to Jackson— almost an entire day each way. He would suffer through the interview with the doctor and come away more disgusted than ever. "All he knows how to do is inquire about my sexual prowess." And then he came as close to humor as he had come in weeks as he asked me how long did I think it would take Sigmund Freud to die.

At home he stayed on the couch except when he would come to the table, drop his head almost to the plate, eat what was placed before him and go back to the couch. Brenda kept his medicine and when it was time for it he would find her, stretch out his hand and accept what she placed in it. He seemed to be flaunting the babyhood we (I) had imposed upon him.

Now it was I who kept the front. Earlier he had made the jokes about the situation. Now it was I. I sang a song called "Hello Walls" about a guy deserted by his woman. But he never laughed.

After several weeks we both knew that the trips to Jackson were bordering on the ridiculous. He was not taking them seriously and I am sure the doctor wasn't. Joe had been right the first visit. The man was a quack.

I was still concerned about the suicidal possibility. On one occasion when Brenda had to rush a neighbor in heavy labor to the hospital she put Joe in the car and took him with her. I *had* to be gone at times and nerves were wearing thin. I began to broach the subject of his going to a nearby Veterans Hospital. He agreed to talk to the Veterans examining doctor in Nashville about it. After I had carefully and secretly discussed the case with the Veterans doctor, when we arrived, he asked Joe two questions: "Do you want to be admitted to the hospital?" and "Would you kill yourself?" The answer to both questions was "No." Next day we received a form letter from the VA saying that it would probably be six months before he could be admitted.

The home situation was much too critical for that. Joe never talked of work. And with good reason. The week before, his partners in the pharmacy in Meridian had called me and had said they had to replace him. When I reminded them that the business was a partnership they responded that a partnership could be dissolved at any time by one or more partners. And the two of them, the hospital administrator and the doctor who headed the hospital, had every intention of doing just that. I discussed it with Joe as best I could but he did not seem to care one way or the other. He did volunteer something which I knew to be the truth—that it was he who had built the business, his work and good will among the patients. Two men who had been friend and buddy to him for more than a decade knew a sinking ship when they saw it. And they were throwing the Jonah overboard. The settlement, a few thousand dollars, was agreed upon, half of which Joe promptly sent to Carlyne, the other half to Brenda to try to satisfy the creditors who by now were barraging us with letters and telephone calls.

Stripped of family, business and pride (by far the hardest to lose,

I think) there was little fight left. So when I told him two days later that a conversation I had had with Senator Estes Kefauver had resulted in an immediate admission to the Veterans Hospital he offered little resistance.

I had talked to a counselor of my own, a professor in a school of social work who was a friend, and he had tried to prepare me for the process to follow. He had explained that the first stage was one of complete dehumanization for the patient. But I was far from prepared.

We drove the thirty miles in his little Karmann Ghia, of which he had once been so proud. He cried more than half the way, begging me not to take him, telling me what the place was like and how he had rather be dead. "I have to do it, Brother. We've got to get well. There's a lot of living ahead." It was a weak argument.

Though he had sunk low he still groomed and dressed immaculately. They immediately whisked him away, telling me I could see him as soon as he was "processed." When he returned in more than an hour I knew just how ill prepared I was. Down the maze of cells and bars and locked corridors I saw him approaching. He came and stood before me as if to be a mocking display of what I had done, clothed in a denim shirt two sizes too small and denim trousers two sizes too large. The sight gave me more doubts than I could handle. I knew I had to get out.

That night the silence of the house, the shadow his well-polished and waxed little car made against the window, a little time to be relieved of the responsibility of the past few months, time which I used to reflect upon the implications of all the happenings overwhelmed me. As I cried Brenda said that I should go and bring him home.

But I knew I couldn't.

I had promised to visit every day. The first few visits were spent in listening to the horrors of being incarcerated in a mental institution. I asked him if he had told them about the pills. "Hell no. Do you think I want to have my license lifted?" I did not doubt the horror. It was obvious. And I also knew that he was not sick enough to be in a veterans mental hospital. But I thought it was a way to buy some time. And I was still playing God. Maybe the horror itself would be therapeutic. Maybe the thought of having to go through this again would restore him to the old brother I wanted so much for him to be.

As we walked around the grounds he did everything but threaten me. "Will, this place is half-filled with niggers." It had been a long time since I had heard him use the word. I protested a bit that I did not know he felt that way about people. He said that he didn't, that I knew how he had supported me in my work and thinking, but that it was different when one was locked up with them. Then he launched into a lengthy monologue, a bitter and abusive critique of what he saw my work consisting of, reflecting previously unexpressed frustration and long repressed hostilities.

"Haven't I supported you in everything you have ever done and said?" I replied that I had no reason to think otherwise.

"Think. You know damn well I have. I've taken a lot of static in Meridian about what my nigger-loving brother is up to. And this is the thanks I get. Locked up!"

I reminded him of the little book he had urged me to read. It seemed so long ago. He didn't remember. "You know. When you were in the hospital at Camp Shelby. You wrote me a long letter about all the suffering of black people. Good Lord, Joe. You got me into all this. That one little book. I had never given it any thought before." Still he didn't remember.

"You know the book. Howard Fast wrote it. *Freedom Road*. The book about Gideon Jackson, the slave, and how he and folks like him, poor white folks and black folks almost took over the country after the Civil War. Almost. Until they were slaughtered by other poor whites, manipulated and controlled by the clean hands and pure hearts of rich whites."

A spark of radiance came to his eyes, as quickly replaced with a scowl. "Yea. O, yea. I remember that. Hell, Will. That guy was a communist. Didn't you ever know that? Howard Fast was a *communist!*"

He began to chuckle in a fashion of ridicule. "You got seduced, Brother. You got converted by a goddam communist. Ain't that a bitch! Yea. I remember that now. But I had forgotten all about it. You remember the damnedest things."

I quickly turned to a repetition of what my interest and involvement in the Civil Rights Movement was—that it was all part and parcel of my Christian commitment, that I could be called a "redneck-lover" as well as "nigger-lover" because anyone who is not as concerned with the immortal soul of the dispossessor as he is with the suffering of the dispossessed is being something less than Christian. I added that I did not deny a certain allegiance to our native Southland, quoting what Faulkner had said in a letter to the Memphis *Commercial-Appeal* when I was at Ole Miss. "I hate to see the South destroyed twice in a hundred years over the same issue." I tried to make the point again, a point he had always so readily agreed with before, that it did not have to do so much with the blacks as it had to do with us.

He chose to respond to the part about Southern loyalty. "Maybe you're the one who needs help. You think you're going to save the goddam South with integration, with putting niggers in every schoolhouse and on every five-and-dime store lunch counter stool, and locking them up in the same nut hatch with white folks. Well, shit! What you're saying is that you're going to use the niggers to save yourself. What's so Christian about that?"

My protest was less than enthusiastic. He knew that he had hit a nerve and moved in strongly. "Well, I thought I was going to save myself with *pills* too. With *speed*. And, man, it worked for a long time. They took me a long way down the road. God, how great I felt. Sailing around in the clouds. Nothing big enough to worry about. But look at me now. A self-admitted nut! Your niggers are like my pills. They prop you liberals up and make you feel good. All fresh and clean inside like a dose of Black Draught. But when you crash!"

His voice was attracting the attention of patients and attendants from far across the yard. But the old facade was gone. He didn't care who heard him and he didn't care what they thought. "When the liberals crash it's going to make my head look like Karl Menninger. Get me out of this damn place, Will. I don't belong in here and you know it. This is plain damn silly. This is a place for crazy people. And I'm not crazy. I just lost my family. My whole world tumbled in around me. Wouldn't you fall apart a little if that happened to you?" I mumbled some words about giving it a chance, unconvincing to us both.

"Will, if you don't get me out of here I'm going to call Mamma. She knows I'm not crazy. She'll get me out of this damn place." I found his words at once pathetic and amusing.

"Joe, Mamma couldn't get a Rhodes Scholar out of kindergarten. You know that. Now just *how* do you think . . . what would she say . . . whatever would go through her head if you called and asked her to get you out of here? Good Lord, Brother. You've *really* flipped!"

His face reddened and his voice rose again. "No, by god! I haven't flipped. And another thing, why are you always putting Mamma down? I don't appreciate it. She's our mother. I don't give a damn what she does. I don't care what she says. She's *my* mother and I love her. Damn right I spoil her. Why shouldn't I? I know you think she's neurotic. Well, so what? You think I'm crazy too but that doesn't make me crazy."

Suddenly he was calm again. His mood turned abruptly from anger to the old protective and patronizing vein. He placed his hand on my shoulder and stepped closer as he spoke. "Will, I love you. You know that. I'm sorry I yelled at you. I know you're just trying to help. And I know I need it. But I want to help you too. I wasn't kidding about your wanting to save the South. I don't care what William Faulkner says about the South. We're the *South*. If there is one. Me and you. You may be the sweet magnolias and mint juleps and I may be the deprivation and degradation. If that's what the South is, to hell with it." He grew solemn and turned to walk back toward the building containing what he called the "cell-block." "Well, I have to go to romper room." It was his term for group therapy. As we reached the door he began to speak again. "Turn it loose, Will. Let it go. It's over, Brother. It's too late. All that's left of the South is a notion. All the South is anymore is a bunch of folks with a different history—folks with grandmas and grandpas who used to live down the road or across the river. But they don't live there anymore, Will. Remember the time Grandpa Bunt told us all the niggers were dead? Well, all the grandmas and grandpas are dead too. And what the hell did the South, when it did exist, ever do for us? Except damn near starve us to death. Find yourself a nice, comfortable job. Go back to being a college chaplain or something. You're going down a dead end street." There was a long pause before the attendant opened the barred door. "Just like I've been doing."

He started to walk away but then thought of something else to say. Forcing a grin he said, "Anyway, Brother, you've got your hands full being brother to me. Don't try to be brother to the whole damn world."

Neither race relations nor the salvaging of the South were on my agenda that day. So I didn't reflect on his prophecy for a long time. I guess I didn't think about it again until the liberal crash he had mentioned did come. And it came when folks began to realize that Lewis and Foreman and Bevel and Nash and the other young black people sitting on those lunch counter stools weren't talking about a hamburger and a cup of coffee. Years before, when we were discussing whether I should accept the position with the National Council of Churches, he had said to me, "Will, this can't be a two-year commitment with you. It has to be a lifetime thing. If you decide to make your stand on the side of equal justice for Negroes there is one thing you had better reckon with. If there is anything, *anything* you don't want them to have that you've got you had best not mess with them." With the traditional white Southerner it was schoolrooms, front seats on buses, wives and daughters and lunch-counter stools. With the liberals, South and North, it was "quality education." It was not surprising that the "crash" to which Joe referred came on school buses. And a lot of us had to sadly acknowledge, though most have not acknowledged it yet, that there was ultimately nothing any more sacred about "quality education" for our children than there had been in the hue and cry of "racial purity" in the fulminations of the Delta planter for his children. Both were idols.

After about four days he got permission to leave the hospital grounds for a few hours in my custody. As we rode he begged to leave. I gave all the arguments I could but he was unconvinced. Suddenly his mood changed. He became cheerful and talked of other things. When we arrived back at the ward the uniformed orderly, a change from the one who had let us out, unlocked the door. Joe had asked to see the permission slip I was given when we left. With the slip in his hand and the other hand on my arm he announced to the orderly that he had brought me back, whereupon the orderly invited me to come on inside the second locked door. It occurred to me that there would be no problem since Joe was wearing the hospital denims. But then I remembered that he wasn't, that his street clothes had been returned to him for the outing. I was in no mood for a joke and apparently the orderly did not take it as a joke. "Now come on in, Mr. Campbell. It's almost time for supper." Joe added, "I hope I didn't keep him out too long. The note said 4:30." "No, you're right on time," replied the orderly. Obviously satisfied that he had made his point, the hospital personnel couldn't tell one of us from the other, Joe entered the room laughing. "I'll see you tomorrow, Brother."

Brother was at it again. And in two weeks from the day he was admitted, the time everyone has to stay for diagnostic purposes, he called to tell me he had been discharged.

He was kind and solicitous. He explained that he wasn't mad at me, that he understood why I put him there but that he tried to explain that he didn't belong there, that the social worker had told him that he shouldn't blame me, that I was concerned but inexperienced in judging such things and probably had confused his worry and fretting over the loss of his family with genuine depression. He had been exonerated at every point. She had told him, he said, that he had only behaved as a *man* in the marital difficulties, and that most *men* would have exploded in a violent outburst long before he had, that he had a kind and gentle face and honest eyes which would tell anyone he could do them no harm.

For weeks he had said that he could not drive his car, not even around the block. Now he was making plans to drive home early next morning. He again expressed his appreciation for all we had done and was thankful that it was over.

I was baffled, confused and not just a little bit mad. I knew that the entire ordeal had been a waste of time for us both. I also felt terribly betrayed by the system. There was no question in my mind but what the position of the hospital administration had been: "Well, by god, he can use the political influence of a United States Senator to get him in here but that doesn't mean we have to keep him." That, coupled with the thorough con job Joe was capable of doing had been enough.

Still I took hope. Maybe the experience had meant something. Maybe if Carlyne comes back things will be different. And Joe left with that in mind. He had told us when he left that he was going to Birmingham.

Next day he called from Meridian to report a most successful evening with his family. Everyone had been cordial. Carlyne, recovering from long overdue surgery, was like a teen-ager on a date. He knew that they would soon be home. And I believed they would.

But something did not go right. His visits from Meridian to Birmingham became more frequent. Mr. Bowen had told him that he would have to win their confidence, that he would have to court her again just like he did before they were married. And he followed the manual. Flowers, candy, all the trimmings. Things seemed to be on schedule. Then he reported a visit which didn't sound encouraging. There was a dramatic and buskined scene in the front yard as he was telling them all good-bye after an overnight visit. As he was starting to get in his car, he said, Carlyne began to cry in a fashion approaching hysterics. She rushed to him and embraced and kissed him. The children followed suit until the four of them stood clutching each other in an uncontrollable outpouring of emotion, no one knowing exactly what was taking place.

Joe saw it as a sign that the time was near at hand. They would return, he said, as they had gone, unannounced and with no fanfare. He would come home from work some evening and there would be the Volkswagen bus under the carport as if it had never been gone.

Brenda and I saw it differently. We saw it as a sign that the act was now final, that the decision to leave had been reinforced by something Joe was doing or saying and that now it was over.

And that proved to be the case. Shortly afterwards Joe did return from work to find that Carlyne had been there. But it was to take the remainder of her personal effects and clothes, dolls, toys and pictures from the walls.

I believe she had intended to return. But I believe she concluded that what he was parading as healing had been nothing but a farce. I never asked. But I believe he said such things as, "I have a letter from the United States government saying I'm sane. Can you prove you are?" And perhaps, even then, a badgering to bring her to an admission that she was wrong in deserting him at his hour of greatest need, a statement he was to make many times in the future. I believe she saw that it would do no good to return, that it would be the same side of the same record played all over again.

And I sadly admitted at the time that she was right. And if not *right*, then correct, in her assessment.

So I simply gave up.

But not quite.

We saw little of Joe for a year. Occasionally we talked and even less often I would stop by. He got a job in another pharmacy and apparently did good work. The reports were that he walked inside his large house at six o'clock in the evening and was not heard from again until eight the next morning when he walked out the same door and went to work. On Sunday mornings he entered the Presbyterian Church, walked to the same seat looking at nothing or no one, and never raised his head during the service. When it was over he walked out with his head bowed, got in his car and left, speaking to no one. And that was the pattern for the year. I think he left the pills in the cabinet, drank little or none at all, and bothered nobody. It was a drab existence. But it was a relief of sorts for those of us who had tried to stick by him during the previous few years of sheer pathos.

And then came a whirlwind. "Hello, Brother! This is Brother! I've got somebody I want you to meet." It was New Year's Eve. "You know, you've been telling me to come out of my shell. Okay. Here's the woman who's going to bring me out. Jo, this is Will. Will . . . Josephine."

I spoke haltingly. It was, after all, New Year's Eve in Tennessee also.

"Hello, Josephine." "Hey, Brother. Joe has told me so very much about all of you. I'm just dying to meet you." She volunteered that she and some of her friends had been watching that beautiful hunk of man walk down the Presbyterian aisle every Sunday morning, that she on several occasions had deliberately stood in the way as he left, but that he had always casually walked around her, and that on a dare they had tricked him into coming to a party. Now she had taken it as her project to bring him out of his shell. I wished her well, saying something to the effect that it was a worthy project, and one in which I had more than passing interest. And that was about it.

Two weeks later they called to say they were coming to see us. We prepared a banquet meal of various Chinese dishes which in turn were ignored and untouched by either of them. But it was a joyous occasion watching two middle-aged human beings, each with more than their share of hurting, holding hands and touching and rubbing each other like two love sick teen-agers.

Each got me aside to tell the story.

"Will, I've had two long lonely years. I don't mean lonesome. I mean lonely. Do you know the difference between lonesome and lonely?" I indicated that I had never given it much thought.

"No, you've never had to. Being lonesome is when somebody isn't there and you know they'll be back after a while. Being lonely is when you don't have anybody to be lonesome for. I was lonesome for a long time after they left. But that was when I thought they were coming back. I'm not blaming them, I'm not saying it wasn't my fault. Most of it was. But they're not ever coming back. Not in a million years. And god, Brother, you don't know what hell is and I hope you never do."

He told me that he had been so lonely that he used to call the electronic time-of-day service just to hear the bank commercial. Or call the weather bureau or dial information and ask for his own telephone number. Once, he said, he had thrown away the bug poison because the roaches, scampering for a hiding place when he got up during the night or in the morning to prepare for work, were better than an empty house.

"Now do you understand why I want to get married?" He spoke as if it were something he had to justify to me. Joe wished me to understand that this woman was not trash but rather a highly cultured and intelligent person with extremely high standing in the community. And I had to give my judgment and estimate of her right on the spot. When I pleaded for time he became impatient. It shouldn't take time to recognize class when you see it. She was, he said, a synopsis of compassion and tenderness. Her former husband had been confined to the state mental hospital for many years, a hopeless and often violent schizophrenic. Singlehandedly she had reared five children. One was a successful engineer in California, one was in medical school, and one was married to a college professor. The other two were still with her at home. There was no doubt that she was an exceptional person. So I said that I was impressed with her and wished them the best. Josephine in turn, wanted it understood that she knew what she was doing, that she was convinced Joe had got his stuff together and that they had every intention of getting married. Furthermore, she had discussed with her pastor the propriety of going out with a man not yet divorced and that he had given his blessing.

After dragging his feet on any divorce proceedings for almost two years, now he could not understand why it could not be settled overnight. He was ready to get married and therefore was ready for the divorce. I put him in touch with the only lawyer I knew in Birmingham, Charles Morgan.

In the fall of 1960 I received a call from the wife of a close friend telling me that her husband was in jail in Bessemer and that I should come down if I could.

Bob Hughes was a saintly young Methodist preacher who had attended Candler School of Theology and had taken them seriously when they talked of racial justice and human equality, yet getting some strange answers when he kept asking in ethics classes why there were no Negroes attending the school. He wanted to be a missionary to Rhodesia but the Methodist Board had insisted that he have some experience in the U.S. before they would appoint him. And it proved to be valuable training for what was to come, for when he finally did get his appointment more than six years later, he was soon to be declared a prohibited immigrant by the Rhodesian government when they discovered that Bob had the strange notion that the Gospel had something to say about racial justice, whether in Africa or America. From there he went to Zambia but, with no hope of returning to his beloved Rhodesia in the near future, he came back to America and works in Seattle for the Department of Justice of the United States government, still under appointment from his African bishop and still hoping one day to return.

During those years when he could not be a missionary to Rhodesia he served in a kindred role as Director of the Alabama Council on Human Relations, a moderate organization of whites and blacks working for school desegregation, voting rights for blacks, and equal rights for everybody. This had not put him in good stead with the pharaohs of Alabama and he was brought before a grand jury and asked for his membership rolls. When he refused to hand them over he was charged with contempt of the grand jury and placed in the Jefferson County jail until such time as he wished to comply with their request.

I got to Birmingham in the late afternoon and checked into the Tutweiler Hotel. In about ten minutes the phone rang.

"Will?"

"Yea."

"Steve."

I didn't recognize the voice. "Who?"

"Steve. Steve Foley."

I didn't know a Steve Foley but I did know a Father Albert S. Foley, a tough Jesuit who taught sociology at Spring Hill College in Mobile and was President of the Alabama Council on Human Relations.

He came up, wearing a turtle neck sweater and about the most gaudy checkered pants I had ever seen. He explained that he had decided to go incognito in view of recent developments. Incognito I knew about. But as he stood there, talking in a near whisper, he seemed a classical study in overkill. A twenty-year-old law student might throw someone off the track with that. But a fifty-year-old Jesuit with an Irish brogue? Hardly.

He explained what had happened to Bob Hughes and said that the Southern Regional Council had succeeded in getting a lawyer.

I knew that not one white lawyer in the state had taken anything even approaching a civil rights case and the black lawyers in Birmingham were both few and poorly trained.

But Father Foley, or Steve, as he insisted that I call him publicly, had made a major breakthrough and by doing so had launched a young Birmingham lawyer on his way to national fame. Steve (it is still awkward for me to call a Catholic priest by his first name) insisted that we go right down to meet the lawyer. Somehow I expected a man looking like Uriah Heep to greet us. Instead I saw this mountainous figure grinning at us from behind a desk, huge books piled high all around him.

"I got this damn thing licked, Father, uh, Steve. I'll have your boy out of there by this time Tuesday." He pumped my hand and laughed. "I'm Chuck Morgan. You another one of them nigger-loving preachers?"

"Tuesday?" Steve said he had hoped to get him out the next day. He was locked up in a cell with all kinds of white toughs and he was fearful of what might happen to him if they found out who he was.

"Hell, they already know who he is. The jailer told them. You know what Hughes is doing? He's preaching to them. Sounds like Paul and Silas in there. When I was over there this afternoon he had eight of them sitting around him, reading the Bible to them. Found out one of them can't read so he's teaching him to read. He's all right. Nothing going to happen to him." Chuck spoke like an automatic rifle.

"Look, Father. Steve. Today is Friday. Tomorrow is Saturday. The next day is Sunday and the next day is Labor Day. I'm filing for a mandamus writ but you can't file a petition without a judge and this circuit is shut down until Tuesday. I'll get him out on Tuesday."

It just wasn't proper for middle class white people to be in jail in those days. Steve told him about how upset Bob's wife was. His father, an aging physician in Gadsden was ill and they were trying to keep it secret from him. And the children were crying for their Daddy.

"Steve, I'm a lawyer. I don't crash jailhouses. If you do, go to it. I'll represent you for nothing. I tell you I'll get him out on Tuesday. Those bastards can't do this. Not even in Alabama. Now let's go eat."

We walked the two blocks back to the hotel where Steve wanted to retrieve some records he had left there lest his room be searched. His fear was not unfounded.

While Steve and I were trying to be as inconspicuous as possible, Chuck was trying to be seen by everyone, a not too difficult task as his two-hundred-and-fifty-pound frame claimed half the sidewalk. "Hello there. How's your Mamma? Hi. How you been? What'cha say, good buddy? How's your wife?" He greeted and waved at everyone we met, explaining as we passed, "Justice comes from bellhops and bartenders, not lawyers and judges. Try your case on the streets, not in a courtroom. There's too much chance of losing it in there. There's your jury, fellows. Twelve of your peers. But how they going to be peers if you don't give a damn how their Mamma is. It's called democracy. I'll do my *voir dire* out here. Let the losers do it in court."

He insisted upon taking us to "The Club," a place and a grouping so exclusive as not to have need of a name, built at the very top of Red Mountain, overlooking what was named "Magic City" in the 1880s and '90s as U. S. Steel squeezed, punctured and pillaged the hills and valleys, finding all three ingredients necessary for the making of steel—coal, iron ore and limestone—in one place. "The Club," sitting beside the world's second largest cast iron statue, Vulcan, god of the forge, presiding over it all from his Dixie Olympus, wondering perhaps at times if even a deity could not make mistakes.

Steve and I felt more than a little uneasy sitting there in the midst of all the splendor, eating strip sirloins and drinking good bourbon while Bob was far below us in the county jail. But not Chuck. "The jury is down there. But the judge is up here. We need them both. Not only that, they can't serve drinks after midnight down there."

Such was Chuck Morgan. He won his case and also proved that a white lawyer could take a civil rights case and still practice law in Alabama. And though he vehemently denied that his interest in the case was anything but the fee, something else was working on him.

Three years later, almost to the very day, four little black girls were murdered at their prayers when the Sixteenth Street Baptist Church was dynamited during the crowded Sunday morning hour. The next day, Chuck, scheduled to speak at a routine meeting of the Young Men's Business Club of Birmingham, stood up and made a stinging indictment, not of the Ku Klux Klan which was summarily accused of the bombing by all the "good" people of the city, but an indictment of himself, of every judge and jury and lawyer, of every white church and office holder and public figure, every junior league and civic club, every last body in the city of Birmingham. Because, he said, *we* did it.

He had proved that a white lawyer could take a civil rights case and still practice law in Birmingham in 1960. But with his speech he proved that you couldn't say these things out loud and continue to practice law there in 1963. And within three months he was gone.

Gone from the bellhops and bartenders and folks on the streets he loved first and cultivated as his jurors second. Gone from the people who had spawned him, reared him, told him about Jesus, taught him things about law and justice, and justice under law, and led him to believe that law and justice were somehow to be equated. Gone from "The Club." And gone too from his determination and ambition—questioned by few who knew him at the time—to one day be governor of his state.

Yet gone *to* as well as *from*. Gone to a modest salary with the American Civil Liberties Union. Gone to defend Captain Howard Brett Levy, a thirty-year-old dermatologist who refused to teach Green Berets the ways of war in Fort Jackson, South Carolina. And Muhammed Ali who refused to go to war at all. And gone to begin, as early as 1971, a campaign to impeach Richard Nixon. Considered by many at the time as nothing more than silly antics, adolescent heckling from the peanut gallery, he, more than any other one person, quarterbacked the swing in public opinion which did finally not only tolerate, but approve and demand the proceedings which led to the first resignation of an American president. And on August 9, 1974, Charles Morgan chuckled, cleaned off his desk and moved on to something else.

And then, gone again. Gone from his post with the American Civil Liberties Union. And for the same reason he left Birmingham, Alabama. In early 1976 at a cocktail party, hosted and attended by what he referred to as "Eastern Establishment Liberals," he overhead someone say, "I wouldn't vote for *anyone* with a Southern accent." Chuck, hurrying by with his Coca-Cola, stopped short.

"Excuse me. What did you say? I didn't understand you."

"I said I wouldn't vote for anyone with a Southern accent. Not Jimmy Carter. Not anyone."

Chuck, an ardent supporter of Fred Harris at the time, replied, "Thank you. That's what I thought you said. That makes you a bigot." And hurried off.

Later the man approached him again. "I beg your pardon, but I resent being called a bigot. My reputation in the area of civil liberties and civil rights and politics is rather well established."

"Never mind your reputation, ole buddy. Reputation is what folks *think* you are. I only listen to who *you* say you are. And if you wouldn't vote for *anyone* with a Southern accent you're a bigot. I got run out of a damn good town by folks who wouldn't vote for *anyone* with black skin. Pigmentation variations, vocal chord vibrations—not much difference in my book. If you don't agree you can kiss my ass. You're a bigot."

The word got around. About that and other occasions of Chuck speaking his mind. Chuck was asked by his boss in the agency to be more discreet in what he said—that people might think he was speaking for the agency. Soon Chuck was gone.

When some of his friends asked him if he tried to reach some compromise, at least discuss it, he replied, "Trying to reason with an institution is like pissing on a turtle."

But when Joe wanted a divorce we didn't know all that. We knew him as a brash young lawyer who would look you in the eye and say, "Okay, Joe, you want a divorce. Some folks are embarrassed to talk money. I'm not one of them. It'll cost you five hundred dollars."

Any delay, to Joe, was distasteful. But to have to wait on the proceedings of so annoying a procedure as a divorce court was intolerable. He would call Chuck every day. And me sometimes twice a day. "Will, I want to get married and I want to get married today, not two years from now. Now what the hell is holding him up?" On one occasion he called long after I had gone to sleep. The harangue lasted for more than ten minutes. Finally, I said, a bit impatiently, "Look, Joe. You're not exactly teen-agers, you know. She has five children and you have two. It's not as if you're virgins. Why doesn't she just move in if you're in that big of a hurry?"

He was morally outraged. "Look fellow. This woman ain't no tramp. I told you that before. She's got class and comes from one of the most respected families in town. Now go wash your mouth out. I'd have to take fifty baths if I did something like that before getting married. Now you tell Chuck Morgan to get on the stick."

Then he said something directly opposite from the position he had just stated. When I was explaining the slowness of court proceedings and the necessity of a legal, financial and property settlement, he said some words which were to drastically change my own views of marriage, the Church, and the State.

"You know what marriage is, Brother?" I said that I sort of thought I did since I had been married for almost twenty years. "No, I mean legal marriage? Do you know what legal marriage is?" Then he proceeded to tell me. "Marriage is when two people get together and give each other the right to sue one another if they ever want to."

My god! He's right. Like so many innocent seeds he dropped from time to time in a moment of passion that notion began to grow in my head. If there is a body, a community, which is truly *Church*, or even claims to be *Church*, why should it be the executor of

Caesar's documents? What is a marriage license but a legal contract? And what does *any* legal contract promise and offer except the right to sue one another at another time and place before another of Caesar's agents? Perhaps such contracts are socially necessary but what does that have to do with us? And even if we are not Church now but want to become Church, free from the demands and legality of Caesar, why not start by returning all of his documents and refusing ever to do it again? "No, Mr. Caesar, that is not our understanding of what marriage is all about. If you must protect yourself and your citizenry in this fashion you may continue to do so. But not with our help and blessing. Let the faithful come before the altar of the One we must serve rather than, and before, you. And acting on His, and only His, authority we will pronounce them man and woman, husband and wife."

I was never again to say, "By the authority vested in me by the State of Tennessee." If my authority as priest comes from the State, then I have no authority at all. From that time on I began all weddings by saying, "Render unto Caesar the things that are Caesar's. If you have a license we will sign it at this time." And then saying to the couple, "Now what we have just done is to endow you with a legal contract. It has nothing to do with Christian marriage. It is nothing more than a contract between you and this state which gives you the right to sue one another if you should ever desire to do so." And the document is tossed casually, and sometimes contemptuously aside. "Now the passage which begins, 'Render unto Caesar the things that are Caesar's' continues. 'And render unto God the things that are God's.' And the *wedding* begins at this point."

Maybe one day I will yet follow my conscience and refuse to sign that document at all, ask the couple to have a Justice of the Peace sign the Contract of Caesar. And on a number of occasions there have been no such documents. And by the authority vested in me by Almighty God I have pronounced them man and woman, husband and wife. And I defy Caesar to question that they are *married*. But those without the document are required to spend an extended period of time with me and with one another in making sure they are ready for such radical trust and commitment. For they do not have the protection that the legal contract would afford them. They cannot sue one another. They have only themselves, the *community* if there be one, and the source of the authority which so joins them. Those who have come with no license have not come flaunting liberation but bearing witness to servanthood. They are not products of a new morality but an anachronism of an old morality, a testimony to "Jesus Christ is Lord. Hallelujah!"

The wedding had to be proper. Parents, local relatives and friends and kin from distant places must be invited and present. A honeymoon had to be planned to a secret destination. The car must be hidden to prevent any chance of prank. It was almost enough to make one play a prank to keep him from being disappointed.

His house was, to me, the same cold, depressing scene. Daddy and Mamma were pictures of sadness and loneliness sitting in the big living room where once their grandchildren had romped and played. Joe kept repeating to Mamma, "I'll be acoming back, Ma" just as he had done at the time of his first marriage. But despite the air of sadness it was a promise of hope for two lonely people.

But in less than six months I received a call from the Presbyterian pastor, a man of unusual skills and insights. He wanted me to come by Meridian whenever I could. He tried not to put it in a setting of panic but I knew what it meant. Josephine also tried to do the same.

I knew we were in for a replay. The pattern was the same—impatience, bitterness, drugs and violence. With the pills Joe could go for days with only a few hours' sleep. The stories were the same as before. Wake up at two in the morning, badger her into a quarrel over the slightest trivia, gain an admission of a casual caress during a dozen years of widowhood, reduce her to a whimpering heap. But when it was over, beatings and all, he could not understand why his simple "I'm sorry" did not result in his wife's cuddling on his arm to get another hour or so of sleep. And if it did not, then the scene had to be repeated.

Josephine was not a fighter. She had suffered enough in her first marriage to a violent paranoid schizophrenic. When it became totally unbearable she had no recourse but to move out. But Joe's charm and persuasiveness seemed to have no limit. Soon there would be a reunion.

There was no end to the incidents leading to temporary separations. And during or following each one Joe thought it necessary that I be summoned.

I had at least learned that I had no magic powers. So my responses became less and less frequent.

And the jobs he could get and hold were less and less desirable. As a new start professionally and a new beginning for the marriage they had decided to move to Hattiesburg. In a matter of weeks the friction had overtaken them. Joe sent one of his mysterious telegrams. "Must have 450 dollars by 3:00 P.M. tomorrow." Signed: Brother. When the 3:00 o'clock deadline expired he was on the phone. "Didn't you get my wire?" "Yes, but I don't have 450 dollars." "Hell, you've got money. I'll pay you back. I've *got* to have it." When I insisted on knowing why he needed the money he said I would just have to trust him. But eventually he told me that he had employed a private detective, whom he wanted me to "check out" with my Nashville contacts, to spy on his wife because he knew she was having an affair with someone. His proof was that he had been over to the apartment where she was living and a window in the living room had been open. When he asked why the window was open she had said it was hot in her bedroom. To Joe that was sufficient evidence. "If you're hot in the bedroom you don't open the living room window." It was as simple as that. The window was open for someone to crawl through. The fact that the apartment window was forty feet above the ground made no difference. When I repeated that I did not have the money he said that he would get it from Daddy. And when I explained and complained in less than patient tones that it was cruel and heartless to ask Daddy, who certainly didn't have it, for money for such a nonsensical purpose, he scoffed. "Shit. He's got money. And so do you."

P. D. East was the illegitimate son of a prominent but promiscuous Mississippi daughter. Under the most mysterious circumstances he came to be cared for, and later adopted by an itinerant sawmill couple who brought him to manhood in the logging camps of southern Mississippi. Joe and I had met him when I was at Ole Miss and he was editor of a short-lived newspaper called *The Petal Paper*. There really was a little town named

Petal, Mississippi, located on the Leaf River and in Forest County. P. D. had worked for the Southern Railroad most of his adult life at several different jobs and one day took his visor off, left the ticket office where he sold tickets and never went back. He bought the little newspaper shortly before the Supreme Court decision of May 17, 1954 on public school education. In a combination Will Rogers-Mark Twain style he began satirizing the state legislature, making fun of the powerful White Citizen's Council, the governor, Senator James Eastland and anyone else he considered deserving of his wrath and wit. He proposed editorially that the state engage in a bit of zestful zoology and adopt the crawfish as the state symbol, replacing the magnolia. He said all magnolias look and smell alike but there are many kinds of crawfish, differing in shapes, colors and sizes. But all of them have one thing in common, the direction of movement—always backward, and generally into the mud from which they came. Advocating, through inferential satire, total and complete integration at every level of society and further advocating the legalization of liquor sales in the state he very early hit upon a journalistic suicide combination which led to the demise of his newspaper as a profit-making venture within a matter of months. He continued to publish his little tabloid but without a single local advertiser. And soon it had to be done in exile as he grew weary of the constant threats upon his life and the lives of his wife and child. With fundraising letters from people like Harry Golden and John Howard Griffin he managed to survive in Fairhope, Alabama, outside Mobile, and continued to send his paper to several thousand folks, not one of whom lived in the county where his paper had originated.

Through P. D., Joe and John Howard Griffin became good friends. Some years earlier John Howard had dosed himself with a combination of chemicals, rubbed his body with various dyes, turned his skin dark enough to travel around the South as a Negro. The resulting book became the widely circulated *Black Like Me*. But the book, despite its success, had not endeared him to Mississippi political figures and whenever he was in the state for business or social purposes he feared for his life. Joe would hide him and P. D. in the back of the pharmacy or in his home and when they left would follow them to the state line, generally in the late night or early morning hours.

When P. D. learned of Joe's problems he called me and said that he was himself "between wives" at the time and was going to ask Joe to come and stay with him. Joe took great pride in an enlarged photograph John Howard, a photographer as well as writer, had made of P. D. sitting in the prescription department of the pharmacy among all the drugs and medications where, as both a sick man and an accomplished hypochondriac, he was always happiest, spraying his monumental nostrils with a nasal mist or taking some empty capsules Joe would feed him. John Howard had entitled it "P. D. East in Paradise" and the picture hung on P. D 's wall. A copy of it had hung on Joe's pharmacy wall in Meridian.

Joe had no difficulty getting a job in Mobile at a pharmacy, but worked less than a week and was discharged. A few days later P. D. called and after much hesitation and apology said that Joe was driving him crazy. He said he knew that going crazy would be a short journey for him but he was deeply worried about whatever it was Joe was taking and how much. "Hell, Preacher Will, you know I love them pills and can't get along without them. But our brother is into something stout." I promised that I would do what I could.

I pulled into Fairhope about five o'clock the following afternoon and found Joe and P. D. lying in the yard, a beer can and two styrofoam cups on the ground between them. Joe, alert and talkative, embraced me and then turned to P. D. "You bastard, how did you know he was coming?" "Well, I missed it a little bit. I told you he would be here at six and it's only five." They teased a bit and then Joe said he would run inside and get something to cool me down.

P. D. began to explain as soon as he was out of sight. "I know you think I was lying, Brother (he addressed each of us as we did each other), but when I called you he hadn't spoken a sentence that made any sense in three days. He was either talking so fast you couldn't understand him or he was mumbling in such low tones that you couldn't hear him." I told him I understood. "Tell me, what the hell is he taking? How does he turn around so fast. Less than two hours ago he was lying in a stupor on the couch. I jokingly said you were coming to see us. He went to the bathroom and, I swear, in thirty minutes he was just as normal as you see him now."

Joe came to the door and called us in. "Brother, you know a Jonathan Daniel?" "Yea. Sure. I know Jon Daniel. Why?" "Well, he's dead." Joe had heard a news bulletin but had no details. It was not hard to believe for I had been with Jonathan at a conference a few weeks earlier and knew what he was about.

He was a student from the Episcopal Theological Seminary in Cambridge, Massachusetts who was involved in registering black citizens to vote in Lowndes County, Alabama. A few days earlier I had learned that Jon was in jail in that county along with a number of others. We waited to hear the national news which carried a detailed account.

Jonathan and Richard Morrisroe, a Roman Catholic priest from Chicago, had just been released from the Lowndes County jail in Hayneville. Because of some confusion in a telephone conversation there was no one there to meet them when they, and twenty-five others, had been released. Jonathan, Richard, and two black students stopped at a small grocery store on the edge of the little town. Despite the fact that the majority of the woman's trade was black people, she became alarmed at their presence and called a special deputy named Thomas Coleman who arrived on the scene before the four could finish their cold drinks and leave. Armed with his own shotgun he fired as the four were leaving the premises, killing Jonathan instantly with the first shot, turning immediately upon Father Morrisroe, the pellets from the second shot leaving him mortally wounded on the gravel outside the little one-room, unpainted shack which was the store. The two young black women fled in terror and were unharmed. Coleman went to the telephone and called Colonel Al Lingo, Commissioner of Public Safety in Alabama and told him, "I've just shot two preachers. You better get on down here."

That was the news. That was all we knew. My young friend Jonathan Daniel was dead and his friend lay mortally wounded, listed in critical condition. I sat in stunned silence. Joe snapped the television off and came over and kissed me on the head. "I'm sorry, Brother." P. D. said nothing.

I made some phone calls to get more details and to see if there was something we should be doing. Joe and P. D. sat in a silent room, mourning with me over the death of a friend, saying little, forgetting to turn the lights on when darkness came. When I re-entered the room they were speaking in whispers, like people do in a funeral parlor when there is a casket in the room. I could see them outlined against the street light which cast a beam through a crack in the venetian blind, reflecting itself in a huge mirror and returning across the room to bring form to these two big men sitting facing each other as if playing chess. P. D. spoke first. "Well, Brother, what you reckon your friend Mr. Jesus thinks of all this?" I allowed that I guessed he was pretty sad about it. He stood up and turned an overhead light on, went to the kitchen and came back with some beer and cheese. He spoke again as his hulking frame sank into a bigger chair. "Brother, what about that definition of Christianity you gave me that time? Let's see if it can pass the test."

Years before, when P. D. had his paper going, he liked to argue about religion. Most of it was satire, but I would often take it upon myself to set him straight on one theological point or another. He had long since deserted and disavowed the Methodist Church of his foster parents, had tried being a Unitarian and had taken instruction from the local rabbi and was considering declaring himself a Jew. He referred to the Church as "the Easter chicken." Each time I saw him he would ask, "And what's the state of the Easter chicken, Preacher Will?" I knew he was trying to goad me into some kind of an argument and decided to wait him out. One day he explained.

"You know, Preacher Will, that Church of yours and Mr. Jesus is like an Easter chicken my little Karen got one time. Man, it was a pretty thing. Dyed a deep purple. Bought it at the grocery store."

I interrupted that *white* was the liturgical color for Easter but he ignored me. "And it served a real useful purpose. Karen loved it. It made her happy. And that made me and her Mamma happy. Okay?"

I said, "Okay."

"But pretty soon that baby chicken started feathering out. You know, sprouting little pin feathers. Wings and tail and all that. And you know what? Them new feathers weren't purple. No sirree bob, that damn chicken wasn't really purple at all. That damn chicken was a Rhode Island Red. And when all them little red feathers started growing out from under that purple it was one hell of a sight. All of a sudden Karen couldn't stand that chicken any more."

"I think I see what you're driving at, P D."

"No, hell no, Preacher Will. You don't understand any such thing for I haven't got to my point yet."

"Okay. I'm sorry. Rave on."

"Well, we took that half-purple and half-red thing out to her Grandma's house and threw it in the chicken yard with all the other chickens. It was still different, you understand. That little chicken. And the other chickens knew it was different. And they resisted it like hell. Pecked it, chased it all over the yard. Wouldn't have anything to do with it. Wouldn't even let it get on the roost with them. And that little chicken knew it was different too. It didn't bother any of the others. Wouldn't fight back or anything. Just stayed by itself. Really suffered too. But little by little, day by day, that chicken came around. Pretty soon, even before all the purple grew off it, while it was still just a little bit different, that damn thing was behaving just about like the rest of them chickens. Man, it would fight back, peck the hell out of the ones littler than it was, knock them down to catch a bug if it got to it in time. Yes sirree bob, the chicken world turned that Easter chicken around. And now you can't tell one chicken from another. They're all just alike. The Easter chicken is just one more chicken. There ain't a damn thing different about it."

I knew he wanted to argue and I didn't want to disappoint him. "Well, P. D., the Easter chicken is still useful. It lays eggs, doesn't it?"

It was what he wanted me to say. "Yea, Preacher Will. It lays eggs. But they all lay eggs. Who needs an Easter chicken for that? And the Rotary Club serves coffee. And the 4-H Club says prayers. The Red Cross takes up offerings for hurricane victims. Mental Health does counseling, and the Boy Scouts have youth programs."

I told him I agreed and that it had been a long time since I would not have agreed but that that didn't have anything to do with the Christian Faith. He looked a little hurt and that was when he asked me to define the Christian Faith. But he had a way of pushing one for simple answers. "Just tell me what this Jesus cat is all about. I'm not too bright but maybe I can get the hang of it." The nearest I ever came to giving him a satisfactory answer was once when I blasted him for some childish "can God make a rock so big He couldn't pick it up" criticism of the Faith. He blasted right back. "Okay. If you would tell me what the hell the Christian Faith is all about maybe I wouldn't make an ass of myself when I'm talking about it. Keep it simple. In ten words or less, what's the Christian message?" We were going someplace, or coming back from some-place when he said, "Let me have it. Ten words." I said, "We're all bastards but God loves us anyway." He swung his car off on the shoulder and stopped, asking me to say it again. I repeated: "We're all bastards but God loves us anyway." He didn't comment on what he thought about the summary except to say, after he had counted the number of words on his fingers, "I gave you a ten word limit. If you want to try again you have two words left." I didn't try again but he often reminded me of what I had said that day.

Now, sitting in the presence of two of the most troubled men I have ever known, I was about to receive the most enlightening theological lesson I had ever had in my life. Not Louisiana College, Tulane, Wake Forest, or Yale University Divinity School. But sitting here in a heavily mortgaged house in Fairhope, Alabama.

P. D. East and Joseph Lee Campbell, as teachers. And I as pupil.

"Yea, Brother. Let's see if your definition of the Faith can stand the test." My calls had been to the Department of Justice, to the American Civil Liberties Union, and to a lawyer friend in Nashville. I had talked of the death of my friend as being a travesty of justice, as a complete breakdown of law and order, as a violation of Federal and State law. I had used words like redneck, backwoods, woolhat, cracker, Kluxer, ignoramus and many others. I had studied sociology, psychology, and social ethics and was speaking and thinking in those concepts. I had also studied New Testament theology.

P. D. stalked me like a tiger. "Come on, Brother. Let's talk about your definition." At one point Joe turned on him, "Lay off, P. D. Can't you see when somebody is upset?" But P. D. waved him off, loving me too much to leave me alone.

"Was Jonathan a bastard?"

I said I was sure that everyone is a sinner in one way or another but that he was one of the sweetest and most gentle guys I had ever known.

"But was he a bastard?" His tone was almost a scream. "Now that's your word. Not mine. You told me one time that everybody is a bastard. That's a pretty tough word. I know. Cause I *am* a bastard. A born bastard. A real bastard. My Mamma wasn't married to my Daddy. Now, by god, you tell me, right now, yes or no and not maybe, was Jonathan Daniel a bastard?"

I knew that if I said no he would leave me alone and if I said yes he wouldn't. And I knew my definition would be blown if I said no.

So I said, "Yes."

"All right. Is Thomas Coleman a bastard?"

That one was a lot easier. "Yes. Thomas Coleman is a bastard."

"Okay. Let me get this straight now. I don't want to misquote you. Jonathan Daniels *was* a bastard. Thomas Coleman *is* a bastard. Right?" Joe the Protector was on his feet.

"Goddammit, P. D. that's a sacrilege. Knock it off! Get off the kid's back."

P. D. ignored him, pulling his chair closer to mine, placing his huge, bony hand on my knee. "Which one of these two bastards do you think God loves the most?" His voice now was almost a whisper as he leaned forward, staring me directly in the eyes.

I made some feeble attempt to talk about God loving the sinner and not the sin, about judgment, justice, and brotherhood of all humanity. But P. D. shook his hands in a manner of cancellation. He didn't want to hear about that.

"You're trying to complicate it. Now you're the one always told me about how simple it was. Just answer the question." His direct examination would have done credit to Clarence Darrow.

He leaned his face closer to mine, patting first his own knee and then mine, holding the other hand aloft in oath-taking fashion.

"Which one of these two bastards does God love the most? Does he love that little dead bastard Jonathan the most? Or does He love that living bastard Thomas the most?"

Suddenly everything became clear. Everything. It was a revelation. The glow of the malt which we were well into by then seemed to illuminate and intensify it. I walked across the room and opened the blind, staring directly into the glare of the street light. And I began to whimper. But the crying was interspersed with laughter. It was a strange experience. I remember trying to sort out the sadness and the joy. Just what was I crying for and what was I laughing for. Then this too became clear.

I was laughing at myself, at twenty years of a ministry which had become, without my realizing it, a ministry of liberal sophistication. An attempted negation of Jesus, of human engineering, of riding the coattails of Caesar, of playing on his ballpark, by his rules and with his ball, of looking to government to make and verify and authenticate our morality, of worshiping at the shrine of enlightenment and academia, of making an idol of the Supreme Court, a theology of law and order and of denying not only the Faith I professed to hold but my history and my people—the Thomas Colemans. Loved. And if loved, forgiven. And if forgiven, reconciled. Yet sitting then in his own jail cell, the blood of two of his and my brothers on his hands. The thought gave me a shaking chill in a non-air-conditioned room in August. I had never considered myself a liberal. I didn't think in those terms. But that was the camp in which I had pitched my tent. Now I was not so sure.

Joe and P. D. came and stood beside me, Joe pulling me to him in sympathetic embrace, P. D. handing me his half-emptied beer. I closed the blind and sat down, taking a sip of the beer and passing it back to P. D. who in turn sipped and passed it on to Joe. And we passed it round and round until it was gone.

The lesson was over. Class dismissed. But I had one thing I must say to the teacher.

"P. D.?"

"Yea, Brother?"

"I've got to amend the definition."

"Okay, Brother. Go ahead. You know you always had them two words left."

"We're all bastards but you've got to be the biggest bastard of us all."

"How's that, Brother?"

"Because, damned if you ain't made a Christian out of me. And I'm not sure I can stand it."

P. D. thought that was just about the funniest thing he had ever heard.

Our three-man wake for Jonathan and mourning for Thomas (funny that these should be their names—Jonathan, lover of David; Thomas, dubious of resurrection) continued, and between trips to refrigerator and bathroom my learning continued as we talked of history, civil rights and Gospel.

At one point Joe asked what we thought the court would do with Thomas Coleman since he had already pleaded guilty, had admitted that he had killed Jonathan and mortally wounded Richard. We all agreed that he would be released, that the climate of fear was such in Alabama at the time that no white jury would convict a man for killing a Yankee agitator.

Now P. D. wanted to argue with the conversion he had led me to. I tried to point out the parallel between the Alabama Court and God. Joe was only listening, and P. D. wasn't buying.

"Look, you stupid idiot. We agree that they're *gonna* turn him loose. But that ain't the same as saying they *ought* to turn him loose. They ought to fry the son of a bitch. You know that! He *killed* a man. A good man."

I agreed that the notion that a man could go to a store where a group of unarmed human beings are drinking soda pop and eating moon pies, fire a shotgun blast at one of them, tearing his lungs and heart and bowels from his body, turn on another and send lead pellets ripping through his flesh and bones, and that God would set him free is almost more than I could stand. But unless that is precisely the case then there is no Gospel, there is no Good News. Unless that is the truth we have only bad news, we are back with law alone.

P. D. saw that as sheer lunacy. And said so with considerable embellishment. Then, turning to Joe, he sighed, "Brother Will wants to play church! Come on, gang. Let's play church!" He motioned Joe to a chair, pulling another up beside him, folding his hands to a position of prayer. "Brother Will is the preacher. Me and you is the congregation."

I decided to play church and began to preach. "Here's all I'm trying to say, Brothers. I'm trying to say what you brought me suddenly to see with two questions. When Thomas killed Jonathan he committed a crime against the State. When Thomas killed Jonathan he committed a crime against God. The strange, the near maddening thing about this case, is that both these offended parties have rendered the same verdict—not for the same reasons, not in the same way, but the verdict is the same—acquittal."

"Shit, Will, you're saying George Wallace is God Almighty. And George Wallace wouldn't even make a good Devil." Joe kicked his foot, missing, then kicking again. "You don't interrupt the preacher, fool. And you don't say 'shit' in church!"

"No. George Wallace frees him to go and kill again. The other liberates him to obedience to Christ. Acquittal by law is the act of Caesar. Render unto him what is his. The State, by its very nature and definition, can do anything it wills to do—Hitler must have proved at least that much. Acquittal by resurrection takes us back to our little definition of the Faith. And takes us into a freedom where it would never occur to us to kill somebody."

The teacher wasn't having the lesson now. "Brother, you're just as crazy as hell! There are a bunch of lunatics out there, absolute madmen! Killers! Hell, maybe you'll be next. Or even worse, maybe *I'll* be next. Mad men have to be restrained! I say, fry the son of a bitch."

"Okay. You say they have to be restrained. Let's talk about that. The truth is, law is not restraining them. If law is for the purpose of preventing crime every wail of a siren calls out its failure. Every civil rights demonstration attests to the courts' inability to provide racial justice. Every police chief who asks for a larger appropriation because of the rising crime rate is admitting his own failure. Every time a law has to be *enforced* it is a failure.

"Sure. The Thomas Colemans must be restrained. Exactly! Then where is the fruit? When *will* he be restrained? Certainly not by legislation and court decisions. Of those we have plenty. And in the legislative and court decisions he watches a truce being signed between his two traditional enemies, black leaders and the Federal government. And that, no doubt, is necessary. But meanwhile, the rejections continue, the killings go on, the hostilities mount and intensify to be set loose wholesale yet again on another day.

"If you want to argue, P. D., on what will work and what won't work then let's put it there. I'll go to the mat with you on that."

Joe sat tight on the chair P. D. had assigned him, clutching the rungs of the seat, staring straight at the designated preacher. P. D. did not move.

We were moving into territory familiar to both of them. Joe stood up and yawned. "I've seen this movie, Brothers. I know about law. I've been divorced." P. D. leaned backward in his chair, burped as discreetly as he could and whispered, "Brothers, we're getting a little bit tight."

Conversion is at once a joyous and painful experience. If it was not the beginning of my ministry it was certainly a turning point. And it was certainly the most significant theological training I had received since we sat at our father's fireside and listened to him read the Bible every night.

And it was a personal lesson as well. For being pushed by P. D. East, in the presence of Joe, to see Thomas Coleman, murderer of my friend, in the light of the Gospel turned me back to where I had once been, years before, a path from which I had strayed. It was the beginning of a process—the process of coming to terms with one's own history, whatever that history might be.

I, like many another Southern liberal, had tried to deny that history, to flee from it, to so insulate myself from it in learning and action and sophistication that it would appear never to have existed. I had become a doctrinaire social activist, without consciously choosing to be. And I would continue to be some kind of a social activist. But there was a decided difference. Because from that point on I came to understand the nature of tragedy. And one who understands the nature of tragedy can never take sides. And I had taken sides. Many of us who were interested in racial justice had taken sides and there were good reasons in history for doing what we did. We who left home, or were pushed from home when Mamma or Daddy couldn't understand, were just a little bit prideful of our alienation from them, and a little bit arrogant in our new-found liberation and assumed sophistication. We justified it in terms of the suffering, the injustices, the blatant hostilities and economic deprivations black people had had heaped upon them. There was drama and romance in the Civil Rights Movement and we who had no home at home sought that home in the black cause. Because we did not understand the nature of tragedy we learned the latest woolhat jokes, learned to cuss Mississippi and Alabama sheriffs, learned to say "redneck" with the same venomous tones we had heard others, or ourselves, say "nigger." We did not understand that those we so vulgarly called "redneck" were a part of the tragedy. They had been victimized one step beyond the black. They had had their head taken away by cunning, skillful and well-educated gentlemen and ladies of the gentry. And so we, my people and Joe's and P. D.'s, picked the wrong enemy. We were right in aligning ourselves with the black sufferer. But we were wrong in not directing some of our patience and energy and action to a group which also had a history. A history of slavery. The redneck's slavery, called indentured servanthood, was somewhat, but only somewhat unlike that of black slaves. He was told that if he would serve the master for five years, or seven years, he would then be free in a new and prosperous and promising land in a new world. But freedom to what, and in what? Freedom to flounder, to drift, to wander west in search of what had been promised but never delivered. Freedom to compete in the wilderness with wealthy landholders, with black labor, to fight a war to defend that system as well as his own peonage, to come back home and watch the aristocrat as he tried to meet the basic needs of those he had formerly owned and the handouts of the Freemen's Bureau to those declared free but still valuable as working property, while he had no assistance at all. No wonder that he had to find a Jonah. And no wonder, as he strived to match the cultural and economic status of the aristocrat he became a living denial of his own servanthood, teaching his grandchildren that his fathers landed at Plymouth Rock. And no wonder that such deception resulted in the paranoia, the hostilities, bigotries and prejudices which he had harbored over the years. It was all in the libretto and scenario.

I thought of those things as I thought of Thomas Coleman, and as I reviewed my ministry and considered my conversion.

My ministry had become one of law, not of grace. While I had tried to keep in mind all along that the central theme of the triumph of grace over law was clear in the New Testament, I had come to act as if I didn't believe it. I knew that while St. Paul stopped short of a rigid antinomian position, a complete disregard for law, he did make it clear that to abide *in* grace was more radical than to abide *by* law. And such law as he did emphasize was not law in the sense of entreaties of the State to make us behave, but an ethos, a condition of being, *In Christ*. I had not quite accepted that freedom before, marching instead under the banner and umbrella of social science and legislation, Caesar and politics, a litigious gospel which is no gospel at all.

I moved to sit facing P. D. as Joe had sat earlier. The beams of light shining between the slats of the Venetian blinds seemed somehow brighter than before.

"Where's Brother?"

It could have been either of us who asked. Then we heard the sounds, sounds meant to be whispers, through the plastered walls. Joe was confessing his misdeeds to Josephine and asking if he could come home. We knew they would soon be back together.

Five years after our theological evening, on New Year's Day, P. D. died of an acute liver ailment. His fourth bride, whom he had married as a nineteen-year-old Wellesley sophomore and whom he said he loved more than any woman he had ever known, called to tell me. "But as you know," she added, "P. D. was not much on religion and funerals and all that, so there will be no service."

But there was. On the final page of his autobiography, *The Magnolia Jungle*, he had suggested some words he hoped Easton King, Clarence Jordan, or I would see fit to say:

These are the remains of P. D. East. He had a heart and he had a hatchet. They were both the same size. One could hardly determine the difference between the two. He lived and died confused and frustrated. He did not know where he came from, nor did he know why. And for years he worried about it. Finally, one day he stopped worrying about it. He realized that where he came from and who he was mattered little. He realized that what he was and where he was going did matter. And that was all he knew. It was about all he cared to know. His beloved Magnolia Jungle needed a path. It needed a clearing so that all of us could look up and see the light of the sky—the face of God. Let it be said of P. D. East: with his heart and his hatchet he hacked like hell!

Easton was dead. So was Clarence Jordan. So John Howard Griffin and I, along with a mutual friend at Koinonia Farm, did the funeral on a telephone conference call. It was a fitting memorial for a man who took delight in being a pagan, befriended my brother when no one else would, and led me to the Lord.

And ten years after our theological evening, almost to the day, I chanced to be in Montgomery in the company of two women whose cousin had been the owner and operator of the store where Jonathan was killed. I asked them to drive me to Hayneville where Thomas, who had been acquitted by the Alabama court as we had anticipated, lived. I did not succeed in finding Thomas. But in front of the little store I picked up a small rock and dropped it in my pocket. I did not select it and did not examine it at the time, simply reaching down and picking it up from among the thousands of pebbles on the parking area. When I looked at it later it so closely resembled a miniature human skull that not one person who saw it failed to see what I saw in it. A portion of the lower face was missing, the indentation a faded red. (Some do not believe in signs and omens.) I sent the rock to Brother Patrick Hart, secretary to another Thomas, Thomas Merton, and asked him to toss it upon the ground near an outdoor chapel which had been erected as a memorial to Jonathan in the deep and remote woods of the Trappist Monastery at Gethsemani, Kentucky.

It seemed as fitting a farewell to Jonathan as the telephonic funeral rites were for P. D. And an appropriate commemoration of an evening in Fairhope, Alabama.

1963 was a Kennedy year in America. It was a hundred years after Lincoln. Race was the prevailing issue and was still seen as a distinctive Southern problem. Government agencies, private organizations and philanthropic foundations with names like Ford, Rockefeller, and Carnegie were pouring millions of dollars into the South for what had become known as Human Relations. And the churches decided to involve themselves in the social scene of the nation in a way they had not done since Prohibition. It was still token—one major denomination gave more than two hundred times as much that year to enrolling converts in foreign lands as for all social ills at home—but there were those who were at least trying.

In January of that year a conference was convened by leaders of the major religious faiths. In the planning stages it was called the Centennial Conference on Religion and Race. Centennial because it was to be held on the very day the Emancipation Proclamation had been signed one hundred years earlier. But the name got changed along the way. Some on the planning committee didn't want to be reminded of the national institution of slavery. Just the institution of segregation. So it was named the National Conference on Religion and Race.

It was intended to be a gathering of thousands of people who would make their voice heard so loudly that it would make any future conference unnecessary. Names like Dr. Abraham Heschel, later known for his leadership in opposing the Vietnam War, Sargent Shriver, then Director of the Peace Corps, but also brother-in-law to the President, and Dr. Martin Luther King, Jr. were prominent on the playbill. And because it was a Southern problem under discussion it seemed appropriate to have at least one white Southerner listed to speak. My name was chosen. The speech would lead to a turning point in my life and would evoke the last battle Joe would ever wage on my behalf.

The conference, held in Chicago, began harmoniously enough with Rabbi Heschel declaring in the keynote address that "at the first conference on religion and race, the main participants were Pharaoh and Moses, when Moses said to Pharaoh, 'Let my people go.' The exodus began, but is far from having been completed. In fact, it was easier for the children of Israel to cross the Red Sea than for a Negro to cross certain university campuses."

His words of humor and wisdom were enough to bring the enthusiastic delegates to their feet. Everyone knew where those university campuses were. A few minutes later the unity was disrupted when William Stringfellow, then a relatively unknown attorney and theologian from New York, and one of three people who had been asked to respond to the address, stood up and calmly stated, "The issue, the only *issue*, at this conference is baptism." The delegates came to their feet again. But not with applause. Boos, jeers and catcalls from outraged Christians filled the hall in apology to the offended Jews who sat in stunned silence. The remainder of the session concerned itself far more with Mr. Stringfellow's words than with the solution of the racial crisis. Nothing can be more hostile and boisterous than 657 liberals bent on solving someone else's problem when the harmony and unanimity of the occasion is threatened. We were not, after all, in agreement as to why we were there.

My own address did little to restore the unity, though the words which led to further discord were never actually spoken. Each speaker was required to send an advance copy of his speech. (There were no women among the major speakers at the Conference in 1963.) The offensive paragraph in the prepared text had been written in all innocence and good faith. I said that if we are to suppose that all people are equally good then we must suppose that they are equally bad. "If I live to be as old as my father I expect to see whites marched into the gas chambers, the little children clutching their toys to their breasts in Auschwitz fashion, at the hands of a black Eichmann."

I tried to make it clear that I was not speaking just to the American scene but to the world, a world in which two-thirds of the people, and all of the emerging nations, were non-white. I did not see them as words of prophecy but as obvious words—something all of us knew already. But two days before my address was scheduled to be presented, my superiors began to pressure me not to make the statement before the conference. Since Stringfellow had offended so many with his remark it was even more important that I not contribute to disharmony within the group. One public relations official wrote and offered me a line which he guaranteed would make me the hit of the conference. "The issue at this conference is not baptism. The issue at this conference is not circumcision. The issue at this conference is segregation in Alabama." It was a good line but it wasn't mine and I declined to substitute it for the offensive words I had planned to say.

"But this is what I think. This is what I believe."

"Fine. Believe it back in Tennessee but don't say it in Chicago."

I really didn't understand. They explained that in their judgment I was doing nothing more than agreeing with the Klan and the White Citizen's Councils. I was, they said, though they knew unwittingly, giving aid to the enemy.

The *enemy*. And who, and what, is the *enemy*?

The enemy is a lynch mob in Georgia.

Can it not also be on Wall Street? Could it be on a street in Springfield, Massachusetts, where there are families with fortunes two centuries old, fortunes made from the sale of rum and slaves?

(I had met the pastor of a big church on that very same street, at a Boston luncheon for religious activists, who complained at length that his most annoying problem was one of eight ushers who insisted upon walking down the aisle in the offertory procession wearing a gray flannel business suit instead of the traditional cutaway coat. Then, turning almost immediately to me, his hand on my knee in patronizing fashion, he asked, "Mr. Campbell, do you think the white clergy of the South will *ever* give any leadership to this race thing?" I had my own notion as to who the enemy was.)

For the first time in many years I felt like a defensive white Southerner. I remembered the conversation Joe and I had when I was considering moving from Mississippi to Tennessee to work in race relations. Was I, despite the truth and justice and fairness of racial equality, somehow betraying my people? Joe had said, after stating all his concerns, reservations and worries, "You have to do what you have to do." I had done it. And I was not sorry. My second thoughts were not that the evil system of racial discrimination of the South may not be so bad after all. Rather that the South had, after all, won the Civil War. For that war was fought, finally, over the theory of racial superiority. And that position had prevailed from one end of America to another—everywhere.

How could one be giving comfort to so baneful a cause with the simple statement that equal justice might also mean equal judgment? But I gave in, backed down. Didn't say the words out loud when I reached that part of the text, standing instead in a moment of silence while the press, with their advance copies in hand, read the omitted lines. *Time* magazine chose to give more coverage to the unspoken words than to any that were spoken.

But it was not the words I did not say that disturbed the folks back home but the words which the Jackson *Daily News*, the McComb *Enterprise-Journal* and other local newspapers reported that I did say.

LOCAL MAN ADVOCATES RACIAL MIXING.
AMITE COUNTY NATIVE CALLS FOR OPEN HOUSING.
These were among the headlines.

When I returned to Nashville from Chicago, Joe called from Hattiesburg where he and Josephine were back together. "Well, Brother, you've shit in the nest again. The natives are restless in Mississippi. Better cool it for a while." He said Mamma and Daddy were getting threatening phone calls and letters. He had received a few himself. Soon I began to get hand scrawled letters from aunts and cousins, begging me to return to the faith they knew I once had—a faith that knew that God was the original segregationist. Joe wanted me to send him a copy of the speech. He knew that the press had distorted it and he wanted to take it to Amite County so Daddy could read it. I was afraid that might make the situation worse. I had, as the press reported, called for total and complete integration and desegregation. But Joe insisted that I send him the speech.

"Hell, Brother. You know how the Hedeman Press does things. If Daddy reads the speech, he'll understand. Daddy isn't a bigot, you know. He's known the Civil War is over for a long time. Just send me the speech." I said that I would.

A week later Joe and Josephine drove up to see us. Joe was at his protective best. He wanted to talk about nothing else. Gentle, reassuring, solicitous, and patronizing.

"Daddy read the speech and didn't see anything wrong with it. He's on your side. He agrees with everything you believe. He just can't say it down there but he agrees with you. And you know I do. So don't worry."

But he admitted that it had created quite an uproar in Amite County.

"But, hell. It'll blow over. Just stay away from down there for awhile. It'll cool. Don't sweat it."

The afternoon and evening were spent in praising and reviewing the speech.

"That was a damn good lick, that part about the Negro woman who worked in the whorehouse. Let's go inside. I want you to read that part to Josephine."

Josephine, of course, had read the speech and neither she nor I cared to rehash it much farther. But Joe insisted. "Come on. Read us that part. I want to hear the way you read it up there." As I began to read he came over and stood behind me, showing me exactly where to begin.

Across the street from where I once had an office in an American city there was a house of prostitution—so they said.

When I read "so they said" Joe slapped his leg and laughed out loud, kissing me on the head and repeating over and over, "So they said. So they said. You're a mess, Brother. I swear you are. Ain't he something, Josephine? Tell him he's something." Josephine told me I was something.

"Go on. I want her to hear this." A bit embarrassed I continued.

A small grocery located in the building was managed by a Negro lady. The establishment proper was owned by whites. We used to go there for take-out sandwiches when we had interracial gatherings and had to eat in the office.

"See, Josephine, the restaurants are still segregated here. Or were then. Just like in Meridian. And Will had a Negro secretary. Didn't you, Brother? Damn right you did. You were the first white man in Nashville to have a Negro secretary, weren't you? Damned if you weren't. Go on."

On one such occasion when I went for the sandwiches, the manager of the grocery was not there and in her place was the white proprietress. When I inquired as to where Mrs. X was . . .

"See, Jo, he didn't want to use their real names in public. Might get their families in trouble or something. Right, Brother?"

Josephine was a little annoyed and told him to quit interrupting.

. . . the white lady began to weep and told me of the sudden death of Mrs. X the night before. And then in fits of tears she told me of her deep affection for Mrs. X. And it was apparent that her tears were not the patronizing tears of the Old South weeping for a passed-on Aunt Jemima or a departed black mammy. Here was genuine grief for a friend and peer. This was in the era of the kneel-ins in our city. And as I sought to console this proprietress of a house of prostitution, I could not help but feel the tragedy of a culture in which this woman would have been unwelcome in the respectable churches in the area, but was deeply mourned for in a bawdy house.

"Get this next part now. This is what I want you to hear." He was looking over my shoulder, reading at times along with me. Josephine didn't comment. Brenda grinned and looked the other way.

No wonder a prophet whom most white council members call Lord said to some of the "good" people of his day that those who sold their bodies for pay and those who cooperated with occupying forces for pay were closer to the Kingdom than they—"Truly I say to you, scalawags and whores enter the kingdom of God before you." Woe unto a generation when a human soul finds more acceptance and community in a whore house than in a church house!

Before Joe had finished with the laurels I began to feel that I had just given the Gettysburg Address. But he wasn't high, wasn't strung out. It was his way of convincing me that I wasn't in any trouble within the family. But the rest of us were wearying of it and tried to turn to other things. Joe wouldn't have it.

"I tell you what. Let's go down and talk to George Barrett. Isn't that his name? Yes, George Barrett. That's the lawyer friend that helped Will get me in the nuthouse that time, Jo. George Barrett. He'll sue the living hell out of the Hedeman Press. Those bastards. They libeled you and you know it. Barrett will tear them apart. Come on. I'm buying everybody's supper. We'll eat in Nashville after we see George."

When I talked him out of that idea he had another one. This time I agreed for it seemed a good way to get us off the monotony of the Chicago conference.

"Hey, Brother. Let's go over and see your old buddy you told me about. He sounds like someone I need to meet. I want to make some pictures of him."

Mr. Bill Jenkins, an elderly black man, owned a farm joining ours and because he lived alone, and because he was an interesting and entertaining man to talk to, I would go over quite often to check on his health. He was almost ninety years old and though his mind was clear the experiences he wanted to talk about were limited and we generally covered the same subjects on each visit. His house was but a few hundred yards through the fields, but we drove there in Joe's car in case he needed to go to the store or run some errands.

"Mr. Jenkins, you've lived around here all your life, haven't you?"

"Yes, suh. Been here all my life. Nearly ninety years."

"Were you born here?"

"Yes, suh. Well, not right here on this place. I bought this place after me and my brothers lost that big place down on the river."

"You lost it?"

"Yes, suh. Big river bottom place. Two thousand acres. It belonged to my daddy. And when he died me and my brother was going to buy out the other heirs and we borrowed some money. But the big 'pression come and we couldn't pay it back so they took it."

"How much did you borrow?"

"We borrowed five thousand dollars."

Joe was not missing a word. He was making as many pictures as the Polaroid camera would snap and develop.

"What would that place be worth now?"

"Ho, I don't know. Lot of money though. They tell me one of them little lots sells now for five, six thousand dollars. And one acre would make two or three of them lots. It'd be worth a lot of money now. 'Course, now, like I told you. We didn't lose the graveyard. We kept the graveyard. Got a deed to it and fenced it off. But they built houses on it anyway. Took a dozer and pushed all the tombstones off and built houses on it. They pushed down the colored graveyard. But they didn't push down the white folk's tombstones. It was right beside the colored graveyard, nothing but a rock fence between them. But they pushed down our graveyard."

Joe put his camera down and entered the conversation. "They

can't do that. It's against the law to build a house in a cemetery. Who did it?"

"You like to go down there and look at it?"

We drove the mile or so to the place he had told us about. Mr. Jenkins sat between us, pointing out every landmark as we passed. The old house where he was raised had been restored by white people, standing in splendor high on a bluff overlooking the Cumberland River and parts of what is now Old Hickory Lake. Hundreds of sub-division houses surrounded it, many of them on sites he remembered as smaller houses which had been constructed by his brothers and sisters as each came of age, married and began families of their own.

"Pull right in here."

He hobbled up the concrete walk, leaning on a sassafras sapling he always carried, and knocked on the door. A middle-aged white woman came out to meet us.

"You standing right on my mamma's grave."

The woman looked stunned and stepped back.

"Yes, ma'am. My mamma's buried right here." He moved forward and stood on the spot where the woman had been standing. "And my daddy right here beside her." He walked about the yard, pointing out where brothers, sisters, cousins and still-born children lay.

The woman spoke again. "They told us there had once been a cemetery here. But we have a clear title to the place."

Mr. Jenkins moved toward her again. Joe stood in silent but obvious outrage.

"Who gived you a title? They couldn't give you no title for they never had no title. We kept to the title when we lost the place." His voice was trembling with hurt and agitation and times gone by.

The woman said that the company they had bought the house from talked to an old colored man and they got all the papers straight.

"What old colored man? I'm the oldest colored man there is and ain't nobody talked to me. I'm the onliest one left. Ain't nobody talked to me. They couldn't give you no title."

He turned and walked back to the car. "Let's go. I don't want to be here no more."

Back at his house we made some coffee and talked some more.

"Mr. Jenkins, was your daddy born here? On that place where we were?"

"No, suh. My daddy rode in here from Atlanta, Georgia. Way over a hundred years ago. Rode in here on a big white horse. I heard him tell about it many a time. He had some little money or nother and he bought that place. Didn't cost much back then and he bought it. Raised every one of us right there. 'leven of us. Not counting two born dead. And we had some times. I'm telling you, on that place, we shore had some times."

Joe was making more pictures, the old man pausing long enough to look and smile approvingly of each one as it developed.

"What do you think of the young people today?"

"Ho. They ain't no count. Young people today ain't worth nothing a-tall."

"What do they do now that they didn't do back then. Back when you were a boy?"

"Nothing! They don't do nothing now. Walk the road. Ride around in some old car. Gamble. Drink whiskey and beer. Wine. Fight and gamble. Kill somebody. Always killing somebody now."

"Mr. Jenkins. You ever been in any trouble?"

"No, suh. Been here might' nigh ninety years and ain't never been in a minute's trouble." He paused for a long time, looking down at his right hand resting on his knee, turning it over and gazing at a long scar in the palm. He looked up and spoke again. " 'Ceptin the time I killed my wife."

Joe turned his head and I could hear him chuckle softly and say under his breath, "Spoiled his record."

"And I never would of done that but she turned bad, got mean. Commenced to drink, run around with mens. Guess you'd call it got mean. An' she tried to kill me or I never would have done that. Hit me with this double bit axe."

He threw his hand up, shielding his forehead again from the blow of the axe, the long scar forming a white ridge in his palm, glistening in the morning sunlight pouring through the window.

"I got away when she cut me. Went down to this other house and got my gun. My hand almost cut in two where she hit me. Judge told me if I'd of had my gun right there I wouldn'a got a day."

"How much did you get?"

"Six years. Uh. Ten to twenty. That's what the judge gived me but I spent six years. All of it down at Fort Pillow. They was good to me down there though. I just run loose. Raised chickens and raised a garden for the warden. Worked on his own place too. He had a big river bottom down there. Only time I ever left from around here."

When we left Joe didn't want to go directly home. We drove back to the property which had once belonged to Mr. Jenkins but was now a sub-division. He wanted to drive up and down every street, counting the houses, appraising the lots, estimating what the place would be worth today. And he vowed that he would get the old man's graveyard back.

"That ain't right, Will. I'm going to get it back for him if it costs me a fortune."

Of course, there would be the delay until the oil well came in. But that would not be long. We talked about Leon, and Corine, and John Walker, and a lot of other black people we had known as children. And then about Amos and Andy.

"I guess that was about the worst thing we ever did to Negroes," Joe said. "You know. There really wasn't much we *could* do to hurt them if we had wanted to. We were about as bad off as they were. But I guess making fun of them was worse, in a way. And that's what Amos and Andy was. Just making fun of them. Were we wrong in enjoying that, Brother?"

I said I guess it was all just part of the times.

"Of course, it *was* funny. Now you'll have to admit that." He laughed and pressed the horn. "Buzz me, Miss Blue," sounding like Andy talking to his secretary when he would holler through the door for her to call him on the intercom.

"But hell, all the characters were actually white. So we weren't really laughing at Negroes. But I guess we were laughing at hearing white folks act like they thought niggers acted. And I guess that was wrong." He was seizing every opportunity to assure me that he was in sympathy with the black cause. And with me. His little brother.

Several states of the South had seen a rapid resurgence of the Ku Klux Klan. That organization had intrigued and frightened me since the group of robed and hooded men had presented the pulpit Bible to the church and Uncle Jessie had walked out on them. I had been faintly aware of the paradoxical symbolism the day I had preached my first sermon, holding that huge book with my nervous hand, my fingers trembling on the large embossed letters, K.K.K., raised on the outside back cover.

Since 1956 when I began my work with the National Council of Churches, a large part of my time had been spent in combating the brush fires of violence for which the Klan was said to be responsible. Even prior to that, Joe and I were more than vaguely aware of their activities. I was still the chaplain at Ole Miss when Autherine Lucy had been admitted to the University of Alabama by Court order. There had been student demonstrations and there had been riots. Since Robert Shelton, Imperial Wizard of the United Klans of America, lived in Tuscaloosa it was assumed that his organization was involved. Meridian is not far from the Alabama line and Joe had followed the incident with great interest. During the upheaval he called one night and said that he had overheard a conversation in the drug store to the effect that several carloads of Ole Miss students were on their way to Tuscaloosa to join the demonstration which was then a full blown riot and completely out of control. He gave me the name of a particular fraternity which had been mentioned and I recognized it as the one to which two sons of the most prominent segregationist in Mississippi belonged. I walked across the campus to the fraternity house, had some coffee with some students and asked if I could use the telephone. There was a notebook by the phone where long distance calls were logged. Casually thumbing through it I saw that there had been several calls made to Tuscaloosa that day and one of the boys had made three calls to his home town. I assumed that what Joe had heard had been accurate when I discovered the next day that several students known to be involved in segregationist activities were not on campus. But neither of us ever knew for sure. Three days later Miss Lucy was suspended for "safety," and that university remained all-white until 1963. (Today every member of the starting basketball team is black, as is the president of the student body.)

It was assumed that the Klan was responsible for many of the acts of violence directed at the Freedom Riders in the spring of 1961. Beginning in Washington with New Orleans as their goal, a group organized by the Congress of Racial Equality had boarded a Greyhound bus with the stated purpose of riding as an integrated group. In Anniston, Alabama the bus was stoned and burned and in Birmingham the group was so harassed with violence and arrests that they gave up. But in Nashville a tough and determined little group headed by John Lewis and C. T. Vivian vowed that the ride would be completed. After days of negotiation between Federal and State officials and the bus company, the trip resumed. With air cover and a military convoy ahead and behind the trip was safe enough. But when the bus reached Montgomery it was the job of city police to protect them. As they left the bus there were no police in sight and for fifteen minutes the riders were beaten and terrorized by the waiting mob. Most of them were friends and acquaintances of mine. Few of them escaped injury. John Seigenthaler, than administrative assistant to Robert Kennedy, and now publisher of the Nashville *Tennessean*, was on the scene as the personal representative of the President. When he saw two young women being attacked he stepped between them and their attackers, announcing that he represented the President of the United States. And that was the last thing he remembered for a long time. A blow to the head left him unconsious where he lay in the sun for more than an hour before being taken to a hospital. Because the National Council of Churches was so unpopular in the South at the time, Seigenthaler had often kidded me about my role. "How does it feel to represent forty million Protestants?" When I walked into his hospital room the next morning, just as the priest who had come to give him communion was leaving, I said, "John, I'm here representing forty million Protestants." "Well, by god, come on in. I'm pretty sure one of your forty million Protestants hit me on the head yesterday. But I have never been so glad to see an old Baptist reprobate in my life. I hope representing forty million Protestants is safer than representing the President of two hundred and thirty million people."

The following year, 1962, James Meredith enrolled at the University of Mississippi, after being blocked physically in the school doorway by Governor Ross Barnett and Lieutenant Governor Paul B. Johnson, Jr. The resulting riot left two men dead and scores injured and the campus was occupied by army troops. When I visited Meredith six weeks later I had to pass through three military check points to reach him and found as his roommate Ramsey Clark.

William Moore, a white Baltimore postman was slain as he walked along a lonely road in northeastern Alabama carrying a sign urging "Equal Rights for All."

In Birmingham that same year, Dr. Martin Luther King, Jr. and several other ministers were arrested, fire hoses were turned on demonstrators with such force that their only defense was to lie flat on the streets, letting the velocity of the water roll them along like seashells at high tide. Police dogs were used on marchers, including school children. It was the year four little girls were murdered at their prayers when a bomb exploded in the Sixteenth Street Baptist Church. President Kennedy expressed Americans' "deep sense of outrage and grief," but the crime was never solved. There was little doubt in the minds of most people that the Klan was involved.

The following June three young civil rights workers, Michael Schwerner, Andrew Goodman and James Chaney, were killed while working in a voter registration drive in Mississippi. Six weeks later their bodies were unearthed from a recently constructed pond levee. All of those charged, including the sheriff of the county and his chief deputy, were said to be Klan members.

It was the same year Joe had wept on the telephone when he, knowing that I was on my way home to visit our parents, called to say that Daddy had asked him to relate to me that it would be best if I not come. It was not because he did not want to see me, not because he disapproved of anything I was doing, not because he did not love me. He had learned from a neighbor that a local racist group had said if I came home that summer I would leave in a box. Joe said it was the hardest thing our Daddy had ever had to do—ask one of his own sons not to come home—and that it was one of the few times he ever remembered seeing him cry.

It was of such things that Joe talked when I told him that I was going to North Carolina to visit with a Klan leader, said by the FBI to be potentially the most dangerous man in the state.

A young television journalist, Peter Young, then living in North Carolina, had read an article I had written concerning the death of Jonathan Daniel in which I had expressed compassion for his killer. Despite the fact that his own racial views were opposed to theirs, he had become so involved in covering Klan activities in the state, had so related to their condition and tragedy that he had suffered serious physical and emotional exhaustion. He wanted to introduce me to some of his Klan friends. Joe wasn't interested in their tragedy, insisting that we had enough of our own without taking on more.

"Will, these people are killers. You don't know what you're getting into. They know who you are. The whole thing is a trap and you're walking straight into it with your hand on the trigger. I really thought you had better sense."

He begged, pleaded, argued and cajoled.

"If you do it it means you don't love me. It means you don't love Mamma and Daddy. You don't love Brenda and the children. Now I'm asking you. Just don't do it. Getting mixed up with the Negroes was one thing. Getting mixed up with the damn Ku Klux Klan is sheer lunacy."

I reminded him of our long conversation in Fairhope.

"Well, hell. That was drunk talk. I didn't agree with all that crap anyway. P. D. is crazy, Brother. He's a nut. Don't be influenced by something he told you. He was just kidding anyway. You know how he is. He just likes to argue. And anyway, he sure as hell has no love for the Ku Klux Klan. You remember what he said about that guy . . . what's his name? Coleman, who killed your buddy Jonathan."

His words were in a fashion reminiscent of the time he had tried to keep me out of the Army.

He tried another tack. "Let's come at it this way then. You're not a nut. You're a respected and responsbile Christian clergyman. Right?"

I said I hoped that was the case.

"Okay. You know it's the case. So what you're going to do is simply give a bunch of hoodlums respectability. Is that what you want to do? Give respectability to the Ku Klux Klan?"

It was my time to score. "Sure. Why not? What better way to neutralize an organization than to give it respectability? Look what respectability did to the Christian Church."

"I don't know, Brother. Maybe you are a nut!"

But he knew my head was made up. That I was going to do it. He went and unlocked a gun cabinet and removed a small, single-shot twenty-two-caliber derringer.

"Here. Keep this in your pocket at all times. It only fires once. But one is all it takes."

"Come on, Joe. I don't want that thing. Nobody is going to bother me and if they did what chance would I have against the experts? Keep it."

But he wouldn't have it, insisting that if I wouldn't listen to reason I could at least be prepared for what he was certain would occur.

I had recently watched a documentary film which the Columbia Broadcasting System had done called "The Ku Klux Klan: An Invisible Empire." It showed such horrors as the murder of the three civil rights workers, the castration of Judge Aaron in Alabama, the death of the four Sunday School children in Birmingham. It took the viewer inside a Georgia Klan Klavern hall where an initiation ceremony was in progress. At one point the candidates were lined up in military formation and the command, "Left face," was shouted. One scared and pathetic figure turned right, bringing confusion to the formation and bringing cheers, jeers, catcalls and guffaws from the audience viewing the film.

I felt a sickening in my stomach. Those viewing the film were a conference convened by the U. S. National Student Association and consisted of representatives of the young New Left radicals of the sixties. They were alleged to be the mad militants. Students for a Democratic Society, the Port Huron group, black and white, men and women who had in recent months taken over campus after campus, burned down buildings, coined and used such words as "establishment" when referring to the social order and "pigs" when speaking of the police. Who were they beyond that? Most of them were from middle to upper class families. They were of Westchester, Ann Arbor and Cambridge. Fortunes awaited them as soon as their daddies deemed them to be sufficiently family facsimiles, which I knew would be soon for most of them. They were students in or recent graduates of rich and leading colleges and universities. They were mean and tough but somehow I sensed that there wasn't a radical in the bunch. For if they were radical how could they laugh at a poor ignorant farmer who didn't know his left hand from his right. If they had been radical they would have been weeping, asking what had produced him. And if they had been radical they would not have been sitting, soaking up a film produced for their edification and enjoyment by the Establishment of the establishment—C.B.S.

I was there to make a speech and lead a discussion following the film. As soon as it was over I stood before them and said, "My name is Will

Campbell. I'm a Baptist preacher. I'm a native of Mississippi. And I'm pro-Klansman because I'm pro-human being. Now, that's my speech. If anyone has any questions I will be glad to try to answer them."

Even before my last sentence a huge black man was on the floor, slapping his hands and screaming loudly, "Out! Out! All blacks out of the hall! Out of the hall! Out! Out! Everybody out of the hall!" He started for the door with more than half the audience following him. The half hour that followed was sheer pandemonium. Bedlam. All of the blacks except two or three departed. Many of the whites went with them, feeling, I suppose, that they would be thought non-radical if they remained. It was one of the few times I have ever been genuinely fearful of bodily harm. And it was the first time I had realized the power of words. I had intended to begin a dialogue, maybe even a heated dialogue, with my statement. But I had not intended to start a riot.

Of those who remained, a hundred or so, most were speaking at once. I could only filter and sift out an occasional thing that was said.

"Pro-human. You think they're human!"

"How can you say you're a preacher and think like that?"

"Fascist pig."

"Insulting to our intelligence."

"No. Don't tell him he's not a Christian. That's what Christians are!"

"Mississippi redneck!"

"I guess you would have helped Hitler. Guess you thought he was human."

As a matter of fact, I did think Hitler was human. Only a human could have been responsible for killing seven million other humans. That was what I wanted to talk about. What does it mean to be human and how do we humans get to be the sort of humans we are.

But it took time to get my little band of radicals settled down enough to point out to them that just four words uttered—"pro-Klansman Mississippi Baptist preacher," coupled with one visual image, white, had turned them into everything they thought the Ku Klux Klan to be—hostile, frustrated, angry, violent and irrational. And I was never able to explain to them that pro-Klans*man* is not the same as pro-Klan. That the former has to do with person, the other with an ideology. I tried to stand patiently, even in the face of fear and danger, because I had so recently learned that lesson myself.

Joe listened as I related to him the events of that evening and what it was that I was trying to say. The film had been skillfully done and it told them a lot. But there was a lot it did not tell them. It did not, for example, tell them the story of the man I was on my way to visit. It did not tell them that his father left him when he was six years old and his mother went to work in a textile sweat shop where for thirty-seven years, she would tell me later when I came in one day wearing a pair of bib overalls, her job was to sew the seam down the right leg of those overalls. The outside right leg, for thirty-seven years. Never the inside of the right leg, never the left leg. The boy was sent to reform school, ran away and joined the Army when he was fourteen, was jumping out of airplanes as a paratrooper when he was sixteen, was leading a platoon in the jungles when he was eighteen. For seventeen years he was taught the fine arts of torture, interrogation and guerrilla warfare.

Shortly before the conference of radicals was held, President Johnson had gone on national television and in a plea for the cessation of racial violence had pointed his finger at the viewing audience and said, "Get out of the Klan, and back into decent society while there is still time."

The closing five words certainly must have been heard by those in the Klan as a threat from an impending police state. And the President did not tell them just how they could get into the decent society of which he spoke, how they could break out of the cycle of milltown squalor, generations of poverty, a racist society presided over, not by a pitiful and powerless few people marching around a burning cross in a Carolina cow pasture, not by a Georgia farmer who didn't know his left hand from his right, but by those in the "decent society" to which the President referred, the mammas and daddies of the young radicals who would soon go home to run the mills, the factories, the courthouses and legislative halls, the universities and churches and prisons they were then threatening to burn to the ground.

The film had said that only the Ku Klux Klan had a record of violence as an organization. It neglected to mention the Ford Motor Company, the textile industry and their own system of violence, the American State Department, the war in Vietnam which was then raging out of all sense and control, the American churches with their vast holdings and investments and power, the University which teaches, fosters and carries out more violence in one semester than the Klan has committed in its history, for it is they who produce the owners, the managers, the governors and presidents, the rulers and the warriors.

The film could have added, but didn't, what my journalist friend had pointed out, that the same social forces which produced the Klan's violence also produced the violence of Watts, Rochester and Harlem, Cleveland, Chicago, Houston, Nashville, Atlanta and

Dayton, because they are all pieces of the same garment—social isolation, deprivation, economic conditions, rejections, working mothers, poor schools, bad diets, and all the rest.

Eventually Joe had heard enough. He said that he understood what I was saying. But he insisted that I keep the gun.

There was, of course, another reason for my wanting to develop a relationship with those who were alleged to be the heart and center of Southern racism. The romance of "black and white together, we shall overcome" was wearing thin and more and more blacks were telling us that if we wanted to do something in race relations maybe we should go and work with our own people. Stokely Carmichael had recently stood on the bed of a farm truck in Mississippi and used the term "Black Power," and the separatist movement was gaining momentum in many quarters. By then I was suspicious of all "movements" but what they were saying did make sense to me. If that is where the problem lies, if one is interested in a solution, that is certainly where he should be investing his energies.

With all these things running through my head I made the trip to what was being referred to by Peter Young as "Klan Country." And I would again be learner more than I was teacher.

As my acquaintances and friendships with various individuals actively involved in the Klan widened, Joe would insist upon an almost weekly report. "You had any crosses burned on your lawn, Brother?" "Nope. No crosses." "Well, you must be lying to them. They must not know what you believe."

But I didn't lie to them. And they didn't lie to me. Neither of us had any reason to distrust the other. I never asked any of them to get out of the Klan and I never asked any of them to get out of any of the respectable and fashionable organizations or institutions of which they were a part and party, all of which, I was learning, were more truly racist than their Klan.

On one occasion I was spending several days with a man who headed up what my journalist friend called the Maoist wing of the Ku Klux Klan—Maoist because he had split with the larger United Klans of America because it was revisionist and too moderate. His wife had had a serious operation and because I had been in the Army Medics I knew how to do such things as change a simple surgical dressing or empty a bedpan. The man was a fairly large tobacco farmer and one of the jobs he had asked me to do was to drive the workers to the huge barn where they were "sheeting" tobacco. He had shown me the houses the workers lived in the evening before. Also the evening before he had exploded during the television news when it was reported that there were demonstrations in one of the North Carolina cities for open occupancy housing. I noted with more than passing interest the color of each worker as they got in my car that morning. The first one was an elderly black man. Not more than a hundred yards down the road a young white woman joined us. The next one was a middle-aged white woman. The last was a young black man who looked to be not more than twenty years old. When we reached the tobacco barn it soon became obvious that the elderly black man was in charge of the labor. He decided when the tobacco was in case, when there was enough in each sheet, when it was time to move on to the next barn. That night when my friend returned from town where he had attended the sale of some of his crop we talked about various and sundry things. At one point I asked him if he paid all the workers the same amount.

"Well, yes. I say, yes but I pay that old man a little more, because, well, he's been here a long time, knows more than the others what to do and all, you know." He couldn't bring himself to refer to him as the foreman but I knew. And he knew.

"We have to pay them minimum wage, you know."

"Well, okay. The truth is you operate a Fair Employment Opportunity agency here. And I noticed that you have open occupancy housing. The houses aren't very big but they all look pretty much the same to me. The truth is you have more integration right here on this farm than those demonstrators you wanted to get your thirty-caliber, air-cooled machine gun and mow down."

He took more than a modest exception to the term integration so I did not press him.

We talked of other things some more. I had come to feel comfortable in his presence and secure in our friendship. So I got around to asking him a question I had wanted to ask for a long time. He spoke often of the Klan and its activities.

"How about telling me what the Ku Klux Klan stands for?"

It was as if he had been waiting for me to ask.

"The Ku Klux Klan stands for peace, for harmony, and for freedom."

I suppose I was not as ready for his answer as he was in giving it.

I was an educated man and he had not even finished high school. But he was extremely bright and read a lot. I thought I would play a little Socratic game with him so I asked, "And what do you mean by peace, harmony and freedom?"

"I just mean peace, harmony and freedom. Those three words. If you don't know what they mean go look them up. There's a dictionary if you want one."

The dialogue was proceeding to my satisfaction. "In other words, *you* define the words. You don't ask others you may not like to define them."

"Of course I define the words. Who defines the words you use. When you use them they're your words and you know what they mean." He meant, I suppose, what I should have known already—that words are symbols and nothing more. Ever.

But I still felt we were moving where I wanted to go. "Okay. Your organization stands for peace, harmony and freedom. You define the words. Now one more question. What means are you willing to use to accomplish those glorious ends?"

"Oh. Now I see what you're getting at. The means we are willing to use are as follows: murder, torture, threats, blackmail, intimidation, burning, guerrilla warfare. Whatever it takes."

And then he stopped. And I stopped. I knew that I had set a little trap for him and had cleverly let him snap the trigger.

But then he started again. "Now, Preacher. Let me ask you a question. You tell me what we stand for in Vietnam."

Suddenly I knew a lot of things I had not known before. I knew that I had been caught in my own trap. Suddenly I knew that we are a nation of Klansmen. I knew that as a nation we stood for peace, harmony and freedom in that war, that we defined the words, and that the means we were employing to accomplish those ends were identical with the ones he had listed.

I remembered an Ivy League Divinity School dean who had invited me to talk about the racial happenings of the South. In our conversation before my scheduled address I had asked him about the recent demonstration at his university intended by the students to stop Dow Chemical from recruiting on their campus. He told me that he was very much in sympathy with what the students felt and believed, that he had stayed up all night in a negotiating session with them. "But," he added, "we can't tolerate that kind of tactics. You can't run a university in the midst of chaos."

They were the identical words I had heard from mayors, governors, and merchants in the South during the sit-ins. "We have nothing against integration but you can't operate a business in the midst of chaos." Each spoke the truth. And each revealed his idol. And ultimately one has to question and doubt if the Almighty holds the University to be any more sacred than F. W. Woolworth or the Mississippi plantation system.

Later in the evening my friend was showing me his new Klan robe. It looked very much like those seen in any academic procession or Sunday morning church parade. It was made of crimson satin and he was very proud of it—like everyone who wears a robe for any purpose is proud. He strolled and strutted about the room for my inspection.

"Whatda I look like, Preacher?"

I said, "You look like a Harvard professor." This he denied with considerable embellishment for he was almost violently anti-intellectual. He had once told me, "You show me a Ph.D. and I'll show you a communist. Show me a Master's degree and I'll show you a socialist. And show me a college graduate and I'll show you a damn liberal."

But I bet him fifty dollars that the next time there was an academic procession at any one of the nearby universities, preferably one with a divinity school, he could go and join it and not be challenged. He thought about that for a long time. Then he said some words which I would never forget. He said, "No, Preacher. You're wrong. They would know the difference."

"How? How would they know the difference?"

"Because," he said, "my robe has a cross on it." He pointed to a golden felt cross sewed just over his heart.

"They'd know the difference because their robe ain't got a cross on it."

I had discovered a strange kind of school. I was learning things I had only suspected before. Or had not known at all. Important things. Things from and about people some of my colleagues referred to as "the Enemy." Things from and about people who were our people—mine and Joe's. Whatever they stood for. Whatever they did. In a strange sequence of crosscurrents we were of them and they were of us. Blood of our blood. Our people. And God's people.

I shared the things I was learning with my brother in Meridian, Mississippi.

And he understood. As he would understand them now to be part of the chronicles of his day and time.

It began as another good visit. Joe was cheerful and alert, making jokes and bringing expensive presents for everyone as he always did. He even teased about his pills. "Take a good look, Sug. Don't I look like an addict? Gaunt and emaciated. Pallid and lethargic. Wanna see me on the nod?" He made a movement with his head like one falling asleep in a chair. I knew the teasing was for my benefit. He came around the table and kissed me on the head. "Come off it, Brother. Everything's fine."

They had been back in Meridian for over a year and we had not seen them often. Josephine, a woman of such strength of character, fierce loyalty to duty, and love for Joe, would go to any length to make the marriage work.

Late that night I realized that it was failing. Not long after we had gone to bed I heard a scream from the room where they were staying. Bounding and tripping through a hallway and two bedrooms which separated us I threw open the door and found Josephine on the floor beside the bed. At the moment I was opening the door I could see Joe jumping back into bed, pulling the covers up, feigning sleep.

Josephine was hysterical, embarrassed and hurting. Still she spoke with dignity and composure. "Will, you'll have to sleep in here tonight. I just can't take it anymore." "I'm sorry," I answered. "I'm really sorry."

She disappeared to go with Brenda and I crawled in beside Joe, hoping that not a word would be said until morning. Instead Joe bolted upright exclaiming, "What the hell was that all about?" My anger overwhelmed me. "You tell me, you sorry bastard!"

For the first time in our lives I was frightened of my own brother. At my words he jumped out of bed and reached for the light. "Now just a damned minute, fellow! What the hell is that supposed to mean?" His speech was loud but distorted.

"It's supposed to mean exactly what it sounded like. You tell me!" The anger embraced and enhanced the fear.

I lay in bed looking up at this towering hulk, wondering what my maneuver would be if he attacked me.

Instead he began to cry. "Will, you never talked to me like that before. You never called me a sorry bastard before. Will, the whole damn world has turned on me. Et tu Brute?" "Cut out the histrionic horseshit, Joe. I'm tired. I'm in my own house. And I want to go to sleep."

"You're in your own house." His speech was as if he would not say the next word at all. "That means I'm not welcome in your house, don't it, Brother?" His crying was a plea. "Brother. I could never . . . I never could . . . I couldn't ever turn you out of my house . . ." The faltering and slurring words were driving me to an emotion I had never felt before. "I couldn't turn you out of my own house . . . Brother . . . I mean . . . I couldn't say that to you . . . turn you out of my house . . . Uncle Sug . . . out of my own house . . . I couldn't do it, Brother . . . if you killed both my babies. If you bashed the heads of Joey and Julie on them rocks down there toward your . . . you . . . know. The . . . that . . . little house . . . where you work. I couldn't." And he couldn't!

Both fear and anger departed. For years I had tried to practice not feeling pity for people. Anything is better than feeling sorry for someone in the fashion of pity.

"You know, Joe. I really feel sorry for you. I really pity you."

"Do you, Brother? Do . . . you really . . . I mean . . . do you . . . sure 'nuff?"

I had meant it as an offense and he was receiving it as words of endearment.

"Yea, Joe, I really do feel nothing but pity for you."

"I'm glad . . . Brother. I knew you didn't . . . mean . . . that . . . what you . . . said."

I should have let it be. But the anger was welling up again. By then I knew the pattern, knew that the amphetamines had speeded him all day and that the seconals he had taken to bring him down were locked in mortal combat in his brain, and that what we were seeing was the resulting firepower as each roared at the other for control of his being—frustration and hostility as the winner sought to turn him around. Exaggerated freedom, seeking sequestration for the night. Yet knowing, I did not stop.

"Boy, you must be mighty proud. Six foot two and two hundred and ten pounds. Straddle a defenseless woman, choking the life out of her and beating her head on the floor."

The words partially shocked him into reality.

"Defenseless hell! You don't know that woman." With that I was afraid once more but this time fearful that it would be I who would attack. But I held on.

"Joe, what are you on?" I had, of course, asked that question many times before and it was useless to ask it again.

"Now don't start that shit again." His words were still rolled but came in more regular sequence. "I worked my ass off all morning and then drove every mile of the way up here. To be with you. To see you. I was tired and took one little sedative to help me go to sleep. Okay. I admit it. I asked her to move over a little bit so I could go to sleep and when she didn't I just . . . I swear it . . . I just pushed on her a little bit and she fell off the bed and started screaming like an idiot and woke everybody in the house up like she meant to. So what am I on? Nothing! But hard work and bullshit twenty-four hours a day."

"Joe. Shit! Now just shut up. You can't even talk and you lie there and tell me you're not on dope! Jesus Christ!"

I snapped the light off and we lay there in the darkness, neither one speaking now. I wished the mind had a switch like the electrical current and then wondered if perhaps Joe wished the same thing, wished and needed such a switch so badly that he had set out to devise one. I wondered how the off switch was working at that very moment—the grounding or short-circuiting effect of a mind coming down with such force and rapidity.

Now I hated myself for the anger, not wanting to go back to my earlier god-role, yet rationalizing that the therapy of kindness and patience, or at least trying, had not helped. Perhaps this would. I knew that I had expressed anger and hostility because I was angry and hostile, not in an effort to heal my brother. Perhaps, yes a definite maybe, this would help—to see the fits and spasms and convulsions of raw naked anger in someone he loved.

My thoughts stumbled backward to a time before his family had gone away—a time when Carlyne could no longer handle the situation and had called me. Our family was vacationing at a south Georgia resort, guest of two medical doctors, Robert and Kay Boatwright. They had invited their priest, also a friend of ours, to join us. The three families had agreed that no one would bring work, worries or problems on the trip. But the second day we were there Carlyne called.

Joe was in the hospital. She reported calmly that it was nothing serious, that Dr. Brown just wanted to have him where she could observe him in a clinical situation for a few days. Then the calm departed and she began to cry. She needed to see me. She needed to talk to me about Joe. Without hearing it I knew that she had been through another episode of violence. There was more fear expressed in her voice than worry over his physical condition. I said that I would come as soon as I could.

After we talked I returned to the Boatwright cabin, headquarters for refreshments at any time after seven o'clock in the morning, and reported what the call was about. Then I related to the priest and two medical doctors some of the history and developments over the past few years and the change I had seen come over my brother.

"Will, let me tell you something." It was Doctor Bob. "Forget it. There isn't one damn thing you can do for your brother. I've seen a thousand just like him. Your brother is a hopeless sociopath and he is never going to be any different. He's a sociopath, man. And not you, nor I, nor Kay, nor ten dozen shrinks are going to change him. So forget it. Have a drink and forget it 'cause there ain't a damn thing you can do."

For a while a strange kind of calm came over me, a restive, locker-room feeling one gets even when the game is lost. I took my guitar out of the case and began to strum and sing. I sang us right on into and past the dinner hour with Dr. Kay coming often with "something for the boys in the band." I was not conditioned for "on the rocks" refreshments, particularly when the rocks were just that—rocks, small porous stones dipped in vermouth and frozen, served then as the sole companion to the more robust stuff she added.

It was my turn to serve as common "Daddy" for all the children that evening, and they had decided to go and see the Florida State University Circus which spent the summer at the resort. As I watched the clowns, the gymnasts and acrobats, the caged and hostile animals my melancholy returned, rising to full-fledged fury as I found myself envying the gymnasts and empathizing with the trapped circus beasts. The liberating diagnosis the doctor had offered was suddenly even more enslaving than what I had felt earlier.

"Your brother is a sociopath. And there is nothing you can do for a sociopath. So don't worry." He had meant to be supportive and kind. But suddenly I didn't feel supported.

Oh! Well now. Thank you, Doctor. I thought there was something wrong. How stupid of me.

But how is this behavior different from the paroxysm of a diverticulated colon? Or the seizure of an epileptic, the bleeding of a hemophiliac, the coma of a diabetic, the calcium deposit in an arthritic joint? Pardon my tentative inquiry, Sir, but who taught us first that one's inability to control the cortex is sin, lack of means to ward off some physical malady a cause for sympathy? Shit, Doctor, you never even saw my brother.

I thought of those things as it began to rain and then remembered another place where we had lain side by side with rain and wind pounding the roof and windows. Joe had remembered it too. He turned on his side, just as he had done that night when Noon Wells had been killed.

"Hey, Dave. Are you scared?" (He had not called me "Dave" for many years.) It was an offer of reconciliation. It was my cue. But I didn't take it.

"Yea, Joe. I'm scared. I'm real scared."

When I awoke next morning, still drained, feeling like a dish rag, Joe was not beside me. I jumped out of bed and hurried to the den where Brenda and Josephine had slept, dreading and fearing the scene I expected to find. Joe, instead, was stretched on the bed between them. He had brought them coffee and was reading the comic strips to them, pulling the covers off first one and then the other with his toes like a playful kitten.

"Brother, I hate to tell you this but you might as well know. Me and Sug are going to run off to Mexico. Tell him, Sug. Ain't we?" "Well," Brenda said, "let's wait until winter. I hear it's mighty hot down there in the summer." "Okay, Sug. Whatever you say. We'll leave you the kids and the chickens though, Brother."

My god! The night had never happened at all. And for the remainder of the day no one mentioned that it had. Joe insisted on going to the market to get doughnuts so no one would have to cook. As we sat around the table he began to tell us about the oil wells that were then being drilled in the vicinity of our home place in Mississippi and predict the amount they would pump out each day from the well they were sure to drill on the forty acres he owned there, offering us jokingly "one more chance to buy in" before "she blows."

When our son Webb was christened and we had asked Joe to be his godfather, we had playfully agreed that one of the duties of a godfather was to deposit a dollar-a day toward his college fund. Joe suggested that with the oil well he intended to increase that to ten dollars a day so that instead of the estimated twelve thousand dollars for Webb to go to college there should be, counting interest, more than a hundred thousand which should be called "Webb's early retirement fund," meaning that Webb would not have to bother with college. We would all quit work, buy two Winnebagoes and travel about the country for a year or so, then build two big houses on a lake somewhere and fish all day. Though he was teasing about all the extravagance he was convinced that there would soon be an oil well on his property, solving his financial worries.

He wanted to make pictures with his late model Polaroid camera and we walked every foot of the farm we had bought and were living on, photographing every rock or tree of interest to him.

We paused on the edge of a field for him to reload his camera. Through the trees we heard a faint hammering sound. It was a light and delicate noise, not like a hammer against metal but more like an object being dropped upon the ground. We moved a little closer in the direction of the sound and suddenly Joe grabbed me by the hand and began to pull me in the opposite direction. I started to speak but he motioned for me to be quiet. We walked back to where he had left his camera.

"Did you see that?"

"No. I didn't see a thing. What was it?"

"It was Webb. He's having a funeral for Mary Ann and I guess you ought to go be with him."

Mary Ann was an old, black mare we had bought for Webb when he was five or six years old. She looked even older than the man said she was when we bought her, hard calluses on her neck and shoulders from long days of pulling a plow, ribs that stuck out and could be counted from a distance, hoofs that were ragged and flattened with wear. But Webb had loved her during the three years we had her, riding her bareback up and down the road, hitching her to an old Amish surrey he and I had bought in Kentucky and driving around the neighborhood, pretending whatever it is that little boys pretend when they are doing things their forebears did for necessity and they do for fun. Three days earlier she had died.

The usual way of disposing of large animals when they died was to call a factory in Nashville which used the carcasses for various products they manufactured. Webb had said we were never to do that when Mary Ann died and so we had a neighbor come with a backhoe and bury her in the middle of a grove.

Webb did not go near her body before she was buried and had not been to her grave. But time had passed and now he was paying his last respects to his friend and companion, experiencing death for the first time. And he had chosen to do it alone.

"Will, you've got to go in there with him. That's a pitiful sight. I started to make a picture of what he's doing, but there's some things you don't photograph."

I moved to the edge of the trees to where I could see Webb. He had taken two pieces of a dead oak limb and tied them together with a piece of wire. It was a cross. The noise we heard was his pounding it into the ground at the spot he had chosen as the head of her grave. Occasionally the rythmic pounding would stop and he would step back to look at it. Not satisfied that it was straight enough, or deep enough into the ground to withstand the wind and rain, he would move back in and pound some more. I stood watching him, not knowing what to do when he had finished.

He walked away for about ten steps and I thought he was going to the house, and was relieved. But suddenly he turned around and fell to his knees, folding his hands together in a position of prayer, facing the cross. I realized how we fail our children. I was not with him. But now I could not be without him. I moved quietly and knelt down beside him. I wanted to say a prayer, maybe give words to what he was feeling inside. But that would be a presumption. This was *his* service. Not mine. Perhaps even my presence was an imposition. I did not rise until he did. And when he walked over and sat down on a log I went and sat beside him, neither one speaking to the other. Finally he broke the silence. In a tender but clear voice he said, "I'm going to miss ole Mary Ann."

I knew it was my time to speak but didn't know what to say. And when I did my own voice was not as composed as his.

"Webb, I know what it is to lose someone you love. There's no rule against crying if you want to." He leaned against me and briefly rested his head on my shoulder. And we were together.

Joe stood casually by the porch when we got back to the house, grumbling about some flaw in his camera. As Webb opened the door to go inside Joe hit him playfully on the rump and then turned to me as if the scene had not happened at all.

Inside the house Joe wanted me to play the guitar. And sing. "Sing Josephine that song you wrote, 'Mississippi Magic.' " It was a song about a young man riding the rails from Mississippi to Chicago when the madness of black folks and white folks hating one another was getting him down. He fell in love with a Chicago whore who chided him for his radicalism when he declared that he liked "the blacks *and* the kluxers," and told him not to go back, even when he was dead because:

> *They ain't never gon' love you.*
> *You better stay up here and lie beside me.*

Joe particularly liked the ending when the boy said to her:

> *O, yea, they gon' love me when I'm dead.*
> *They gon' come in for miles around—*
> *That ole Hartman Funeral Home in McComb City.*
> *They'll stand round my coffin all night.*
> *They'll say, "Ole Will was a good ole boy.*
> *He just had some crazy ideas."*

And even more the final chorus:

> *Then that Mississippi madness, be Mississippi magic again.*
> *That Mississippi madness, be Mississippi magic again.*
> *'fore we was born we was all kin.*
> *When we dead we'll be kinfolks again.*

We sat around the table as I sang, Joe following along, always a word or two behind and far off key. He came and stood directly behind me and when I reached, " 'fore we was born we was all kin. When we dead we'll be kinfolks again," he kissed me on the head, squeezing my shoulder until it ached.

After the singing we drank a little wine. And ate. And then they departed, each of us in love and charity with the other.

Calls came almost daily. Joe's creditors were closing in. The house in Hattiesburg would be foreclosed if he didn't raise three thousand dollars. And even then he would be sued for what he owed on the mortgage. But to Joe none of it was his fault. Constables began showing up to serve legal credit notices when he reported for work. One repossessed an expensive watch from his arm, right in front of the pharmacy. But Joe simply went and bought another one even more expensive to deny the humiliation.

He had continued to tell Josephine that he was going to let the creditors harass him for just so long and then he would bring in Will and George Barrett. Now the time had come to make his move. He called on Sunday afternoon. He wanted me to talk to his father-in-law, a sainted man of near eighty who had suffered a stroke and had trouble articulating his words. He reported that Joe was in bad shape, that he feared some dishonesty on the part of some of the creditors but that wasn't the real problem. Joe could possibly be sent to prison for fraud because he had mortgaged a house which was already mortgaged.

Then it was Josephine's time. But instead of repeating the words she had been coached to say, as her father had done, she told me the reality of the marital situation. She could not, she said, take it any longer. She would stay with him until the financial crisis had been resolved through bankruptcy proceedings and then a divorce was inevitable. She told of the scenes, the violence, the running through the night to get away, the horrors of a gentle man gone mad. When it was Joe's turn he had to check all phone extensions because, he said, "they have stripped me of all my privacy." Now he had decided that his father-in-law was a part of the conspiracy. So were the creditors, some of whom he was sure were having affairs with his wife. And all the lawyers in Meridian were a party to it and could not be trusted. So it was time for George and me to come down. He outlined a picture of how all of them would go scampering, abandoning the ship like drowning rats once the name of George Barrett was heard in the courtroom.

I tried to explain that it was not quite so simple, that George had no legal magic and probably could not come down next day anyway, that it was impossible for me to come soon and that he should trust his own bankruptcy attorney and come out of it as best he could and make a new start. The prison threat was weighing heavy upon his mind, though the probability of imprisonment was extremely remote. He addressed me in a fashion I had never heard from him before. In all the hostility and violence, directed at others close to him he had never raised his voice to me.

"Do you want me to go to Parchman? I feel betrayed! I never thought *you* would let me down. Every time you have ever needed help I have been there. Now I need help and you have deserted me."

My protestations that I would come in a minute if there were anything I could do were futile.

To Joe I was refusing to perform a simple miracle. He did feel betrayed and deserted. And I felt something I didn't recognize.

Sunday, February 12, one week later, had been a good day for our family. We had driven a hundred miles to meet some friends for lunch. We sang and played travel games. Brenda complained about the cramped conditions of the ride in the pick-up truck, Penny and Bonnie laughed at her, Webb took it in stride.

A note on the door from George Barrett awaited our return. "Will, I'll be back at 5:30. Don't leave. George." I knew what it meant. Brenda tried to dissuade me but I did not have to wait until 5:30. I knew.

At 5:30 he was back, motioning from the door for me to join him outside. As we walked along, going nowhere, he slipped his arm around my shoulder.

"Will, Joe is dead."

"How did he do it?" But he had not "done it." At least not in the sense of using a gun or rope or hose from an exhaust pipe. George explained that it was a heart attack, that he had gone into his room about midnight. He did not come out in the morning, Josephine could not open the door so she had summoned help and when the hinges of the door were removed they found him beside the bed. They called it a massive coronary. But he had willed it. It might as well have been a gun or rope or hose from an exhaust pipe. He had to die. Life had become too much.

It was our father's birthday and Abraham Lincoln's birthday. I had known what George had come to tell me. But it is never believable news. It was as if a cruel and monstrous projector had flashed a scene upon a giant screen and would not change the frame. I tried to see good times past, childhood antics, things that used to be. But the machine was stuck. Only our last conversation remained in focus. It was one of the few times there had ever been real anger between us. I tried to explain the hurt to George in terms of the alienation. "We lived together all these years and then he had to die without me."

"Will, you can't blame yourself for this. We both know it's a lot more complicated than that."

"I'm not *blaming* anybody! I'm just stating a fact. He died without me."

I went inside and called Meridian. Josephine was able to talk and asked me if I could come directly there. She said that Paul had already gone to East Fork to be with the folks. I said that I would.

"Will, your mother said he called her last night. That was the last thing he did. After he went in the room and locked the door he called her. I know she thought it was strange because it was a lot later than he usually called. She said he sounded cheerful though." Then she began to sob. "You know . . . how . . he always . . . you know . . . teased her . . . tried to cheer her up . . . with that saying?" There was a long pause before she continued. "Will, he said it!" Her crying became uncontrollable and I knew what she meant. Joe had said to Mamma, "I'll be acoming back, Ma." It was the last words he spoke. On earth.

I played at completing the fire in the fireplace which I had started while waiting for George to come back. When I stood up twelve-year-old Penny slipped her arm around me. "Daddy, don't you go blaming yourself about Uncle Joe. You did all you could do." I didn't even know that she was aware of our last conversation and still do not understand how she knew what I was thinking. But she did know and gently led me by the hand to her room. Bonnie, Webb and Brenda joined us with their silent presence. They knew what to do and they did it.

But I knew I couldn't cry long. Somewhere, some way, a long time ago the change had been made. The leadership role had been reversed. Joe who led us through the economic deprivation of the depression, who laughed us through childhood crises, who had so generously shared his worldly goods with us all had somewhere along the way ceased to be the leader. And now he was dead. And I knew I had to be the leader in the sad task of laying him down, knew in fact that I had been his leader for a long time, and wondered in those moments if the root of his problem might have been as simple as the leadership. But that kind of self-doubt and pity had to be a fleeting thing.

I thought of our beginning, our history—those four. It seemed an all right genesis:

Grandpa Bunt:
Never lost his temper,
Nor a fight.

Noble Stoic.

Grandma Bettye:
Wore her bathrobe to church
Because it was pretty
And
Jesus deserved the best.

Knew the Lord.

Grandpa Will:
Old rats like cheese too.
Worked the fields.
Read history books as the end approached.

They called him Tough.

Grandma Bertha:
I don't care if he's a darkie.
He's fourteen years old.
And they ain't gonna beat him.

Passion compounded.

The strain was good enough.
But hybrids? What about hybrids? Never mind hybrids! Let the dead rest. And now add another.

A friend, Elbert Jean, a former Methodist preacher who said he left the Church to enter the ministry, would drive me to Meridian. At four o'clock in the morning when we arrived Josephine was awake, near hysteria. "Oh, Will, he just never had a chance." And it was true. He didn't have a chance. But I don't know why. I don't know when along the way it happened. Something to smash whatever chance there was. Whatever it was, elusive, consumptive and portentous, here was its codicil.

Just at daybreak someone knocked on the door. Josephine asked me to answer it. I did not know the man standing there. He was a little man, young and well dressed. His speech was not that of the South.

"You must be Joe's brother. He spoke of you so often. He was a dear friend, and I'm so sorry." He shook my hand and handed me a sealed envelope. "Please give this to Mrs. Campbell." He was visibly shaken and forgot to tell me his name. And I didn't ask.

When I came back in Josephine was crying. "That was Rabbi Schlager. He loved Joe so much. And Joe loved him. But Joe was so rude and insulting to him yesterday, said such nasty things to him. The last time they were together. I hope he can forgive him, knew that Joe was sick."

I knew in part what she meant. In our last conversation Joe had lashed out at everything and everybody who came to mind as being responsible for his plight. He singled out the Jews. Joe was dark in complexion, his hair was jet black and wavy, almost kinky. He had a big nose, slightly hooked. Some of his fellow soldiers in Panama used to tell him he "looked like a Jew."

Three times someone put a copy of the book, *The Little Jew*, on his bunk. He became quite sensitive to discrimination against Jews and used to write me about how he had deliberately made friends with a red-headed Jew, a blond Jew and a Jew named Smith. If he had ever had feelings of anti-Semitism they were never expressed to me. But in that conversation he had said, "It's the goddam Jews in this town. The greedy bastards . . . they try to own the whole world." It was out of character, like a cancer fighting with every benign cell around it for its own destructive survival. I didn't take it seriously. Apparently neither had the rabbi. For when Josephine asked me to read the letter to her they were not words one would use to mourn a bigot. They were hand written:

Through the valley of tears, let us search for light, for some word. Where else shall it be? It will be in the source of all solace—in Sacred Scripture! How fitting and proper does the sublime Biblical verse apply to our dearly departed: "I am Joseph your brother" (Gen. 45:4). He represented many things to many people; but above all, with his genial personality and the generous instincts of a Christian and a gentleman, it was easy for him to build himself into the hearts of all who knew him. Yes again, "I am Joseph your brother." He lived in deeds, not years; in feelings, not figures upon the dial. He counted time by heart throbs, practicing daily his spiritual exercises. I saw daily that exercise of his heart—his reaching down and lifting someone up. I heard that heart pound with empathy towards all peoples and causes. Even in death he teaches us, reminds and points us to the enduring values that transcend it; showing the indestructibility of the human spirit, the urgency which the limitations of life's span impose on its travelers.

God paints the picture in the frost, and the sun melts it away. Yet the picture had purpose and fulfilled its mission. "I am Joseph your brother." He said it often to me. He was with us too short a while. But his mission is fulfilled. Might nature arise now and announce to the world, "This was a man, a brother, a friend, a valiant spirit." And might the still small voice echo in refrain, "I am Joseph your brother."

It was not the end of the letter but it was as far as I could read. Josephine followed me to Joe's room and we had our time together. And with him. Then one of us said to the other, "Let's go bury him." And the day began.

There were the usual funeral chores. Joe had been prominent and popular and there was no dearth of sympathy and offers to serve. The funeral director was the finest in professional courtesy. Joe had often said that he wanted to be buried in a plain pine box. Certainly I never believed him. (Joe liked magnificence in everything.) But Josephine and I agreed that the casket should be the most inexpensive one available. We explained this to the funeral director and he led us to those in the middle price range. "What of the one by the door in the back?" "That's for paupers." He stared straight ahead. "That's the one we want."

His mood changed. The professional sweetness was gone. He reminded us that the price of the coffin was the price of the entire service. We knew already.

But it was a mistake. I knew it when we viewed the body in the afternoon. It was as if the mortician were saying, "This is what you wanted and this is what you get!" While a corpse that has come to death through the greatest months of agony and pain is usually made to smile and look as radiant as a bride, the expression of fright and worry was left intact upon the face of Joe. Obviously no effort had been made to disguise any part of it.

All material things for Joe during his adult life had to be the finest. He just didn't fit without the extras—the satin and padding and trimming which could have been had for an additional thousand dollars. The morticians know their trade. Pay enough and they will make it look pretty. And they have pulled it off. We should have paid the extra money to make Joe look pretty. For pretty was one thing he always was.

I stood at the head of the grave in East Fork cemetery. There was Joey, now sixteen and handsome. And Julie, lovely at thirteen, standing with complete composure beside her brother whose body shook with sobs. Carlyne, standing far in the background with casual acquaintances, dutifully permitting the present wife to claim the public grief. The tired, sad eyes of Lee Campbell, placing his firstborn son beside four generations of his flesh and blood. Mamma, staring in hopeless disbelief, asking out loud if it could be true that her favorite, most loyal and most doting child was gone. And Sister, seated between the grave of her own son and her brother, professing aloud her protest of it all. Paul, Bunyon, baby brother, whimpering softly. Josephine, suffering still.

And I.

Sister had said the night before. "He loved us all but he worshiped you."

"Worshiped me!" My god! Could that be it? Had I become his idol as he had once been my idol? Elbert Jean, with whom I had so often discussed Joe and his problems, and my own, had cautioned me during the period when I was dragging him through the psychiatric sessions that it is very, very difficult to tell where illness begins and sin leaves off, and had warned me to make sure which side of the line—obviously doubting that there really was one—I was dealing with. When Sister said, "He loved us all but he worshiped you," I thought of some words Elbert had said to me one time when we were discussing Joe's latest episode. Maybe he spotted what Sister had just said and was trying to warn me.

We had been talking about how difficult it is to know just what to do and suddenly Elbert spoke some words which seemed to me at the time to be totally unrelated to the subject. He said, "You know, an idol is a dangerous thing, no matter if the idol is your own integrity or that pretty gold calf the Children of Israel made while Moses was up on the hill cavorting with the hind end of God." Then he began to laugh and preach with dead seriousness at once—a way he had of doing. "Yea," he sighed, "Moses came down the mountain and found that the people had got tired of Yahweh and had decided to build themselves a god. One more to their liking. So they took all their wives' and girl friends' earrings and bracelets and made a gold calf out of them, a real pretty thing, something they could see and admire and touch and not have to speculate on. But when Moses saw it—look out! He put the gold calf through the grinder and sprinkled it in the water and made'um drink it. I'm sure they didn't know what the old boy was up to. That is, not until the next morning."

We were far back in the woods hunting quail. He leaned his gun against a tree, turned directly toward me and began to urinate, beginning his sermon anew as he wet the ground at my feet.

"And next morning when they all left their tents and went out back to relieve themselves Moses was there waiting for them."

Pointing to the urine trickling from the leaves and soaking into the ground he concluded his preaching with the words he supposed Moses had used. "All right. You wanted to build yourself a god. Well, there he is. Take a good look at him. You just pissed him out."

It was a sermon I did not soon forget. And at Sister's words I remembered it anew.

Epilogue

Was that where it all began? Was it somehow all wrapped up in that Bayer aspirin box and the wings of a dragonfly, fluttering in a hot summer breeze forty years earlier? Had he been such an idol to me that I had unwittingly, unconsciously set out to turn it around and become his idol? Had he really worshiped the idol he had built and I had let him build and perhaps even helped him to build? An idol who reached idol stature by courting and even flaunting success in the face of the worshiper who had never known success such as he had known? Not success epitomized by the evil of this world's goods, for graven images neither need nor want this world's goods. Epitomized rather by the evility of this world's *goodness*. Forever center stage, yet not even god enough to enjoy center stage, basking instead in the humility of not quite fame? An idol who would keep his own clay feet so well concealed that an assumed perfection on the part of the idolator was inevitable. An idol, like all idols, who would hear confession but never make his own? Who would give absolution in abundance but never seek it? Forgive even the Biblical seven times seventy but never once ask forgiveness, the idol feeding and feasting forever upon the idolator?

But there was still not time for such questions. And such certainties. Suddenly, as I stood waiting for the last of the mourners to gather, it was the summer of 1941 and I was standing on this very ground, giving this particular plot a bit more attention than the rest of the cemetery which East Fork Church gave me fifteen dollars a month to keep clean. Joe had been very proud that I was starting at the bottom for it gave him occasion to assure me over and over that I would make it to the top. And as far as he was concerned, despite the fact that I had not succeeded in holding any job for very long, I *had* made it to the top. For he would have it no other way.

Ah, Brother 'Skeeterhawk. I remember. The barn, the Moore Pasture, and the fields. I remember all the things you taught me and all the love you gave. O, Dragonfly, why did you fly so fast? And so high? Where did it all begin? I still don't know. But I remember. I remember you. I remember us. Some day I'll write it all down. I'll write that book you were always going to write. But never did. It'll be your story, Brother—the story of Joe. I remember the time you went out and bought a new typewriter, and three reams of paper. Carbons too. Josephine said you wrote half a page and never went back. I'll finish it, Brother Dragonfly. All of it. You wouldn't want me to make it up. So I'll write it down the way it happened. I'll be tempted to write it down the way I wished it. I'll be tempted to write it the way you wished it too. The way you wished it before it was too late. Before the world took you. But I won't do it that way, Brother. I remember how you used to joke on birthdays and Christmas and anniversaries, "All I want is a few kind words." They'll be there too. A few kind words will be there. Kind words for the dragonfly. I'll make them as pretty as I can. You always liked pretty words. I remember the ghost stories and the poems. How you used to take chickens to the store when I was supposed to take them, so I wouldn't be embarrassed. I remember the day you joined the CCC Camp. And the way you cheated at Eeny, Meeny, Miney, Moe so I wouldn't be the one chosen for unpleasant chores. I remember the grave you dug for me when they thought I was going to die with pneumonia, so I wouldn't be way up there at East Fork, away from you. And the way we sat huddled close together in the dark of that pit when I was well again. You were never ashamed to weep. And I'll cry too, later, when they have all gone away. But not yet. Not now. For I'm the preacher here, the technician practicing his trade. And technicians don't cry. Technicians don't have kinfolk. I remember ole Leon and the day Noon Wells got killed. And Rover, who just showed up one day and then left. The way you are gone. I remember it, Brother. I remember it all.

The pastel picture on the tomb of Will Edward loomed like a life-sized poster. Names and faces whirled through my head like a movie gone wild. I imagined that the hundreds of surrounding graves had shrunk to miniature mounds, tiny heaps of fresh dirt, just big enough to cover a Bayer aspirin box. Stones with names like Nunnery, Spurlock, Newman, Tarver and Wells were gone. Only the Campbell stones remained. Flowers had vanished too. And somehow I couldn't establish what day of the week it was.

And then back to some kind of reality. A hundred awkward faces were turned toward mine, uneasily awaiting my prayer of committal and benediction.

We have gathered, O Lord, to say good-bye to our brother. Our Campbell brother. Our East Fork brother. Our Christian brother of all humanity.

Then I mumbled some words about his being now in better hands than ours, and some other words I don't remember, and the burial was over.

It was the day of St. Valentine.

No, it's further down the path. I know it's further down the path."

Joe had buried the dragonfly on Sunday and said that if it were alive on Wednesday I would come home and we would be together.

Valentine's Day was on Tuesday.